UNIVERSITY LIBRARY
UW-STEVENS POINT

W9-BIY-526

A NEW PARTNER IN GLOBAL ENERGY

Global energy markets are undergoing fundamental change. Liberalisation and privatisation mean that organisations are facing new challenges that require a variety of innovative solutions. At PricewaterhouseCoopers, our Global Energy and Mining Group (GEM) provides professional services to organisations working within the Utilities Petroleum and Mining Sectors. We operate world-wide, combining the skills of global energy and mining specialists with the business knowledge of locally based expertise. Clients needs are complex. PricewaterhouseCoopers delivers a range of business advisory services that address these client needs from acting as leading financial advisors through to regulation, tax and legal issues IT solutions and change integration.

For further information, contact Kenny Hawsey, Territory Senior Partner, 48 Nizami Street, Number 24, Baku 370001, Azerbaijan.
Telephone: +99412 97 25 15 Facsimile: +99412 98 99 32

www.pwcglobal.com

PricewaterhouseCooper refers to the individual member firms of the worldwide PricewaterhouseCoopers organisation

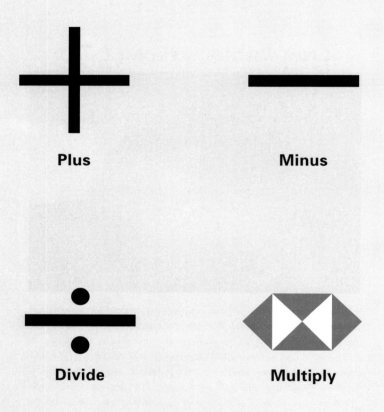

Plus

Minus

Divide

Multiply

HSBC. It's a sure sign that you're dealing with a world-class financial services organisation.

We've been around for more than 130 years. Now we're in 79 countries and territories, serving over 20 million customers.

Those are the numbers. But it's our integrity and common sense solutions that you can truly count on.

Wherever you are in the world, wherever you are in your life, HSBC will be there for you.

Azerbaijan - Tel: (994-12) 970808, Fax: (994-12) 971730

HSBC

YOUR WORLD OF FINANCIAL SERVICES

Issued by HSBC Bank Middle East.

Doing Business in
Azerbaijan

THE DOCUMENT COMPANY
XEROX

XEROX

Digital docuworld
is Your world

The digital revolution is transforming the business landscape...
All the rules are changing.

EXPLORE

DISCOVER

CONNECT

Every Business Needs Professional
Document Production

D
I • BLACK & WHITE COPIES
G • COLOUR LASER PRINTING
I
T • ENGINEERING SYSTEMS
A • SCANNING
L • FINISHING

XEROX
DOCUMENT
CENTRE

Baku Office:
Azerbaijan 370000
38/3 U. Gadjibekov Str.
Tel   : /994 12/ 92 43 13
Fax   :/994 12/ 98 52 70
E-Mail :Xerox@azeri.com

Baku Office:
AZERBAIJAN 370001
4, M.S. Efendiyev str.
Tel   : / 994 12 / 97 37 08
                        92 34 18
Fax   : / 994 12 / 92 34 18

Doing Business in
Azerbaijan

Consultant Editors:
Nadine Kettaneh and Jonathan Wallace

In association with

TRADE
PARTNERS UK
www.tradepartners.gov.uk

KOGAN
PAGE

Publishers' note

Every possible effort has been made to ensure that the information contained in this handbook is accurate at the time of going to press and neither the publishers nor any of the authors can accept responsibility for any errors or omissions, however caused. No responsibility for loss or damage occasioned to any person acting, or refraining from action, as a result of the material in this publication can be accepted by the editor, the publisher or any of the authors.

First published in 2000

Apart from any fair dealing for the purposes of research or private study, or criticism or review, as permitted under the Copyright, Designs and Patents Act, 1988, this publication may only be reproduced, stored or transmitted, in any form or by any means, with the prior permission in writing of the publishers and the relevant author, or in the case of reprographic reproduction in accordance with the terms of licences issued by the Copyright Licensing Agency. Enquiries concerning reproduction outside those terms should be sent to the publishers at the undermentioned address:

Kogan Page Limited
120 Pentonville Road
London N1 9JN

Web site: www.kogan-page.co.uk

© Kogan Page Limited, and contributors, 2000

British Library Cataloguing in Publication Data

ISBN 0 7494 3166 0

Typeset by Saxon Graphics Ltd, Derby
Printed and bound in Great Britain by Bell & Bain Ltd, Glasgow

Established in June 1998, Aon-Azeri Insurance & Reinsurance Brokers Co is a joint venture between local Azeri Partners and the Aon Group Limited*.

Registered on the 5th June 1998 with the Ministry of Justice, Aon Azeri was subsequently licensed by the State Insurance Supervision Department at the Cabinet of Ministers of the Republic of Azerbaijan to perform all insurance related activities as from the 9th July 1998.

With the full support of Aon's world-wide resources behind us Aon Azeri is now able to offer advice and assistance on all classes of insurance and/or risk management services including but not limited to:

★ Commercial Risks	★ Energy
★ Marine	★ Construction Risks
★ Aviation Hull & Liabilities	★ Motor
★ Cargo	★ Banking
★ Life	★ Personal Accident
★ Travel	★ Medical
★ Property	★ Employee Liabilities

Aon Azeri is staffed by experienced and knowledgeable personnel with a mixture of local and international employees who are able to provide immediate and effective assistance to your needs.

As an example of our client base Aon Azeri (as part of the Aon Corporation) have been appointed as brokers to:

Azerbaijan International Operating Company (one of the largest corporations with Azerbaijan and being a joint venture with BP, AMOCO and a number of other major oil companies including Azerbaijan's state oil company SOCAR).

* (part of the Aon Corporation, one of the two largest insurance and reinsurance broking houses in the world, with 40,000 employees in more than 80 countries world-wide.)

20 Islam Safarli St, Baku 370005 Tel: 97 71 15 / 94 25 96 ; Fax: 97 71 10

AMEC

AMEC serves the oil, gas and energy markets offshore and onshore.

AMEC aims to create wealth by developing and providing innovative business solutions for our clients and industry in order to optimise long term benefits and returns for customers, shareholders, employees and suppliers while contributing to the well-being of the communities in which we operate.

AMEC in Baku
Azerbaijan
Tel: +(99412) 973115

www.amec.co.uk

I Golden Lane, London
EC1Y ORR, UK
Tel: +44 (0) (171) 574 3000

HG
5706.3
.A3
D644
2000

Acknowledgements

We would like to thank:

His Excellency Mahmud Mamed-Kuliev, Ambassador of the Republic of Azerbaijan to London for his support of this project; George Riches, ABTIC, for his kindness and advice; Mr Altai Effendiev, Counsellor, and Rena Gandilova, Commercial Attaché, Economic and Commercial Affairs, Embassy of Azerbaijan in London, for their patience and invaluable help; John Slate and Fern Horine, Trade Partners UK, for their support of this project; Linda Cross, Sabina Gadzhieva and Lala Babayeva, The Commercial Section of the British Embassy in Baku, for their tireless assistance and friendliness; Mr Mohammad Chalabi and Intizam, Racers, for their welcome and help in Baku; Jack Durkin, KP Sales, London, for his patience and farsightedness in supporting this project; and The Hyatt Regency Hotel in Baku.

Hyatt Regency Baku Established First Five-Star International Standards In the "City of Legends"

The 160-room hotel is managed by Hyatt International and owned by the Baku Hotel Company.

The hotel offers 145 Deluxe rooms, eight Junior Suites, six Executive Suites and a Presidental Suite, all designed with soft colours and classic furnishings.

The Hotel offers a 230-m^2 ballroom and foyer with a capacity of 400 guests for cocktails and 200 guests for a banquet.

Understanding that business travellers need time to relax and unwind, the hotel offers a variety of restaurants and a health club. With its soaring stained glass windows, *Kishmish* is open throughout the day and serves a wonderful mix of regional and local favourites. *Beluga Bar* offers light meals, vintage wines, fine cigars, a wide variety of iced vodkas and delicious caviar that is its namesake. *Britannia Pub* offers an authentic English atmosphere, beer on tap and pub-style comfort food.

Hyatt Business Centre offers comprehensive office services for international business travelers providing translation, interpretation and secretarial services.

Hyatt International To Open Second Hotel In Baku in 1999

Hyatt International have opened a Park Hyatt Hotel in Baku, Azerbaijan on 10th of August 1999.

The hotel is adjacent to the well-reputed and successful Hyatt Regency Baku and part of a complex that includes the Hyatt International Centre and the Hyatt Meeting & Conference Centre.

The cosy lobby is inviting and refined, furnished with a luxurious mix of art, thick carpets and fireside club chairs.

Park Hyatt Baku will house 159 guestrooms, including six Executive, two Ambassador and two Presidential suites.

The Regency Club Hyatt's "hotel within a hotel" concept, offers floors of exclusive and privately accessed rooms and suites. A regency Club Lounge serves complimentary continental breakfast, all-day coffee and tea service as well as evening cocktails and hors d'oeuvres

Lemongrass, the hotel's 60 seat main restaurant, offers ecletic global cuisine with a hint of Asian flavour.

Club Oasis fitness centre is located in the Hyatt International Centre, and features a gym, saunas and steambaths as well as an outdoor pool, squash and tennis courts, high-tech gym, aerobics studio, massage, saunas, spas and steambaths as well as a café.

1033 at Izmir Street, a dazzling entertainment club that features an enormous video wall, dance floor, featuring contemporary & classic music and the longest bar in the Caucasus.

Contents

Part 1: Business Context

Part 2: Market Potential

Part 3: Business Development

Part 4: Building an Organisation

Part 5: Case Studies

Part 6: Appendices

Preface

The Azerbaijani–British Trade and Industry Council (ABTIC) was established in November 1995 by a protocol signed by the President of Azerbaijan and by the then President of the UK Board of Trade for the Department of Trade and Industry.

The Council meets twice a year in London and in Baku, to discuss all matters affecting trade and investment between the two countries including privatisation strategies, legal issues, taxation matters and any other items which may be of concern to Azerbaijani or British members. The co-chairmen report all major issues to the President of Azerbaijan.

British Council members represent all sectors of investment and trading activity between the two countries while Azerbaijani members represent both public and private sectors and speak for policies affecting mutual commercial activity.

With low inflation, a stable currency, an active privatisation programme and a growth economy fuelled by oil and gas, Azerbaijan represents an exceptional opportunity for investment and trade. Both the Embassy of the Azerbaijan Republic and Trade Partners UK would be happy to assist in welcoming you to this vigorous and expanding economy.

Mahmud Mamed-Kuliev (Co-chairman) and
George Riches (Co-chairman)

BP *Amoco*

THE EIGHTH INTERNATIONAL CASPIAN OIL&GAS EXHIBITION AND CONFERENCE INCORPORATING REFINING & PETROCHEMICALS

SPEARHEAD EXHIBITIONS LTD

Organisers of the International Caspian Oil & Gas Exhibition and Conference in partnership with the Azerbaijan Chamber of Commerce & Industry, are pleased to announce that the Eighth International Caspian Oil, Gas & Petrochemical Show will be held

5 - 8 JUNE 2001

For further information please contact:
Spearhead Exhibitions Ltd
Ocean House, 50 Kingston Road,
New Malden, Surrey KT3 3LZ, UK
Tel: +44 (0)20 8949 9222
Fax: +44 (0)20 8949 9868/9869
Email: caspian@spearhead.co.uk
Website:
http://www.caspianevents.co.uk

"XƏZƏR NEFT, QAZ, NEFTAYIRMA VƏ NEFTKİMYASI" 8-ci BEYNƏLXALQ SƏRGİ VƏ KONFRANSI

SPİRHED EKSİBİŞNZ LTD.

"Xəzər neft, qaz və neftkimyası" beynəlxalg sərgi və konfransının təşkilatçıları Azərbaycan Ticarət-Sənaye Palatası ilə birgə bildirirlər ki, "Xəzər neft, gaz və neftkimyası" 8-ci beynəlxalq sərgisi

5 - 8 İYUN 2001- Cİ İLDƏ KEÇİRİLƏCƏKDİR

Əlavə mə'lumat almaq üçün aşağıdakı ünvana müraciət edin:
Spearhead Exhibitions Ltd.,
Ocean House, 50 Kingston Road
New Malden, Surrey KT3 3LZ, UK
Tel: +44 (0)20 8949 9222
Faks: + 44 (0)20 8949 9868/9869
El. poştu: caspian@spearhead.co.uk
VEB-səhifəsi:
http://www.caspianevents.co.uk

"НЕФТЬ, ГАЗ, ПЕРЕРАБОТКА НЕФТИ И НЕФТЕХИМИЯ КАСПИЯ" 8-я МЕЖДУНАРОДНАЯ ВЫСТАВКА И КОНФЕРЕНЦИЯ

СПИРХЭД ЭКЗИБИШН ЛТД

Организаторы Международной выставки и конференции "Нефть, газ и нефтехимия Каспия" в сотрудничестве с Азербайджанской Торгово-промышленной Палатой уведомляют, что 8-я Международная выставка "Нефть, газ и нефтехимия Каспия" пройдет

5 - 8 ИЮНЯ 2001 ГОДА

За дополнительной информацией обращайтесь в
Spearhead Exhibitions Ltd
Ocean House, 50 Kingston Road, New Malden, Surrey KT3 3LZ, UK
Тел: +44 (0)20 8949 9222
Факс: + 44 (0)20 8949 9868/9869
Эл. почта: caspian@spearhead.co.uk
ВЕБ-страница:
http://www.caspianevents.co.uk

List of Contributors

Azerbaijan Environment & Technology Centre (AETC) is the trading name of RSK Environment Ltd in Azerbaijan. It is registered in Scotland with a representative office in Azerbaijan, which has been operating since 1995. Since then numerous onshore and offshore environmental studies have been successfully carried out and permits obtained for a range of clients from major oil companies to small private enterprises. The services AETC provides spans the complete range of environmental works.

AMEC is a major international engineering, construction and development group. AMEC Process and Energy, the operating subsidiary company responsible for operations in Azerbaijan, serves the upstream and downstream oil, gas and petrochemical industries offshore and onshore.

Arthur Andersen has been a leading provider of services to the domestic Azerbaijani market since 1997. In the Baku office, professionals and expatriates from the USA, UK, Australia, Turkey and Russia have been providing professional services related to exploration and development of the Caspian oil and gas fields. Other services the company provides include assurance, business, consulting, corporate finance and tax.

Azerbaijan Entrepreneurs' (Employers) Confederation co-ordinates the activity of businesses and business men and women involved in entrepreneurial activities in order to protect their legal and economic interests and to promote the development of entrepreneurship in Azerbaijan. The Association acts in close co-ordination with entrepreneurial bodies and organisations, national and international financial/credit organisations and related state executive organisations.

The **British Embassy Commercial Section** gives informative and realistic views to visitors of what they can expect during their stay in Azerbaijan. It provides services for administrative arrangements such as visas, airport arrangements, hotel bookings, and trips. The Commercial Section also provides tailored market reports that include market research and market analysis.

Ernst & Young was the first international professional services organisation to recognise the importance of the newly independent states by establishing practices in Russia, Ukraine, Uzbekistan, Kazakhstan, Azerbaijan, and Georgia. The firm advises on all aspects of corporate and personal tax planning and compliance, including investment structuring and assistance with reporting and filing requirements. It also provides statutory and international audit and accounting services, including helping companies to convert Azerbaijani statutory accounts to comply with western reporting standards.

The **European Bank for Reconstruction and Development (EBRD)** was established in 1991 and has its headquarters in London. It is a multilateral development bank which fosters the transition towards open market-oriented economies and promotes private and entrepreneurial initiative in 26 countries of central and eastern Europe and the Commonwealth of Independent States (CIS).

GlaxoWellcome plc is one of the world's leading research-based pharmaceutical companies. The group was formed in March 1995, following the integration of Glaxo and Wellcome. Both companies had long traditions in the field of prescription medicines and the merger of their operations created the second largest pharmaceutical company in the world. GlaxoWellcome has been operating in Azerbaijan since March 1999 and is primarily involved in the sales and marketing of its key products.

Dr Edmund Herzig is a Senior Lecturer in the Department of Middle Eastern Studies at Manchester University and a founder member of the Manchester University Research Group on Central Asia and the Caucasus. Since 1994 he has also been affiliated as a Senior Research Fellow to the Russia and Eurasia Programme of the Royal Institute of International Affairs, where he is Series Editor for the programme's research publications on the Caucasus and central Asia.

A specialist on the history, politics and international relations of Iran, the Caucasus and central Asia, Dr Herzig is a regular contributor to academic, business, and policy-orientated conferences on the region.

Akif Akbar oglu Kerimov is President of the Union of Insurance Companies of the Azerbaijan Republic, and Chairman of the Board of Aon-Azeri Insurance & Reinsurance Brokers Company. He graduated in Economics from the Azerbaijan Economic Institute in 1973 and has been working in the insurance sector for more than ten years. Mr Kerimov is the author of a number of articles and the first book to cover the insurance sector in Azerbaijan. He participated actively in the preparation of legislation, including the Law on Insurance in the Azerbaijan Republic.

Ledingham Chalmers, one of Scotland's leading law firms, was the first foreign law firm to open an office in Baku in October 1995. Its presence in, and continued commitment to, Azerbaijan is known to a wide cross-section of the government and business community in Baku, making it an integral part of the business scene there. It has strong working relationships with other law firms working in the region as well as those based in the UK and USA.

The firm's energy team has developed a practice from its North Sea base and now represents clients on business in several Commonwealth of Independent States (CIS), eastern and central Europe and African countries.

Morrison International Ltd is the overseas operating company within the Morrison Construction Group plc – one of UK's leading construction and property development companies. The company has over 25 years of international construction experience and has been operating in Azerbaijan since 1992.

Murphy Shipping and Commercial Services operates a multitude of services in the Caucasus and Caspian regions, all of them associated with transportation and logistics. It has been handling heavy lifts and wide gauge cargos in the Commonwealth of Independent States (CIS) since 1993. In 1994, it became the first foreign freight and logistics company to be registered in Azerbaijan. The company also provides ships' agency services originally with Lara Express Lines, and later with CMBT.

Soheil Ramanian is the Managing Director of Trade Development Ltd, a trade consultancy firm based in London with offices in Baku and Tashkent. It specialises in representing and advising engineering companies and manufacturers on engineering products and chemicals for general business activity in the former Soviet Union, especially in Caucasia and central Asia.

Royalton is a firm of interior contractors offering turnkey solutions for office space. It operates in Azerbaijan in two capacities – oilfield services offering engineering and technical supplies, and services to support oil and gas operating companies within the region.

Salans Hertzfeld & Heilbronn is a multi-national law firm of over 300 lawyers with offices in Paris, New York, London, Moscow, St Petersburg,

Warsaw, Kiev, Almaty and Baku. It represents clients from all over the world in a broad range of cross-border transactions and disputes.

James E Hogan is a partner in the Paris office of Salans Hertzfeld & Heilbronn who specialises in commercial transactions in the countries of the former Soviet Union.

Glenn S Kolleeny is the resident partner in the St Petersburg office of Salans Hertzfeld & Heilbronn, specialising in trade and commodities transactions and finance in the countries of the former Soviet Union.

Kamal Mamedzade is an associate of the Baku office of Salans Hertzfeld & Heilbronn.

SOCAR (State Oil Company of Azerbaijan Republic) is the only state-owned oil company in Azerbaijan. With over 150 years' experience in producing industrial crude oil and refined products, it was established as an oil company of the independent Azerbaijani Republic in 1992. The company has, over the last few years, signed 19 production sharing agreements with a huge number of foreign companies, thereby increasing the production of crude oil in Azerbaijan by more than five million tons in 2000.

Trade Partners UK is the British government organisation responsible for the promotion and development of British companies' goods and services overseas. It has a regional network in the UK as well as commercial sections of British embassies world-wide.

MURPHY SHIPPING & COMMERCIAL SERVICES LIMITED

Your very own shipping department!

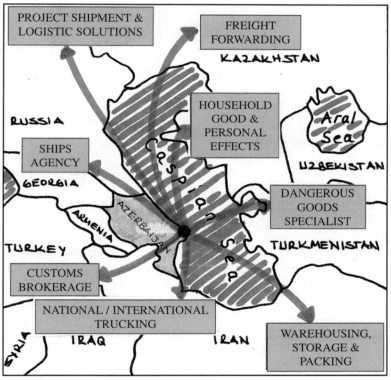

Satisfaction guaranteed!

LONDON OFFICE
TEL: 44 (0)208 5715710
FAX: 44 (0)208 5715711

E-MAIL:
general.office@murphyshiiping.com

BAKU OFFICE
TEL: 994 12 980 151
FAX: 994 12 939 315

E-MAIL:
Frieght@murphy.baku.com

ASHKABAD-BAKU-BISHKEK-HOUSTON-LAGOS-LAUANDA-PORT HARCOURT-POTI-TBILISI-WARRI

Pioneering Energy

Charles Remp and his family at home in the Coalinga oilfields, California - 1913

The Remp family's involvement with the oil industry began a century ago in California, at the same time Baku oil began flowing to world markets. Four generations later, our pioneering spirit was as strong as ever when Steve Remp first visited Azerbaijan in 1989. Today, we are proud of our long association with Azerbaijan and look forward to doing business there for many years to come.

Ramco Caspian Limited, 9 Boyuk Gala Street, Baku 370004, Azerbaijan Republic
Contact Lisa Newman, Public Relations Manager - lisa.newman@ramco-plc.com
For more information about Ramco, visit our web site at www.ramco-plc.com

Foreword

Since becoming an independent state in 1991, Azerbaijan has worked hard to transform its economy from one of central command, linked to the Soviet interdependent-states system, to one of free market orientation. A reform programme, begun in 1995, has ensured sustained economic growth for the country, financial stability with inflation under tight control and a booming private sector, now accounting for approximately half of Azerbaijan's GDP.

There are many excellent reasons for businesses to consider investing in Azerbaijan. A developed legal and business framework assists entrepreneurs and investors in the establishment of businesses while the country's integration in the international community favours smooth trade relations. As a result, foreign direct investment has continued to increase every year and is expected to reach US$1,550 million in 2000.

Azerbaijan's favourable geographic location gives it a key strategic position in the area, making it a major participant of planned infrastructure developments such as TRACECA, the communications and transport network for the Trans-Caucasus region.

Vast natural resources, especially of oil and gas, have hardly been tapped, and privatisation of the country's most attractive state-owned assets is only just beginning; these two areas will provide extensive investment opportunities for foreign investors for some time to come. Other sectors such as agriculture, manufacturing, tourism and construction also hold great potential for investors seeking to establish a presence in Azerbaijan or the region as a whole.

Trade Partners UK has launched its initiative for Azerbaijan and hopes that this publication will provide businesses contemplating investing in Azerbaijan with all the information they will need to do so.

John Slate
Trade Partners UK

MAN'S BIGGEST ENEMY.

(Magnified approximately 30,000 times.)

This is the bacterium which causes tuberculosis. Every year diseases, such as tuberculosis, account for 9 out of every 10 deaths worldwide. Glaxo Wellcome, working with universities and hospitals, spends £1.2 billion a year and employs 9,000 researchers in the fight against disease.

GlaxoWellcome DISEASE HAS NO GREATER ENEMY.

Complete Support Strategy

Applied Technologies Incorporated

Azerbaijan Representative Office
Adil Iskenderov St. 2, Apt 1, Baku, Azerbaijan
Tel: +(99412) 98-09-59 / 98-83-16 Fax: +(99412) 97-21-12
E-mail: office@ati.co.ae

Dubai Representative Office
PO Box 24458, Dubai, UAE
Tel: +(9714) 62-73-98 Fax: +(9714) 62-90-24

www.britishairways.com

Great cabin crew are born, not made.

At British Airways we like to nurture what comes naturally. Every one of our cabin crew is chosen for their natural desire to help other people. And that's why we hope that, when baby Isabella here grows up, her helpful ways will be making life easier for passengers on British Airways.

BRITISH AIRWAYS
The world's favourite airline

The Only British Owned & Managed Hotel in Azerbaijan!

262 room 4 star hotel on the shore of the Caspian Sea 10 minutes from the heart of the Capital.

The most comprehensive leisure, business, conferencing, entertainment & transport facilities in the Caucuses

Modern, spacious rooms design by British Business Traveler
AC / Voice Mail / Sat. TV (BBC World & Prime) / $2m^2$ work station.

Guaranteed lowest prices for all of your business needs.

http://www.hot.key.com/crescent   crescent@hotel.baku.az

The Crescent Beach Hotel & Leisure Resort
++994 50 213 1457 / 8++994 12 974 777   Fax: ++994 12 974 780

Gateways

BAKU'S MOST CHOSEN ESTATE AGENT

Real estate management

Residential brokerage

Office brokerage

Investment Counseling

Construction & Refurbishment

15, Z. Tagiev Str. (Fountain Square)
370000 Baku, Azerbaijan
Tel.: (99412) 983 041
Fax: (99412) 938 728
E-mail: gateways@azeurotel.com

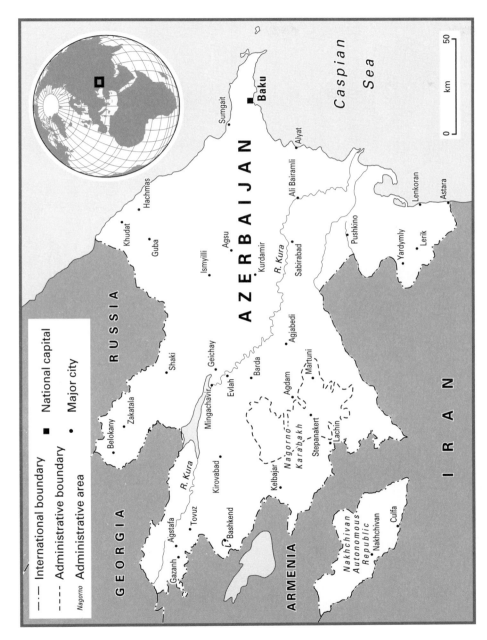

Map 1: Azerbaijan and its neighbours

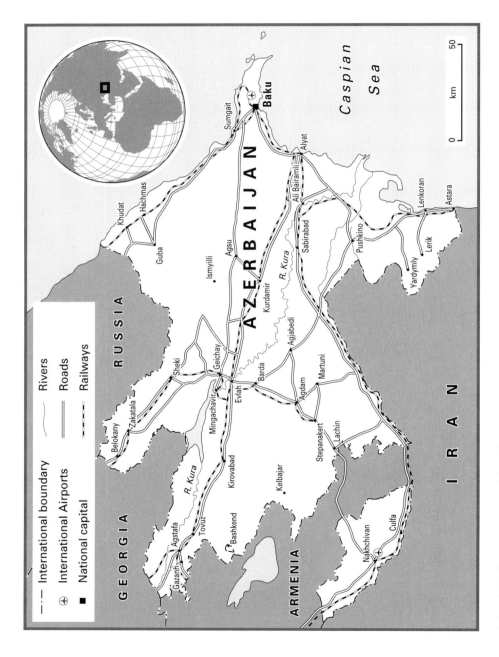

Map 2: Infrastructure of Azerbaijan

Part 1

The Business Context

1.1

The Political Environment

Dr Edmund Herzig, Department of Middle Eastern Studies, University of Manchester

Introduction

The last decade of politics in Azerbaijan has been dominated by the processes of nation- and state-building. These processes began prior to the attainment of independence in 1991 and remain far from complete today. Nation-building has required the attempt to define and affirm the national identity of the Azerbaijani people, their inalienable claim to independence and to the territory within their country's internationally recognised borders. State-building has centred on the establishment of viable government institutions capable of controlling and administering key resources (territory, coercive power, wealth) and of sustaining themselves beyond the political lives of individual office-holders.

Historical background

Today's politics have developed out of the late Soviet period politics, which pitted the national independence movement against the republican communist elite and the ultimate authority of Moscow. In the late 1980s dissident nationalists exploited the new freedoms of *glasnost* (openness) and *perestroika* (restructuring), and the communists' loss of ideological conviction and political will, in order to mobilise mass popular support.

Azerbaijan's nationalist movement shared with its counterparts in other Soviet republics the rejection of colonial or imperial rule from Moscow, the assertion of the primacy of national language and culture, and resistance to Moscow's economic exploitation and environmental degradation of the motherland.

The catalyst for Azerbaijan's independence movement was the rejection of Azerbaijani authority by the Armenians of Mountainous Karabagh (an autonomous district of Azerbaijan, the majority of whose population is Armenian). In February 1988 the Mountainous Karabagh district council voted to transfer from Azerbaijan to Armenia, a claim that was immediately supported by a vocal mass campaign in the neighbouring republic of Armenia. The Karabagh issue, which steadily escalated from a political to a military conflict (until hostilities were brought to an end by a 1994 ceasefire), has remained a central concern for Azerbaijan's politicians.

The leading role in the national independence movement was played by the Azerbaijani Popular Front (APF). In 'Black January' 1990 Soviet security forces used rioting and a massacre of Armenians in Baku as the pretext for a brutal suppression of the APF, killing at least 120 civilians and forcing the movement to go underground. In August 1991, however, Azerbaijan's communist president Ayaz Mutalibov lost the external support on which his power was based when communist power in Moscow collapsed. He was able to hold on to his position when Azerbaijan's parliament voted to restore the country's independence (31 August 1991), but when Azerbaijani civilians were massacred in Khojali in the Karabagh war in February 1992 he was forced to resign. In May of the same year the APF seized power, confirming and legitimising its hold on government with the victory of Abulfaz Elchibey in a presidential election the following month.

But the APF government proved unable either to recover territory lost to the Armenian separatists, or to establish control over the coercive and material resources of the state. In the absence of an established national army, the Karabagh war was conducted by militias and paramilitary groups. President Abulfaz Elchibey initially cultivated links with Suret Huseinov, the most prominent Azerbaijani militia commander of the time. Later, in winter 1993, the Azerbaijani forces suffered defeats in the war and Elchibey dismissed Huseinov. The latter led a rebellion from his home town of Ganje, and Elchibey, lacking any loyal troops, was forced out of power.

President Heydar Aliyev

The coup against Elchibey allowed Heydar Aliyev to return to power. Aliyev (born in Nakhichevan in 1923) had become Communist Party First Secretary in Azerbaijan in 1969 and had enjoyed a career at the pinnacle of the Soviet elite until he had fallen out of favour under Gorbachev and had gone into semi-retirement in his native Nakhichevan. After 1993, as president of independent Azerbaijan, he in turn faced problems with insubordinate security forces. There were coup attempts against him in October 1994, March 1995 and autumn 1996, all involving disaffected elements in the security forces. Far from being weakened by these crises,

Aliyev was able to use them to remove officials whose loyalty was suspect and to consolidate his own control over the security forces through the ministries of the interior and defence.

Aliyev's current dominance over Azerbaijan's political scene has been strengthened through the appointment of loyalists, many of them members of his extended family or of the Nakhichevan 'clan', to key positions in the administration, security services and economy. Potential rivals, such as Rasul Guliyev (former speaker of Parliament) and Hasan Hasanov (former foreign minister), have gradually lost their power, leaving no minister or pro-government parliamentarian with a strong independent political profile or power base. In Azerbaijan, as in other oil-based economies, the oil industry lends itself to political control through a state oil company and assorted government agencies – the state oil company SOCAR is no exception.

If Aliyev shows few scruples in removing possible political challengers, there can be no doubt that his political acumen is matched by a vision of a wealthy and independent Azerbaijan. At home Aliyev projects the image of a wise elder statesman with the experience to steer his young nation through the troubled waters of independence. When he returned to Baku in 1993, many expected him to revert to Soviet type and reorient his country towards Moscow. Instead he showed his grasp of prevailing national and international political and economic forces by taking over much of the ideology and policy agenda of the APF, not least the pro-western foreign policy orientation and the use of oil as a tool in winning international support for Azerbaijan's independence. He has proved far more adept than Elchibey in managing relations with Russia and Iran, Azerbaijan's two most powerful and threatening neighbours. Even opponents grudgingly recognise Aliyev's achievements. In his mid-70s Aliyev embarked on a further five-year term in office following victory in the October 1998 election. Illness and heart surgery in 1999, however, have placed a question mark over his long-term prospects as president.

Transition to democracy?

The government and all the major political parties in Azerbaijan espouse the ideal of creating a multi-party secular democracy and the 1990s have seen the enactment of numerous political reforms. Yet critics both at home and abroad suggest that the commitment to democracy is no more than skin-deep, intended primarily to placate the international community.

A new constitution, adopted by referendum in November 1995, establishes Azerbaijan as a presidential republic. It has been criticised for concentrating excessive powers in the hands of the president, but perhaps more significant is the fact that in reality Aliyev's exercise of power appears unfettered by constitutional constraints.

While Azerbaijan has experienced a number of changes of government since becoming independent, none has come about through elections. Both the parliamentary election of 1995 (in which Aliyev's New Azerbaijan Party and its allies won an overwhelming majority) and the presidential election of 1998 (in which Aliyev won 76 per cent of the vote) were condemned by international observers as falling far short of international standards for democratic elections. In both elections, significant parts of the opposition either refused to take part or were prevented from participating.

Azerbaijan's diverse political parties are mostly weak and small and do not play a central role in national political life. The pro-government parties are vehicles by which to mobilise support for the president in parliament, while the other parties serve the same purpose for leading opposition politicians, readily splitting and realigning to keep up with the disputes and divisions that take place on a more or less personal level between their leaders. Few parties have succeeded in articulating clear and consistent policy programmes that differentiate them from their rivals, or have developed nationwide party organisations or large memberships. There are exceptions. Parties that are either direct successors to the old republican Communist Party, or that have inherited part of its assets, property, membership and networks, or that are the successors to the nationalist independent movement, tend to be better organised and equipped. Among these are the Communist Party, the New Azerbaijan Party, the Azerbaijan Popular Front, the Musavat Party and the National Independence Party.

With a president who is made strong both by constitution and through his own leadership qualities, an array of weak and bickering political parties and the president's own party enjoying a large majority, it is not surprising to find that the Azerbaijani parliament is unable to offer an effective check on executive power.

Civil society

Azerbaijan's constitution contains explicit guarantees of human rights and provides a blueprint for a law-governed society. Constitutional provisions, however, are not always respected or enforced. A serious weakness exists in the corruption and susceptibility to political influence of the judiciary. The government controls key judicial appointments and there is no evidence that the court system is capable of bringing the government to book when it behaves unconstitutionally, or of protecting citizens' rights against arbitrary government action. Domestic and international human rights organisations have monitored numerous cases of arbitrary government action contravening citizens' rights. While there has been some progress – the death penalty was abolished in 1998, for example – the situation remains one of persistent abuse in certain areas that are covered by specific constitutional guarantees and explicit government commitments. Government control of the electronic media and of most newspaper publishing facilities prevents the media from fulfilling its role as an independent source of information, a forum for national debate and a channel for raising issues and expressing grievances.

However, newspapers covering a wide spectrum of political views are available, and the gradual trend is towards greater freedom of expression. For a privileged few there is growing access to international media via satellite television, and to electronic mail and other Internet sources.

The independence period has seen the creation of numerous non-governmental organisations (NGOs) dedicated to a range of causes and issues spanning human rights, political reform, conflict resolution, media freedom, humanitarian assistance and the environment. With few exceptions, however, NGOs are dependent on western financial support, so while their growth is a step in the development of civil society, so far they have not developed deep roots in society. This inevitably inhibits their ability to mediate between state and society.

Prospects for political stability

Compared to the early 1990s Azerbaijan today has achieved an impressive degree of political stability. A durable ceasefire has replaced the armed conflict with Armenia that raged between 1988 and 1994. Independence does not currently appear to be exposed to imminent internal or external threats. External factors, particularly any major change in Russian policy and behaviour, could still have a profound impact on Azerbaijan, and the unresolved conflict over Karabagh retains its potential to destabilise politics, as has already been the case on several occasions since 1991. Renewed hostilities and defeat would jeopardise the survival of any government, while a negotiated settlement that was viewed as a sell-out or surrender would also encounter strong domestic opposition.

The most serious threats to the country's stability are internal. As shown above, serious weaknesses in political development persist. The political economy is characterised by the dominance of patronage networks centred on senior government figures. Competition between these networks constitutes a parallel dynamic to the constitutional politics of political parties and elections. How far this intra-regime competition constitutes a threat to political development and cohesion remains uncertain, but such rivalries are more likely to come into the open when the time comes for Heydar Aliyev to step down. The concentration of power in the hands of the president and his dependants has created a regime in which there is a marked split between insiders and outsiders. Apart from the presidency, political institutions remain weak, and to date elections have done little to develop mechanisms for the smooth and legitimate transfer of power.

Aliyev bases his claim to rule on his proven capability in securing stability and promoting national interests, in addition to the promise of future prosperity. This claim may carry considerable weight in a country that has recently experienced violent political turmoil, military defeat and massive social and economic dislocation, but in the medium to long term, political stability must be underpinned by the delivery of sustained economic growth bringing tangible benefits to ordinary Azerbaijanis. While there can be little doubt that oil will generate significant revenues in the coming decades, the challenge will be to ensure that the majority of citizens will enjoy a share of that wealth.

International recognition has been forthcoming with the June 2000 recommendation by the Committee of the Council of Europe to accept Azerbaijan as a full member of the Council. A decision on full membership will be taken in Autumn 2000.

The Investment Climate

European Bank for Reconstruction and Development (EBRD)

Introduction

Azerbaijan has achieved a remarkable turnaround in the last few years as a result of significant foreign investment in the oil sector, the development of new export markets and the ceasefire in Nagorno-Karabakh. The country's accelerating pace of change will increasingly generate investment opportunities, especially in the energy sector. However, as with all transition economies, it is important that investors are fully aware of both the opportunities and the risks that exist so that they can target their investments accordingly. This chapter looks at some of the most promising areas for investment as well as the challenges that lie ahead.

Economic background

The reform programme begun in 1995 succeeded in achieving sustained financial stability and prolonged economic growth, making Azerbaijan one of the strongest economies in the Commonwealth of Independent States (CIS). Inflation fell from a peak of 1,664 per cent in 1994 to negative figures in 1999 due partly to a contraction in government spending and a tight monetary policy, although a slight inflation rate of 2.9 per cent is projected for 2000. Gross domestic product (GDP) growth has been positive for the past three years, rising from 1.3 per cent in 1996 to 7.4 per cent in 1999.

Due to the strength of the country's performance in the oil sector, Azerbaijan was affected less than some of its neighbouring countries by the Russian crisis of August 1998. Although oil price fluctuations are expected to continue to affect growth prospects over the next few years, the growth rate is not expected to go below 4–5 per cent. In 1998 the private sector accounted for approximately 45 per cent of GDP and 60 per cent of employment (including agriculture).

Foreign direct investment

Foreign direct investment (FDI) has increased from US$20 million in 1993 to US$1,051 million in 1997 and US$948 million in 1998, but fell to US$355 million in 1999.

To date, most FDI has been invested in the oil sector. The first oil production sharing agreement (PSA) between foreign investors and the Azeri State Oil Company (SOCAR) was signed in 1994, granting development rights to an international consortium. Since then, a large number of similar agreements have been signed (in addition to the AIOC deal) regarding both oil production and exploration, bringing the total volume of foreign commitment to the oil and gas sector to around US$50 billion.

Foreign investment rose in the non-oil sector from 15 per cent of FDI in 1994 to 33 per cent in 1998. The sectors attracting the largest levels of investment are construction, service industries, manufacturing, transport and telecommunications. The largest investors in the non-oil sector are from Turkey and the USA. Other leading investors are from Germany, Russia, Iran, the UK, Japan, France, Israel, Switzerland and China.

The privatisation process has attracted a high level of interest, with foreign investors buying more than half of the vouchers distributed to date. Further opportunities are expected to be offered through the privatisation by international investment tender of potentially lucrative stakes in the telecommunications, utilities and financial sectors.

Reasons to invest in Azerbaijan

Extensive deposits of oil and gas

Azerbaijan's rich oil reserves in the Caspian Sea Basin offer extensive investment opportunities. During the Soviet era the country's oil reserves were underexploited because priority was given to the Siberian oil fields; consequently, the country's major off-shore oil reserves remain largely untapped and will remain an area of great potential for foreign investors for some time to come.

A developed business structure

Important progress has been made in implementing the reforms needed to transform Azerbaijan into a market economy. The foreign trade regime and domestic prices have been liberalised, small-scale privatisation has been completed and restructuring of the banking sector has begun. A new tax code is expected to be in effect before the end of 2000. In addition, an effective treasury system has been introduced to improve expenditure management.

Major privatisation programme

The forthcoming privatisation of large-scale enterprises offers attractive opportunities for prospective investors. While small-scale privatisation is largely complete, voucher privatisation has been stalled for over a year and a new programme for large-scale privatisation, stressing cash sales of strategic enterprises has still not been passed by parliament. Only 10 per cent of vouchers due to expire in August 2000 had been redeemed by the end of 1999. However, since the voucher privatisation of medium- and large-scale enterprises began in 1997, over 950 enterprises have been transferred to majority private ownership. While this represents roughly 25 per cent of all medium and large firms slated for privatisation, the largest and most attractive firms have so far not been included in the voucher programme. The new privatisation programme is expected to become valid before the end of 2000. Under the Privatisation Law 1993, foreigners are allowed to participate in the voucher auction process, although they are required to buy options to do so first. These are sold by the State Property Committee and simply allow holders to participate in the auctions. In addition, the government is currently planning the privatisation of 50 large-scale enterprises, for which strategic investors are being sought.

A favourable geographic location

Azerbaijan's geographic location gives it a key strategic position in the development of the southern Caucasus, as well as the integration of Central Asia with Turkey and Europe. Major infrastructure projects are currently under way.

Integration in the international community

An EU Partnership and Cooperation Agreement provides the country with most-favoured nation status for trade in goods. Trade liberalisation is progressing towards the requirements for accession to the World Trade Organisation.

A legal framework for investment

Foreign participation in the economy is encouraged by the Government of Azerbaijan. The Law on the Protection of Foreign Investments generally provides foreign investments with the same legal regime as local investments. In addition, efforts have been made to simplify some local documentation requirements; for instance, companies with more than 30 per cent foreign capital do not require a licence to export their goods and services.

Main challenges

The government's main aim over the medium term is to diversify the economic structure in order to reduce the country's dependence on oil-related income and to prevent an excessive appreciation of the manat. Changes in the legal business environment are needed to improve the functioning of the courts, to reduce overlapping jurisdictions within government and to raise the level of public sector transparency.

Further improvement is needed in the implementation of bankruptcy procedures. Action cannot be initiated against enterprises in the privatisation process, and privatised companies often neglect responsibility for inherited liabilities. One of the major reform challenges is the establishment of effective post-privatisation corporate governance. So far, privatisation has led to the transfer of ownership to enterprise insiders, with little control exercised by outside shareholders. The development of sound corporate governance is hampered by the lack of a securities market. This prevents the tradeability of shares in privatised firms and limits the financial discipline that would derive from a functioning market. Securities market legislation has been passed but is yet to be implemented. For example, SOCAR was audited in 1999, but refused the auditors access to the country's main refinery, raising more concerns over financial transparency in the all-dominating oil sector. Proposals to set up an oil fund, which would manage oil-related balance of payments surpluses, are under discussion. However, the accountability of such funds remains unsolved.

Another major challenge for the Azerbaijani government lies in the problem of cash collections in the energy sector. Power shortages in early 2000 highlighted Azerbaijan's serious energy crisis, with many suppliers unwilling to deliver fuel oil to the country's ailing energy sector, given a history of non-payments. Reform proposals, including the unbundling of Azerenergy and Azerigas, the creation of an independent regulator, and the privatisation of regional power distribution, have been stalled for several months.

The consequences of the Nagorno-Karabakh conflict remain a significant challenge. The World Bank is helping to reconstruct areas affected by the war, but the country has been left with many social problems, including an unemployment rate in 1998 of 13 per cent. In 1995 it was estimated that 60 per cent of the population lived below the poverty line, although the actual number may be lower due to unreported earnings.

Investment opportunities by sector

Although economic growth in Azerbaijan remains driven by the oil sector and the related boom in construction activity, there were clear signs in 1998 of a broadening of the recovery to other sectors. Some of the sectors with the best opportunities for foreign companies are outlined below.

Oil

Azerbaijan has played a key role in the development of the oil sector in the Caspian region. Proven reserves total about 3 billion barrels, but it is estimated that the ultimate potential is as much as 40 billion barrels. About 60 per cent of the country's territory is oil-bearing, according to the Baku Institute, and nine-tenths of the petroleum reserves are offshore, in the Caspian Sea.

Investment opportunities in the oil sector will increase significantly over the next few years. By 2010 Azerbaijan plans a five-fold increase in annual crude output, from 11.6 million tonnes extracted in 1998 to about 47 million tonnes. By June 1999 the government had signed contracts worth nearly US$50 billion over 25 to 30 years with companies from Canada, Italy, Japan, Norway, Saudi Arabia, Spain, Turkey, the UK and the USA. In 1998 alone it signed six contracts with consortia worth nearly US$17 billion.

The largest contract to date was signed in 1994 with an international consortium known as the Azerbaijan International Operating Company (AIOC). The US$8 billion, 30-year contract aims to develop three fields, with total reserves estimated at 3 billion barrels. Dominated by UK and US companies, the AIOC has already spent over US$1 billion and committed itself to contracts requiring additional expenditure of several hundred million dollars. The consortium pumped its first oil – from the Chirag offshore field – in 1997.

Gas

In the early 1990s natural gas accounted for over 60 per cent of primary energy supplies in Azerbaijan, making it one of the most gas-intensive economies in the world. Gas production amounted to 4.2 billion cubic metres (bcm) in the first three-quarters of 1999 and is expected to increase to about 20 billion cubic metres by 2010. This is partly due to an expected increase in oil production in the Caspian Sea since most of Azerbaijan's natural gas production comes from associated gas from offshore oil fields.

A complete overhaul of the gas supply system over the next few years is expected to lead to significant investment opportunities. The modernisation programme includes replacing worn-out compressors and upgrading gas pipelines. Local gas production still falls short of demand, but the country aims to become self-sufficient in gas over the next few years.

Agriculture

Azerbaijan is well-endowed with fertile land, with most farming taking place in the central lowlands and along the Kura and Araz rivers. The government took the first steps in promoting the development of agribusiness by privatising most enterprises of the State Bread Complex, cotton ginneries, the Food Concern and the Poultry Concern. Foreign investment opportunities are widespread as both agriculture and the processing sector are in need of extensive capital.

To date, foreign companies have invested in a number of diverse areas, such as cotton processing, canneries, tobacco and tea. For example, the German company Janke has supplied manufacturing equipment for the Guba Canning Factory and is providing annual working capital of US$1.4 million. The main foreign companies engaged in the processing of tea are Intersun (United Arab Emirates), Beta (Turkey) and Saro (Turkey).

Privatisation has prompted Azerbaijani farmers to move increasingly away from growing wheat towards the cultivation of fruit and vegetables, which are more suited to small plots. Increases in agricultural productivity are expected to give a boost to investment in agribusiness enterprises, such as food processing plants and textile companies, and in rural services, such as the leasing of farm equipment.

Manufacturing

The manufacturing of oil equipment is Azerbaijan's oldest major industry and along with related sectors, such as instrument engineering and radio-electronics, constitutes some 20 per cent of the country's industrial potential. The need to upgrade obsolete equipment and to modernise the industry offers significant potential for foreign investment.

Privatisation is expected to lead to a number of possibilities for foreign investors in the light industry sector, which includes food processing, textiles and wine production.

Construction

Foreign investment in the development of Azerbaijan's energy sector had led to a construction boom from 1994, with the sector growing from 3.7 per cent of GDP in 1995 to 15.1 per cent in 1998. Foreign investors include companies from Canada, China, Germany, Iran, Japan, Singapore, Turkey, the UK and the USA.

Most activity is related to crude oil and gas development and to projects linked indirectly to the oil boom, such as the construction of offices, hotels and luxury houses. Continued inflows of foreign investment in the oil sector over the next few years is expected to lead to sustained double-digit growth in construction.

Tourism

Azerbaijan has considerable potential for tourism, which is yet to be fully developed. With its blend of medieval and 19th-century architecture, a well-preserved old town and a magnificent mosque overlooking the Caspian Sea, Baku is one of the most attractive cities of the former Soviet Union. The country has many other historical sites dating from early times as well as numerous beaches and mountains. Investment opportunities exist in hotel construction and the development of tourist services.

Transport

In September 1998, 27 nations signed the Baku Declaration, confirming their support for the Great Silk Road programme. This will create a Europe–Caucasus–Asia transport corridor, giving Caucasian and central Asian nations access to trans-European and trans-Asian networks.

Under the programme, which was originally established by the European Union (EU), participating nations will work together to upgrade the existing infrastructure and to establish a new transport network, including railways, air-traffic routes, pipelines and telecommunications lines. The future corridor will connect Almaty, Bishkek, Ashkhabat, Baku and Tbilisi to Japan and China in the east, and France, the UK and Spain, in the west.

In 1998 an estimated 4 million tonnes of cargo was transported via the existing Eurasian transport corridor. According to EU estimates, annual freight turnover via the new Silk Road is expected to rise to 18 million tonnes in 2000 and 34 million by 2010. Estimated to cost US$1 billion, the programme will create a wide range of investment opportunities for foreign investors.

Financial sector

The private banking sector comprises just over 70 commercial banks, which have a market share of approximately 10 per cent of total lending to companies and consumers. This market share is expected to expand considerably with the scheduled privatisation of the International Bank of Azerbaijan and the restructuring of another three state-owned banks (Savings Bank, Industrial Investment Bank and Agroindustrial Bank). The International Bank of Azerbaijan has made considerable progress in implementing restructuring plans. A 20 per cent stake in the International Bank of Azerbaijan, the largest and best-capitalised state bank, is to be offered for tender to a strategic investor, although the timing of this remains unclear. The Savings Bank will benefit from the merging of its performing assets and liabilities with those of Agroprom and Prominvest, which are both to be closed.

A number of foreign banking institutions have already made investments in the Azerbaijani financial sector. As of the end of 1998, banks with foreign majority ownership operating in Baku included financial institutions from Iran, Russia, Turkey and the UK. As the private banking sector continues to expand, foreign institutions will have further opportunities to invest in this area.

Conclusion

A number of serious challenges face Azerbaijan over the coming years as it continues to make progress towards a market economy. As already indicated, the country has much untapped potential, but investors should not expect a quick return on their investment. However, long-term projects are likely to lead to positive results as the country continues to accelerate its pace of change.

1.3

International Trade Relations

Hussein Bagirov, Minister for Trade

Introduction

Since independence, Azerbaijan has been developing its foreign trade relations and trade liberalisation measures have been carried out. Azerbaijan is one of the former Soviet republics with the most liberal trade regimes. Between 1992 and 1994 the Commonwealth of Independent States (CIS) countries accounted for the largest share of Azerbaijan's foreign trade turnover, in great part due to the historic ties that meant close economic relations. Since 1994, however, and especially since the signing of contracts with leading western oil companies, the influence of Europe, the USA and Far Eastern countries has begun to be felt in the foreign trade account.

Foreign trade

The foreign trade indicators of Azerbaijan for the first half of 1999 are shown in Table 1.3.1.

Table 1.3.1 Foreign trade indicators for Azerbaijan

	1998 (US$ million)	*1999 (US$ million)*	*% change*
Import	1,077.2	1,033.5	-4.1
Export	606.2	928.6	53.2
Goods turnover	1,683.3	1,962.1	16.6
Balance of foreign trade	-471.0	-104.8	366.2

Table 1.3.2 Foreign trade partners of Azerbaijan

Country	1998 (US$ million)	% of total goods turnover	1999 (US$ million)	% of total goods turnover	% change
Turkey	355.9	21.1	211.5	10.8	-40.6
Russia	299.6	17.8	308.9	15.7	3.1
Great Britain	109.3	6.5	77.9	4.0	-28.7
Ukraine	105.0	6.2	62.1	5.8	-40.9
Georgia	102.1	6.1	81.2	4.1	-20.5
Iran	87.0	5.2	70.0	3.6	-19.5
USA	53.6	3.2	112.7	5.8	110.3
Italy	54.1	3.2	321.3	16.4	493.9

The basis of Azerbaijan exports is petroleum products. Since the 19th century, the Azerbaijan oil industry has developed at a high speed and, after independence, over 20 contracts were concluded attracting some US$60 billion in investment.

The volatility of world oil prices has a direct influence on Azerbaijan foreign trade and export volumes. In 1998, decreases in exports and a fall in the price of oil led to a negative trade balance, but the increase in oil prices in 1999 has led to positive changes in the foreign trade indicators.

Other than oil, a number of products such as cotton, chemicals, machinery and agricultural products are high export earners for Azerbaijan. In the first half of 1999, the main export partners of Azerbaijan were Italy, Russia, Turkey, Georgia, Iran and France.

Table 1.3.3 Main commodities exports from Azerbaijan

Commodity	1998	% of total exports	1999	% of total exports	% change
Crude oil	149.5	24.7	396.2	42.7	165.0
Diesel	161.2	26.6	186.0	20.0	15.4
Petrol	29.8	4.9	26.6	2.9	-10.0
Kerosene	26.0	4.3	68.8	7.4	164.7
Chemical industry	11.3	1.9	22.8	2.5	101.6
Electricity	24.9	4.1	26.0	2.8	4.3
Cotton	49.3	8.1	21.7	2.3	-55.9
Alcoholic and non-alcoholic beverages	12.4	2.0	6.2	0.7	-50.3
Tobacco	10.9	1.8	20.8	2.2	91.2
Ferrous and non-ferrous materials	13.4	2.2	24.7	2.7	84.9

Table 1.3.3 *continued*

Commodity	1998	% of total exports	1999	% of total exports	% change
Machinery, mechanisms, electronic-technical equipment	33.4	5.5	34.7	3.7	3.6
Other products	84.1	13.9	94.1	10.1	11.9
TOTAL	606.2	100.0	928.6	100.0	53.2

Table 1.3.4 Main export partners of Azerbaijan

Country	1998 (US$ million)	1999 (US$ million)	% change
Turkey	135.8	69.1	-49.1
Russia	105.8	83.1	-21.8
Georgia	76.9	71.7	-6.8
Italy	45.1	313.0	594.5
Iran	44.5	22.6	-49.2
Great Britain	40.4	10.8	-73.1
France	11.7	58.1	395.3

Between 1992 and 1995, foods accounted for a high ratio of Azerbaijan's imports, but that was soon corrected when land reform and land privatisation led to an increase in the domestic production of food and agricultural products.

Favourable conditions were created for foreign investment activity and by 1998 the total level of foreign investment had increased to US$1.4 billion, the highest level among ex-Soviet republics. The growth in foreign investments led to an increase in imports of investment-related products such as machinery and equipment technology. For the first six months of 1999, the level of machinery and equipment as a ratio of total imports was 31.7 per cent and that of food was 19.1 per cent. The main import partners of Azerbaijan are Russia, Turkey, the USA, the United Kingdom, the Ukraine, Iran and Germany.

Table 1.3.5 Import of main commodities to Azerbaijan

Commodity	1998 (US$ million)	% of total imports	1999 (US$ million)	% of total imports	% change
Meat and meat products	15.5	1.4	13.5	1.3	-13.4
Sugar and confectionery	15.4	1.4	20.1	1.9	30.4
Wheat	51.6	4.8	67.8	6.6	31.5
Wheat flour	24.5	2.1	21.8	2.3	3.1
Salt, sulphur, stone lime and cement	22.5	2.1	23.3	2.3	3.1
Electricity	34.9	3.2	44.9	4.3	28.8
Chemical industry	79.4	7.4	57.6	5.6	-27.5
Ferrous and non-ferrous materials	129.7	12.1	111.1	10.8	-14.3
Machinery, mechanisms, electronic-technical equipment	348.3	32.3	342.2	33.1	-1.7
Overhead, air and water transportation facilities	87.1	8.1	90.4	8.7	3.9
Other products	268.3	24.9	240.9	23.3	-10.2
Total	1,0770.0	100.0	1,0330.0	100.0	-4.1

Table 1.3.6 Main import partners of Azerbaijan

Country	1998 (US$ million)	1999 (US$ million)	% change
Turkey	220.1	142.4	-35.3
Russia	193.8	225.9	16.5
Ukraine	92.9	38.4	-58.7
Great Britain	69.0	67.1	-2.8
Germany	46.7	46.1	-1.4
UAE	45.6	12.3	-73.0
Kazakhstan	44.4	24.6	-45.5
Iran	42.6	47.4	12.1
USA	39.8	82.9	108.4
Georgia	25.2	9.5	-62.4

International trade associations

One of Azerbaijan's main objectives with regard to foreign and trade policy is to forge close co-operation with international organisations – and with international trade organisations in particular. This co-operation should help achieve high standards in Azerbaijan's trade system. The organisations that Azerbaijan is a member of are listed below, with the date of joining:

World Trade Organisation	Observer status since 1997
(The Memorandum on Foreign Trade	
was presented to the WTO Secretariat	
and negotiations with the working	
group are to begin soon.)	
Black Sea Economic Co-operation Organisation	1992
Organisation of Economic Co-operation	1992
Islamic Centre of Trade and Development	1992
UN Economic and Social Commission for Europe	1992
UN Conference for Trade and Development	1992
UN Economic and Social Commission for Asia and Pacific Ocean	1993
UN Industry Development Organisation	1993

As previously mentioned, Azerbaijan is one of the former Soviet republics with the most liberal trade regime and reforms in this area continue to be implemented. The export licensing quota system and customs duties on exports from Azerbaijan were eliminated. Customs duties of 15 per cent are levied on imports and a reduction in this figure is expected shortly. Goods, credit, deposit, letters of guarantee and other facilities are used to facilitate foreign trade. All of these create reasonable guarantees for the future of Azerbaijan's foreign trade development.

You handle the oil and gas,
we'll take care of the messy stuff.

THE BUSINESS OF LAW

LEDINGHAM
CHALMERS
SOLICITORS

For more information please contact Mike Walsh at our Baku office on +994 12 936 669

Scotland Edinburgh, Aberdeen, Inverness, **Turkey** Istanbul, **Azerbaijan** Baku, **Falkland Islands** Stanley
UK contact: Brian Cassidy or Gavin Farquhar on +44 131 200 1030
or visit us at www.ledingham-chalmers.co.uk

1.4

The Legal Framework

Ledingham Chalmers

Introduction

The legal system in Azerbaijan is in a state of transition as the country transforms itself from having a command economy controlled by Moscow from the time it was a Socialist Republic of the Soviet Union, to operating a more market-oriented economy, controlled by an independently elected executive and legislature.

The process of such historic change is complex and this has been reflected in the laws of Azerbaijan. Despite the adoption of a new constitution in 1995, certain laws and regulations of the former Soviet Union remain partially in force, although this situation is slowly but steadily changing. The constitutional authority and the status of legislation or of bodies enacting legislation may not always be clear. Furthermore, formalities in relation to the enactment of legislation may not always have been followed and all of this may affect the validity of legislative acts.

Problems may also arise when considering the relative hierarchy of laws where there are inconsistencies in two or more laws. Even with the enactment of new legislation, there can be a lack of coordination between the Parliament, the various ministries and the president's office, resulting in some laws being passed which may appear to conflict with one other. A further complication is that new laws are not consistently published or reported and thus it can be very difficult to confirm whether certain legislation is in existence or not.

The European Bank for Reconstruction and Development, the UK Know How Fund and the European Union's Technical Assistance for the CIS (TACIS) Scheme have been providing guidance to the Azerbaijani government, helping it to consolidate a sound legislative structure. Their aim is to create a legislative framework that effectively responds to the current pace of economic development, in addition to providing a solid base for the future development of a more market-oriented economic system.

Protection of foreign investments

The 1992 Law on Protection of Foreign Investments establishes the basic principles of foreign investment in Azerbaijan and guarantees unconditional legal protection to foreign investors. The basic tenet of this law is that foreign investment may be made in any type of business activity unless that activity is prohibited by Azerbaijani law. The legislation provides that foreign investments will not be subject to nationalisation by the Azerbaijani government (except where there is harm to the population or to state interests). Foreign investments will not be the subject of state requisition except in cases of natural disaster, accidents, epidemics, or other national emergencies. In the event of such nationalisation or requisition, compensation reflecting the true value of the investment at the time of the project's nationalisation or requisition will be paid in foreign currency and remitted abroad at the instructions of the foreign investor. Additionally, provision is made to guarantee a foreign investment where legislation is enacted that affects investors adversely compared to treatment under previous legislation. This provision guarantees that the investment will be regulated under the previous legislation for a further period of ten years, although this provision does not apply to changes in the tax regime, spheres of finance and credits, protection of public order, environment, public health and morals.

Azerbaijan and the United Kingdom have signed an Agreement for the Promotion and Protection of Investments. This sets out the principle that neither state shall subject the other's citizens, companies or investments to treatment less favourable than that which it accords to its own or any third parties. The Agreement provides for specific recourse to the International Centre for the Settlement of Investment Disputes, which may be seen as a more effective dispute forum for foreign investors than the Azerbaijani courts as envisaged by the domestic Law on Protection of Foreign Investments. The USA and Azerbaijan have recently signed a Bilateral Trade Agreement and an Investment Treaty that is broadly similar to the Treaty with the United Kingdom.

Constitutional guarantees

The Azerbaijan Constitution (adopted 12 November 1995) provides general protection for foreign investments and specific protection for private property (Articles 13 and 29), and contains a mandate for the 'system of free enterprise' (Article 15).

Who is considered a foreign investor?

The following persons and entities are considered as foreign investors:

- foreign legal entities;

- foreign citizens;

- persons with no citizenship;

- foreign states and international organisations;

- Azerbaijani citizens who are permanently resident abroad and registered there as subjects of business/entrepreneurial activity.

They may invest in Azerbaijan through a number of routes. They may:

- participate in a company established with Azerbaijani legal entities or
individuals (ie in a joint venture);

- establish a company in Azerbaijan that is wholly owned by foreign
investors;

- purchase companies, property, buildings, shares, bonds or other securities in accordance with Azerbaijani legislation;

- acquire rights to use land and other natural resources or other proprietary rights;

- conclude agreements with Azerbaijani legal entities or individuals spec-
ifying other forms of realising foreign investments.

There are three main ways in which a foreign investor may establish a
direct trading presence within Azerbaijan: through a joint venture, through
a wholly foreign-owned Azerbaijani legal entity, or by establishing a branch
or representative office of the foreign legal entity. These entities are looked
at in further detail in Chapter 3.7 Establishing a Business Presence.

Ownership of property

The ownership of land and buildings is dealt with in more detail in
Chapter 4.7, Property Law and Security Aspects, but the following is a
summary of who may own property in Azerbaijan.

Table 1.5.1 Property ownership in Azerbaijan

	Ownership of land permitted	Ownership of buildings permitted	Lease of land permitted	Lease of buildings permitted
Foreign citizens	no	yes, but impractical	yes	yes
Branch/representative office	no	yes	yes	yes
Wholly foreign-owned Azeri entity	yes	yes	yes	yes
Joint venture	yes	yes	yes	yes
Azeri citizens	yes	yes	yes	yes
Azeri-owned entities	yes	yes	yes	yes

Banking and currency regulations

Repatriation of profits

After tax and any other charges have been paid, all other sums legally obtained by the foreign investor are entitled to be repatriated in foreign currency according to the 1992 Law on the Protection of Foreign Investments.

The Constitution states that manats should be the only currency in use within Azerbaijan, although foreign companies may convert manats into hard currency. This may be carried out at the Baku Interbank Currency Exchange Rate and at other authorised banking establishments for foreign trade transactions, subject to some restrictions. A foreign entity or an individual may carry out their activities with the use of foreign currency after the obtaining of a foreign currency licence from the National Bank.

Azerbaijani legal entities may only open offshore bank accounts with the permission of the National Bank.

Currency restrictions

Sales and purchases within Azerbaijan by joint ventures and by wholly foreign-owned Azerbaijani entities and representative and/or branch offices of foreign companies can only be handled in manats unless a special permit has been granted by the National Bank. All hard currency must be remitted to an authorised Azerbaijani bank account, or, if the Azerbaijani entity wishes to use an offshore account, then permission from the National Bank must be sought. Export may be made on the basis of advance payments to a local bank or where an irrevocable Letter of Credit has been issued by a buyer in the name of the Azerbaijani entity. Customs restrictions only permit export of foreign currency if certain requirements are met.

As a branch/representative office has non-resident status, it has the ability to contract with both residents and non-residents in hard currency for certain transactions. There are no restrictions on the branch/representative office receiving or transferring hard currency, provided that this is remitted to an offshore account. There are certain detailed restrictions on a branch/representative office transferring hard currency out of Azerbaijan. In order for the office to receive hard currency in a local authorised bank for use in the provision of goods and services in Azerbaijan, it must obtain a permit from the National Bank.

Severe penalties for failure to comply with currency regulations apply.

1.5

Privatisation: Recent Developments and Future Perspectives

Glenn S Kolleeny and Kamal Mamedzade,
Salans Hertzfeld & Heilbronn

Azerbaijan has yet to begin the process of privatising its largest blue chip companies, the most attractive to foreign investors. Privatisation in Azerbaijan continues to be governed by the State Privatisation Program for 1995–1998 (the '1995–1998 Program'), pursuant to which many small and medium-sized companies, as well as a few larger enterprises such as the Garadag Cement Plant, the sole domestic producer of cement, were privatised. A new 'Law on Privatisation of State Property' was passed by the Milli Majlis (National Assembly) in its third reading on 16 May 2000 and is expected to come into force soon. A draft of the new 'State Program for Privatisation of State Property' (the 'Program') was submitted by the Minister of State Property to the Prime Minister earlier in May 2000 and is expected to be approved shortly.

Privatisation in 1999 and 2000

Applying the 1995–1998 Program, the State Property Committee (SPC) undertook the privatisation of several large-scale enterprises in 1999. The largest of these was the Garadag Cement Plant, a privatisation that was, for a long time, embroiled in controversy. The investment tender for Garadag Cement was won by Garadag Holding, a company established by the principals of the Baku Group, a group of US investors active in Azerbaijan for several years. Nonetheless, the SPC ultimately entered into a sale and purchase agreement to sell the 56 per cent interest offered in the investment tender to Holderbank Financiere Glaris, which also prevailed in the cash tender for the state's remaining 30 per cent interest. Garadag Holding and the Baku Group are contesting Holderbank's acquisition of Garadag Cement in the Supreme Court of the State of New York, and Garadag Cement was hit by labour unrest, including a strike and seizure of the plant. Other large enterprises privatised in 1999 include Baku Steel and Baku Plant for Non-Liquid Transformers.

The slow pace of privatisation in 1999, as well as allegations of wrong-doing in connection with the privatisation of Garadag Cement, led to the decision to disband the SPC and establish a new Ministry for State Property (MSP). The MSP might have the authority to actively promote privatisation of the blue chip companies. On 25 April 2000 President Aliyev signed a resolution authorising the MSP to transfer a unit of the State Concern Metallurgy, engaged in the processing of ferrous metals, and specifically provided for participation of foreign investors in the course of this privatisation. Also, on 14 June 2000 the President signed a decree on the establishment and management of the joint stock company (JSC) Baku Electricity Network. Under the same decree the MSP was authorised to hold an open tender to place newly established JSCs under long-term external management.

New Law on Privatisation of State Property (the 'Law')

Under the Law, announcements of privatisation of state property shall be disseminated through official mass media (which, for example, may be state-owned TV stations, official newspapers such as *Azerbaijan*, *Respublika* or *Khalq Qazeti*) at least 30 days prior to the proposed date of sale of property.

Under the Law the following groups are authorised to take part in privatisation:

- citizens of the Azerbaijani Republic and foreign states, as well as stateless persons;

- all legal persons registered under Azerbaijani legislation (except for legal persons, where more than 20 per cent of the share capital is owned by the state, central and local executive authorities and municipalities);

- foreign legal persons.

The Law defines 'foreign investors' as citizens of foreign states, foreign legal entities and their representative offices, as well as Azerbaijani legal entities with more than 50 per cent foreign investment. To participate in the purchase of state property, foreign investors are required to submit a number of privatisation options corresponding to the number of privati-sation vouchers to be submitted for cancellation. This contrasts with the previous general view that Azerbaijani legal entities, even with 100 per cent foreign investment, would not be required to submit privatisation options to participate in privatisation of state property.

The Law also determines state property, which will not be privatised and will remain in the ownership of the state as, *inter alia*, including:

- soil, forests and water reserves;

- patent, standardisation and measurement enterprises;

- natural reserves and preservations;

- highways, bridges and tunnels of state importance.

Under the Law, sale and purchase agreements to be entered with purchasers of state property shall, along with terms and conditions established by each specific tender or auction, include the following:

- information on both the seller (which, in the text of the Law is referred to as 'the central executive authority', but will most probably be the MSP (this matter will be clarified by a presidential decree on implementation of the Law), and the buyer;

- name, place of location, land covered by, composition and value of privatised property;

- number, category and nominal value of shares of joint stock companies;

- methods of payment for and rules of transfer of property into buyer's ownership;

- obligations of the parties and terms and conditions for execution thereof.

The Draft Privatisation Program (the 'Program')

For the first time the Program will introduce a special committee. This will be the State Committee for Control over Privatisation, composed of top officials of various ministries. Exact composition of the Committee, as well as regulations applicable to its operations, will be approved by the President.

Unlike the 1995–1998 Privatisation Program, the Draft Program is not designed to cover any specific period and, upon becoming effective, will be in force for an indefinite period of time starting from 15 May 2000.

The Program distinguishes between four types of property:

- property, privatisation of which is prohibited;

- property owned by the state prior to the date of decision on privatisation;

- property to be privatised by Presidential decree upon proposal of the MSP;

- property to be privatised by decision of the MSP.

The Program also distinguishes between seven forms of privatisation of state property:

1. Privatisation of state enterprises by individual projects. This method will be applied to large state enterprises and 51 per cent or more shares of the company will be privatised by a strategic investor. Enterprises to be privatised under this method will be determined by the President.
2. Privileged sale of shares to employees. This method implies the submission of a certain number of privatisation vouchers for shares of the company. The number of privatisation vouchers to be submitted by each employee shall be calculated as follows:

   - price of one privatisation voucher is established through dividing total value of state property sold at previous two consecutive check auctions by total number of privatisation vouchers submitted at these two auctions;
   - total number of privatisation vouchers to be submitted for acquisition of shares to be disposed of under a privileged scheme is determined through dividing total value of shares to be privatised by price of one voucher;
   - total number of privatisation vouchers to be submitted for acquisition of shares by each employee is determined through dividing total number of vouchers into overall number of employees of a particular enterprise.

3. Sale of state property through specialised voucher and cash auctions.
4. Sale of state property through auctions. Unlike sale through specialised voucher and cash auctions, where each participant acquires certain number of shares either for cash or vouchers, there is only one winner in sale through auctions – the person bidding the highest number of vouchers or the largest amount of cash. Where no offers have been received or the property has not been sold at the first two auctions, the MSP shall have the right to reduce the sale price of the property by 10, 25, 50 and 75 per cent, respectively, for the third, forth, fifth and sixth auctions.
5. Sale of state property through investment tenders. Generally not less than 50 per cent of the property of the privatised enterprise will be sold through the investment tender. Conditions to be satisfied during implementation of the investment plan will in each particular case be determined by either the President or the MSP. Right of ownership of the property will be transferred to the winner of the investment tender only upon fulfillment of all conditions of the investment plan, and the winner will not have any right of disposal of the property in question.
6. Sale of leased state property. Where the lease was made before 1 January 1993, sale of the company shall be carried out as follows:

   - small enterprise: 60 per cent (sale at nominal value for cash to lessees), 15 per cent (privileged sale to employees), 25 per cent (transferable to employees);

- joint stock companies: 55 per cent (sale at nominal value for cash to lessees), 20 per cent (privileged sale to employees), 25 per cent (transferable to employees).

Where the lease was made after 1 January 1993, state property shall be offered to employees of a leased enterprise at 100 per cent value.

Leased state property other than leased enterprises (eg, buildings, facilities, equipment etc) shall be privatised by the MSP under the following procedure:

- leased property is first to be offered at 100 per cent value to lessee. Where lessee consents to purchase the property, he should pay the value within 30 days from the date of the offer;
- where lessee refuses to purchase the property or fails to pay value thereof within said 30 day period, such property goes to privatisation through voucher or check auctions or is sold with the enterprise.

7. Declaration of the state enterprise bankrupt and subsequent sale. Decision on this form of sale is to be adopted either by the President (upon proposal of the MSP) or the MSP itself (upon consent of state committee exercising control over the course of the privatisation process.)

Like the 1995–1998 Privatisation Program, the Program reserves 15 per cent of the shares of a privatised enterprise for purchase by employees (and, as mentioned above, 15 per cent and 20 per cent for small enterprises and joint stock companies established on the basis of leased enterprises). Both the 1995–1998 Program and the Program generally mandates a 55 per cent voucher/30 per cent cash split of the remaining shares. However, depending on whether the President or the MSP privatises a particular entity, a different division of state shares to be sold for vouchers as opposed to cash can be established on a case-by-case basis, particularly for larger enterprises. This is intended to give the Government a considerable amount of flexibility in maximising revenues from the privatisation of Azerbaijan's blue chips.

However, investors and investment funds which have already purchased large numbers of privatisation vouchers, and the options required for their exercise in privatisation tenders, may not be able to use them in tenders for the most attractive companies. If a purely cash tender for one of the major enterprises were announced, the market might well adopt the view that vouchers would not be accepted at tenders for the most attractive companies, leading to a further collapse in the already very low value of vouchers and options. The fact that privatisation vouchers and options have dropped to record low prices apparently reflects the market's scepticism on the likelihood of privatisation of blue chip companies.

Unlike the 1995–1998 Privatisation Program, the Program distinguishes between only two categories of enterprises – small and large, as Table 1.6.1 illustrates.

Table 1.6.1 The Draft Privatisation Program's division of small and large enterprises by number of employees

Field of Operations	Division based upon number of employees	
	Small	Large
Industry	Up to 150	Over 151
Transportation, communication & construction	Up to 75	Over 76
Trade and services	Up to 50	Over 51

Participation of foreign investors

The Program still requires submission by foreign investors of options for taking part in privatisation of state property. However, it makes clear that no options are to be surrendered in course of sale of vouchers and/or state property between foreign investors, as well as foreign investors and local players. Also, under the Program foreign investors have the right to participate in privatisation with net profit obtained in Azerbaijan without any requirement for submission of options.

Land and debt restructuring

Under the Program, owners of privatised enterprises are entitled to exercise a right of first refusal with respect to the purchase of the land underlying such enterprises. Of course, it should be noted that while privatised companies may purchase land subject to these and other restrictions, foreign investors (and stateless persons) are not permitted to own land in Azerbaijan. This discriminatory regime is also unfortunate in light of the importance which foreign investors place upon ownership of land as evidenced by recent experience in other states of the CIS, such as the failed privatisation of the blue-chip, Almalyk Copper & Lead Plant in Uzbekistan, which was tendered without its real estate assets and raw material base.

An additional condition to the purchase of many state-owned enterprises is assumption of outstanding loans and debts, which must be repaid within a stipulated period of time. Under the Program, debts of privatised enterprises outstanding on 1 January 2000 can be restructured for a period ranging from 25 to 99 years.

Regulations on the circulation of privatisation vouchers and options

Under the 'Rules On Regulation of the Circulation of State Privatisation Vouchers' effective 28 January 2000, sale and purchase of privatisation vouchers may only be effected by licensed professionals. Persons who possess more than 400 privatisation vouchers and do not have receipts for the purchase of the privatisation vouchers were obliged to register their privatisation vouchers with the State Securities Committee (SSC) within 45 days. Vouchers may only be used to purchase shares in privatising state enterprises if they have been deposited with the National Depositary Center (NDC). In order to participate in voucher auctions or investment tenders holders of more than 100,000 privatisation vouchers must present them to the NDC, at the latest, 30 days prior to the last day on which vouchers will be accepted as payment for the enterprise being privatised.

New rules have also been adopted to regulate the sale and use of privatisation options, which foreign investors are required to use to participate in investment, voucher and cash tenders as well as in connection with purchases of shares of privatised companies in the secondary market. The 'Rules On Regulation of Issuance, Circulation and Cancellation of State Privatisation Options' (effective 29 January 2000) provides that at registration, a buyer of options must present, *inter alia*, a receipt for the prepayment of 5 per cent of the value of options (on the date of the filing of the investor's application to acquire the options). Submission of bids to purchase shares in privatising companies must be considered by the SSC within 3 working days, and if the bidder is accepted the whole option price is paid. If the bid is rejected the 5 per cent deposit is returned to the bidder.

The official price of an option is defined as equal to the average market price of a privatisation voucher on a given day (as of 28 June 2000 the price of an option was AZM6,750 or US$1.5).

The number of options required to be submitted at privatisation tenders as well as in connection with purchases of shares of privatised joint stock companies on the secondary markets has also been clarified as follows:

- voucher auctions for shares of joint-stock companies – 1 option for each voucher tendered;
- cash auctions for shares of joint-stock companies – the minimum share/voucher ratio set for the voucher auction for shares of the particular enterprise;
- the secondary market – the minimum share/voucher ratio set for the voucher;

- privatisation of small enterprises or purchase on the secondary market of small enterprises – option price set on the date of the sale-purchase agreement with respect to the enterprise based on the entire value of the enterprise determined by the MSP;

- investment tenders etc – as determined on a case-by-case basis by the MSP in conjunction with the SSC.

Delivery of options is not required for the purchase of small enterprises or transactions involving shares of privatised companies among foreign investors.

Conclusion

The 1995–1998 Program was relatively successful in quickly privatising many smaller enterprises. The Draft Program holds much promise for the successful privatisation of many state-owned enterprises, including large blue chip ones. However, the government of Azerbaijan has not yet demonstrated its determination to actually privatise its major state-owned enterprises. According to a recent interview of the President of the state concern, Azerkimya (Azeri Chemistry), it is expected that various companies of the chemical industry will become open for privatisation upon a special presidential decree to be issued in the near future. With hydrocarbon resources at record prices, it is clear that Azerbaijan could successfully privatise its largest and most attractive assets.

However, foreign interest has been deterred by the discriminatory practice of requiring only foreign investors to deliver privatisation options in cash, voucher and investment tenders as well as for the purchase of shares of privatised companies in the secondary market, and the ban on foreign ownership of land. Finally, the privatisation process has been tarnished by allegations of impropriety in connection with the Garadag Cement privatisation.

Only privatisation of the blue chip companies will provide the foundation for their commercial viability. Elimination of market-distorting, discriminatory measures would enable Azerbaijan to maximise its budgetary receipts from the sale of state-owned enterprises, which may also become substantial taxpayers – both of profit taxes paid directly by the enterprises, and of payroll taxes generated by increased employment at higher wages.

The Financial and Banking Sectors

The National Bank of Azerbaijan

Introduction

Since 1995 the economic reform programme in Azerbaijan has successfully achieved macroeconomic stability and the liberalisation of economic activity. This success has created favourable conditions for economic growth in the country. The radical reforms instigated by the government have been instrumental in gaining the co-operation of international financial institutions that, having witnessed the Azerbaijani government's determination to rapidly introduce a market economy, offered financial assistance. In doing so, the pace of reform has been greatly accelerated and today, approximately 100 countries are trading partners with Azerbaijan.

Financial reform

The radical transition of the Azerbaijani economy to a free market system was instigated by the president of the Republic, Geidar Aliyev, in 1994. The reforms were given impetus by the surge in investment that accompanied the growth of international participation in exploiting Azerbaijan's rich oil resources.

Financial sector reform

Reform of the financial sector is fundamental to the successful transition to a liberal market economy. The Azerbaijani government is well aware of the need to create a robust financial framework for the reforms. At the core of the transition to a market economy should be a financial system that is capable of effectively mobilising resources for economic use, imposing strict financial discipline in the economy, and providing a wide range of services for entrepreneurs. Creating such a system is of paramount importance in the context of broadening international relations, attracting investment, and achieving full participation in the world economy. For this reason, reforming the financial system was a prominent feature of the reform programme that began in 1994 (considerably later than in other FSU (Former Soviet Union) countries). This programme contained a package of measures to help save Azerbaijan from social and economic crisis and to help bring about the transition to a market economy.

The reforms, however, were hindered by the actions of the Armenian government, who supported the separatists of the Nagorno–Karabakh region, which had severe social repercussions – more than one million people were injured or killed during the conflict. This meant that resources had to be diverted to solving the immediate problems such as the relocation of refugees. Nevertheless, Azerbaijan was able to make quick progress in the first stages of the reform programme, thanks to stability in the domestic political arena, the government's well-balanced foreign policy and strict budgetary and monetary policy. These policies in turn resulted in macroeconomic and financial stability in the country and were accompanied by price liberalisation and the opening-up of the country's foreign trade and currency regimes.

Monetary policy

The stringent monetary policy adopted by the National Bank of Azerbaijan (NBA) put a stop to the growth of the money supply, thus slowing the rate of inflation and significantly bolstering the national currency, the manat (AZM). The anti-inflationary measures taken by the NBA included tighter controls on credit issue, stricter demands on banks, and a reduction in the financing of the budget deficit. As a result, inflation fell and the manat stabilised. This improvement in the basic indicators of socio-economic performance attracted greater investment in the national economy.

It is well worth noting that the process of price and exchange rate stabilisation has been remarkably consistent. Since 1994 the rate of inflation has steadily fallen year-on-year. In 1994 annual inflation was 1880 per cent; by the beginning of 1996 it had fallen to a mere 2 per cent. The devaluation of the manat in 1995 played an important role in reducing the inflation rate. In 1997 the exchange rate of the manat to the US dollar rose by 5.1 per cent; in 1998, the rate was up only 0.1 per cent. These statistics are the best of their kind compared to the rest of the former Soviet Union. With inflation under control and the manat stable, a sound basis was created on which economic growth could continue. Thus in 1999 the country's GDP rose by 7.4 per cent compared to the previous year.

Also on the increase is the level of industrial production (a growth of 3.5 per cent on the figures for 1998) and agricultural production (up by 7.1 per cent). In 1999 the amount of capital invested by the Azerbaijani government in various sectors of the economy was down 3 per cent on the previous year. In the same year the amount of foreign investment totalled AZM2.371 billion (53.6 per cent of all capital investment).

The oil and gas industry has been a key factor in attracting foreign investment. Large-scale petrochemical projects have rejuvenated the influx of investment into the country, and have created favourable conditions for growth in related areas of the economy. The growth and restructuring of these and other important sectors has been the central focus of the government's reform programme.

The policy of strict but measured monetary control has featured heavily throughout, with the National Bank taking decisive steps to implement further means of both monetary and credit control. In 1999 the NBA effectively managed the country's money supply through credit auctions, a market in short-term government bonds, a currency market, and by introducing norms for the management of international reserves. In 1999 the NBA, encouraged by positive economic trends over several years, relaxed its monetary policy in an effort to stimulate production. While centralised control of interest rates remained the fundamental instrument with which the NBA regulated the money supply, the basic rate was cut on 1 January 1999 from 14 per cent to 10 per cent. The corresponding reduction in the rates offered by lending institutions resulted in a drop in the average rate on a short-term credit from 25 per cent to 20 per cent (as of 1 January 2000) and on long-term credit from 20 per cent to 19.3 per cent. This cut in the interest rate led to a substantial growth in borrowing: as of 1 January 1999 total borrowing amounted to AZM2126.5 billion.

However, credit extension must be kept under control: the more unbacked credit that is issued, the greater the risk of financial collapse. The National Bank's aim in issuing more credit is to actively manage liquidity in the banking sector. In order to carry out activities in the real sector of the economy, the banks need lending resources, which are essentially formed out of the savings of the country's population. However, people have been reluctant to deposit their savings in the commercial banks because of the lack of a deposit insurance scheme. In an effort to rectify this, the NBA has set up a deposit insurance fund, which, it is hoped, will stimulate the influx of savings into the banking system.

Liberalisation of foreign trade and currency exchange

The government is determinedly pursuing a course towards liberalisation of foreign trade and currency exchange. The law entitled 'On Currency

Regulation in Azerbaijan', which was passed in 1994, laid the foundation for the liberalisation of the currency regime in the country. Consequently, the requirement for the compulsory sale of foreign currency earnings by enterprises to a special government fund was abolished. In practical terms, this meant that the manat became a convertible currency. The liberalisation of the currency regime was a key factor in attracting foreign investment into Azerbaijan.

The stabilisation of the manat was a major achievement of the economic reform programme. The decisive factors in achieving this stability were, as has already been mentioned, the liberalisation of the currency regime, the creation of a versatile currency market and the accumulation of sufficient reserves. As has been the case in previous years, in 1999 the NBA managed to effectively regulate supply and demand on the foreign currency markets. The total volume of trading on the foreign exchange markets was US$496.6 million. On the Baku Interbank Currency Exchange the trade turnover was US$290 million, and on the Open Interbank Currency Exchange the volume of trade reached US$206 million. Across all the currency markets the total amount of currency traded exceeded US$1 billion. Thanks to the interventions by the National Bank, supply and demand of foreign currency on these markets was effectively managed. However, over recent years the market for foreign currency has become much more self-regulatory, and the interventions on the part of the National Bank have become significantly less frequent. This has enabled optimal use of the official reserves.

In August and September of 1999 the country's foreign exchange market went through a stability crisis in the wake of the devaluation of the Russian rouble. A sharp increase in the volume of imports from the Russian Federation, together with a shortage in the supply of foreign currency earnings from exports resulting from the collapse in oil prices, led to a trade deficit of US$450 million. As the demand for foreign currency grew, the pressure on the country's foreign exchange market increased. Demand exceeded supply by more than US$120 million. Luckily, however, the measures implemented by the NBA were successful in averting a fall in the exchange rate of the manat and stabilised it in relation to the US dollar. It is a tribute to the effectiveness of the National Bank's policy that it has consistently maintained sufficiently high levels of foreign currency reserves. Azerbaijan's official gold and foreign currency reserves are currently in line with international norms – that is to say they are sufficient to finance imports for six months.

As previously mentioned, an important facet of Azerbaijan's economic policy is the liberalisation of the currency regime: there are currently no restrictions on buying and selling foreign currency. This applies to the local population, as well as to people from the rest of the world – there is complete freedom to convert the manat into other currencies and vice versa. Moreover, foreign exchange is facilitated by the sufficient numbers of foreign exchange bureaux in the country. Thanks to the liberalisation of currency controls, foreign investors can now repatriate their profits without hindrance.

Government borrowing

A further important factor in regulating the country's money markets has been the creation of a market in government securities. Government borrowing is not high – it is currently at AZM78.1 billion, and covers 22.4 per cent of the budget deficit. This is typical of the general policy of restraint on the accumulation of government debt. In 1999 the earnings received from the issue of government short-term bonds were predominantly used to pay off government debt accumulated by the early redemption of other securities that had reached maturity. This has been possible because the budget deficit is covered by other sources, namely oil dividends, earnings from privatisation, and lending by the World Bank. The yield on government securities is maintained at a level close to the rate of refinancing by the National Bank.

Securities

As far as a market in corporate securities is concerned, it is virtually non-existent because of shortcomings in its infrastructure (including the regulatory framework), the lack of technology and the small numbers of private enterprises that are able to issue securities with high enough ratings. In spite of this, a good basis has been established on which to address a whole range of issues associated with the creation of a stock market. In 1999 a securities commission was set up, whose task it is to co-ordinate and encourage efforts in this area.

The banking sector

Reform of the banking sector

The importance of the need for a developed banking system to ensure the proper workings of the financial markets has already been mentioned. As with all the post-Soviet economies, Azerbaijan's financial system has had to cope with the legacies left to it by central planning and artificial distortions in the economy. Despite the radical transformation of the role of banks in the economy, the creation of a two-tier banking system (with the National Bank as the first tier, regulating the commercial banks in the second tier), the many laws passed to regulate banking activity and the independence of the National Bank, Azerbaijan's financial system still remains relatively undeveloped. Originally the four specialised government banks dominated the banking system, controlling over 80 per cent of all operations, but by 1999 this figure had dropped to 60 per cent. The main reforms of the banking system began in 1996, covering the following areas:

- the creation of an appropriate legislative framework;

- a special programme for the reorganisation of government banks;

- tougher requirements on the consolidation of capital; and

- alignment with international standards in banking affairs.

There are currently 70 banks in Azerbaijan, of which 13 are partially backed by foreign capital – four of these, moreover, are backed wholly by foreign capital. Foreign banks in general show a great deal of interest in opening subsidiary and filial banks in Azerbaijan.

Due to the underdevelopment of the stock market and the lack of investment funds and insurance companies, the banking system in Azerbaijan is the sole embodiment of the country's financial system. The money and capital markets, insurance markets and trust funds are still in their infancy. In light of this, the government and the NBA have developed a multi-faceted programme of reform to address the shortcomings in the country's financial sector. The main aims of this programme are reforming the banking system, achieving a much greater rate of growth in the financial markets and creating a wider variety of institutions and markets.

With these priorities in mind, the National Bank is concentrating on the following:

- restructuring state banks;

- addressing the problem of payment default and bad debt;

- creating a stable and reliable private banking system in order to inject resources into the development of the private sector of the economy;

- further liberalising banking activity and speeding up the development of financial markets; and

- training and developing human resources.

Bank privatisation

It is clear that the restructuring of the state banks is a fundamental part of the financial reforms. The four state banks are undergoing a special programme of fundamental restructuring and management reform designed to improve their position in the changing financial landscape.

Ultimately these banks will be privatised by the sale of the shares held by the government. The preparations for the privatisation of the International Bank of Azerbaijan – the largest of the state banks – are now in their final stages. This bank has significantly improved its financial position and consolidated its place on the markets. Its proposed sale in the year 2000 is attracting the attention of many foreign investors, including those with strategic interests, such as the European Bank for Reconstruction and Development (EBRD).

In the year 2000 the remaining three banks, the Azerbaijan Commercial Savings Bank, the Azerbaijan Agricultural Industrial Bank, and the Azerbaijan Industrial Investment Bank, are set to merge. This move should help improve the financial position of these banks as well as solve the problems related to credit given to the government sector, which occurred as a result of state intervention in the lending policies of these banks.

A key feature of the banking reforms is the agglomeration of the commercial banks' authorised capital stocks. Currently the minimum capital requirement for a commercial bank already operating is US$2 million; for a start-up bank the minimum is US$5 million. These requirements will naturally be accompanied by a greater concentration of capital in the banking system. At present the consolidation of capital by the private commercial banks is approximately AZM500 billion (US$125 million).

Banking services

In an effort to encourage competition and promote the entry of new banking services and technologies into the market, the NBA has liberalised access to the Azerbaijani banking sector by foreign banks. 1997 and 1998 were particularly active years in terms of the inflow of foreign capital into the Azerbaijani banking system. According to data from 1 January 2000, the total amount of foreign capital invested into the banking system was 20 per cent of all capital, or AZM113 billion (approximately US$30 million). Financial institutions from Turkey, Russia, the UK and Iran are currently the main foreign investors in the Azerbaijani banking system.

Since 1998 there has been a noticeable change in the institutional make-up of the banking sector, with the appearance of the first 'non-bank' lending institutions in the form of credit unions. Currently over 100 non-bank institutions have been awarded licences to operate, mostly in the farming sector.

Several changes have also occurred in the regulatory framework of the country's banking system. As an active participant in the Basel Committee on Banking Supervision, the NBA is actively drawing on world experience of banking and banking systems. New standards are being adopted on the classification of assets, dividend policies and liquidity requirements. Furthermore, from the year 2000 the Azerbaijani banking system will start working to international accounting standards.

Today the Azerbaijani banking system, while still experiencing quite natural teething problems, is in a position to offer a comparatively good range of banking services to foreign investors. For example:

- the majority of the country's commercial banks have a broad network of correspondent banking arrangements with foreign banks, including the leading banks of Europe and the USA, and successfully carry out foreign trade operations and other transactions in both local and international currencies;

- the banks can carry out currency conversion operations through the various institutions of the foreign exchange market without restrictions of any kind; and

- the banks carry out investment repatriation operations in accordance with the law. Enterprises may freely transfer profits from their investments in Azerbaijan to their home country after all their tax obligations have been met.

International financial institutions such as the International Financial Corporation and the EBRD have declared an interest in co-operating with the private banking sector in Azerbaijan. They have already taken the decision to open lines of credit to selected local banks and to assist the development of small and medium-sized enterprises.

1.7

The Securities Market

Heydar Babayev, Chairman of the State Committee for Securities

Introduction

One of the principal components of the economic reform programme in Azerbaijan is the development of the securities market. Little attention was paid in the past to the securities market, but the experience of East European and Commonwealth of Independent States (CIS) countries has shown that the health of the securities market is a good indicator of the state of the economy as a whole.

At present, Azerbaijan's securities market is in the initial stage of formation. In terms of capitalisation, defined as the total volume of securities in circulation in relation to GDP, then Azerbaijan's securities market is at 3 per cent of GDP – a level noticeably lower than the level in developed securities markets but somewhat higher than found in other CIS countries.

According to experts' estimates, the market's capitalisation should reach US$20–25 billion, based on the following line of reasoning. SOCAR, the state oil company, is expected to have an annual income of US$1 billion, or by western standards a capitalisation of US$20 billion. Aztelecom, the large telecommunications group, has 250,000 telephone lines, each of which is worth US$1,000 in terms of capitalisation. The mobile telecommunications companies Bakcell and Azercell have over 100,000 telephone lines in total, each estimated at US$3,000 in the West. Correspondingly, the initial level of the market's capitalisation in Azerbaijan can be estimated at US$500 million.

The structure of the market

The securities market in Azerbaijan can be separated into three sections: the government securities market, the market for privatisation vouchers and the corporate securities market.

Government securities

The government securities market is represented by the government's short-term T-bills. However, the volume and duration of their distribution are not attractive enough for investors, especially not international investors.

Privatisation vouchers

The market for privatisation vouchers and options is more active. Each citizen of Azerbaijan has been given four vouchers, bringing the total number of vouchers in circulation to 30 million. Practically more than 40 per cent of all issued vouchers are at the disposal of foreign investors, who have invested tens of millions of dollars into these securities. But this is of limited duration as activity was due to cease in August 2000.

Corporate securities

The most promising area for the near future is the corporate securities market. Its development is related to the pace of privatisation. At present, over 10,000 small enterprises and over 500 medium-sized enterprises have been privatised. The privatisation of five large-scale enterprises and banks follows, including the International Bank of Azerbaijan, the shares of which should be classed as the country's first 'blue chips'.

The government securities market and trade of vouchers at present comprise the greatest part of the volume traded on Azerbaijan's securities market. Together with the increase in privatisation activity, the sales volume of corporate securities will also increase.

Regulation and future development

The basis for the regulation of the securities market is the Law on Securities, signed by Aliyev on 9 September 1998, and the Presidential Decree of 30 December 1998 on the establishment of the State Committee on Securities, which answers to the president. This committee will carry out the regulation of all relations on the securities market in Azerbaijan and create a legal basis for the securities market.

There are currently over 10 licensed investment and brokerage companies as well as over 30 banks operating in Azerbaijan. Besides these, over 200 independent brokers are operating (trading mainly in privatisation vouchers). Although the share of trading volume of the professional firms that are part-foreign-owned is only 20 per cent, this 20 per cent comprises the greatest part of the volume of securities transactions. This is why the effective development of the securities market will depend on how well the rights and interests of investors are guaranteed and protected.

Another important element in the development of the securities market is related to the development of its infrastructure, including the creation of structures for the trading, registration and custody of securities.

In February 2000 the Baku Stock Exchange (BSE) was founded. The founders of BSE include some banks and investment companies. BSE plans to organise trading of government securities, privatisation vouchers, corporate securities and promise renotes.

Custody activities are carried out by the National Depository Centre and Partner Investment company, which carries out all kinds of depository and custody services.

The further development of the securities market in Azerbaijan will depend not only on the development of the infrastructure of the market, but also on lessening the risk involved and on protecting the rights and interests of investors and participants in the market.

This can be achieved through the realisation of the principles of transparency of information in the securities market, through the improvement of the operating rules for the sale of securities and their accounting, and through the further development of a system of taxation to regulate the securities market.

Scottish Caspian Trade (SCT) is an industry led initiative, supported by Scottish Enterprise Energy Group, which provides Scottish based companies with a shared office facility in Baku, Azerbaijan.

SCT operates on a membership basis and eligible companies can join for a fee of £5,000 per annum. Services to non-member companies (including market research, translation and arranging meetings) are also available on a one-off basis.

For further information, please contact:
Pauline Geddes
Scottish Enterprise Energy Group
10 Queen's Road
Aberdeen AB15 4ZT
Tel: +44 (0) 1224 626 310
Fax: +44 (0) 1224 627 006
Email: pauline.geddes@scotent.co.uk
Website: www.se-energy.co.uk

Business Culture

Tom McKeown, Export Promoter, Trade Partners UK

Friendship

There are two adages which encapsulate the British attitude to business: never mix it with pleasure and never do it with friends. In Azerbaijan the attitude is different; it is a pleasure to do business and business is much easier to do with friends since they are already friends – they are known to you.

The British, on the other hand, tend to find it difficult to make friendships with business acquaintances. We tend to be rather 'standoffish', to keep things separate. In this way we hope not to expose our vulnerabilities, thinking that this will keep others from exploiting us. This approach is inappropriate for successful business in Azerbaijan, where business is nearly always better conducted with friends.

Negotiation

In order to conduct business successfully in Azerbaijan, relationships must first be built. Though this is contrary to all that we learn at home it is the first important step. The second is to remember that you should never sit down to negotiate without being ready to get up and leave the negotiating table without giving notice. This may seem an unnecessary caution, but it cannot be overemphasised. You should be ready to exercise the principle of being 'ready to leave' at any moment, whether it be before any business has been concluded, or after three years of business, when unreasonable demands are being made. This is never an easy option to exercise, even in your native tongue, and so is all the more difficult in a culture foreign to ours. It is, however among the most valuable of negotiating skills, along with the 'power of silence'. The power of silence can be a valuable asset when doing business in Azerbaijan, but many foreigners find it alien to their culture and therefore difficult to use as a negotiating tool.

Employees

In the UK we tend to expect an employee to undertake more than one task. Unfortunately, this is not a common expectation of employers of any workforce in the former Soviet Union, and Azerbaijan is not yet an exception – although there are encouraging signs.

Under the Soviet system, an employee had one, and only one, task to undertake; in order to undertake another task, authority had to be given. Such authority could be granted by few, and often required counter-signing. This procedure of 'license' had to be repeated for each and every occasion that an 'extra' task was required of the individual.

Clearly, such an attitude is more than a little foreign to UK business practices hence the importance of understanding the recent history of Azerbaijan so that the basis for change from single to multi-tasking can be presented fairly to employees. We are all nervous of change, even when we know that change is for the better. Change from single to multi-tasking is not seen as good or bad – it is regarded as being in uncharted waters and resistance can therefore be enormous.

Employee sustenance

In the Soviet era, employees were not only fed, but also housed by their employers and it is still common for workers to be fed by them. However, a word of caution: new tax laws suggest that such generosity will soon no longer benefit from the tax-free status it has enjoyed to date.

While feeding staff at work may seem a little strange to us, one should remember that it is not so very long ago that employees were housed by their employers in the UK. This is still the case of some farm-workers and tied cottages are not yet a thing of the past.

Out of hours

One of the more unusual business practices when working in Azerbaijan is that on many occasions you may be invited to participate in activities that appear to have little, if any, relationship to business. These may include joining colleagues on a picnic, playing football one Saturday afternoon, and all manner of games or social events. Participation is regarded as honourable; all too often, foreigners are seen as being aloof, unwilling participants. Activities are often organised especially for foreigners and it is easy to see how offence can be taken when offers are turned down.

Corruption

One of the greatest worries for an investor, foreign or national, is the question of corruption. This is a throwback to Soviet times. While officially hostile to it, the system actually fostered corruption. Of course this is denied by those who were then in power.

It is not necessary to look as far as Azerbaijan for examples of corruption; we have had many cases in Brussels, and have even appointed a commission to look into the question. Indeed it is arguable that the European system, while also officially opposed to it, similarly fosters corruption.

What is different is the fact that since we are operating in a different environment, our response to corruption is less assured. We are nervous of any negative outcome and are uncertain of the repercussions of any course of action we choose to follow. It is this 'weakness' that is exploited, ruthlessly and understandably, by those who can sense frailties and vulnerabilities. This has happened simply as a result of the demise of the Soviet system where, until the break-up, all was provided; now it is not. It now costs much more to live than the average salary provides for. The shortfall must somehow be made up and what easier target than the businessperson?

There are encouraging signs that the government is rising to the challenge, and it is developing a programme to address the issue of corruption. Getting rid of corruption will take time, and it will not happen overnight, but the initiative is a start and should be encouraged.

On a more practical note, there are ways to counter corruption. Not paying up is one way. Obtaining the name, rank, number and all other details – supervising or commanding officer's name, rank, etc – of the soliciting party is another way, so that if you are required to pay, at least there are records as to who and what amount has been paid. In my experience, such an approach has normally ended the matter with no money changing hands. I have also found that a greater respect is earned as a result.

Choosing the right partner

Of all the important issues in starting a business in Azerbaijan, the most important by far is to have the right partner. This is somewhat less important if you are going to be in the country and running the business yourself. But in order to be able to leave the day-to-day operation of the business, you must have complete confidence in the staff you employ. The right partner can be trusted to look after your affairs during your absence, take care of all the issues that tend to alarm the foreigner in us and generally do things in your best interests. Of course finding such a partner is difficult enough on home ground, let alone abroad, but it is well worth taking the time to find the right partner.

Seeking the right partner

To help with the problem of finding the right partner, there are various agencies which are able to introduce parties. Some specialise in such introductions and will act as intermediaries. Although they are not cheap, they are often an extremely reliable way to gain a foothold in the new market. They act as the partner, they know the ropes and have offices in Baku. However, they may not be able to represent your company if they already represent a competitor – even if you had wanted them to do so.

There are several advantages of such an arrangement:

- your exposure is kept to a minimum;
- the levels of commitment are reduced – there is no need for a continuous presence;
- effort in the new market is kept to a minimum.

Of course, every option has its disadvantages:

- you lose some control over the way in which your business is conducted;
- levels of commitment shown by others may not match your needs and/or expectations;
- effort given to the new market may not be sufficient.

On balance, however, the most sensible approach to any new market is one of 'committed caution'. Representation is chosen to introduce the company to the market, and depending upon the success that is reached through such an arrangement, full company offices can later be established. This is by far the least costly way to establish a presence in the new market.

Operating costs

The costs of setting up an office in Azerbaijan are not inconsiderable. And the contemplation of doing so is not for the faint-hearted. Office rental can be anything from US$500 to US$5,000 per month. Expatriate staff, where used, are often far from inexpensive. If expatriates are hired, they should be sensitive to the culture and preferably speak a smattering of Azeri, or at least be willing to learn.

Accommodation costs for expatriate staff can vary as much as office space costs.

Table 1.9.1 shows the staffing costs for five categories of occupation during 1999.

Table 1.9.1 Staffing costs, 1999

Occupation	Cost per month
Secretarial	US$250–300
Drivers	US$250–300
General workers	US$300–500
Skilled workers	US$500–700
Managerial	US$500 +

Thus operational costs can be estimated as being somewhere in the region of US$200,000–US$250,000 per annum.

These figures and estimates are provided as guidelines only and should in no way be taken as the recommended rates. It is not uncommon to find much higher rates of salaries, rent, etc, particularly in the larger international companies. The rates for Azeri companies are usually lower.

Buying a former state company

The State Property Committee is responsible for the disposal of state companies. There have been numerous stories of problems encountered, corruption being but one issue. It is not the intention of this chapter to highlight any one problem but it is fair to say that the issue of corruption has consistently been mentioned in this context. Whether this corruption is real or imagined, the perception that it exists is nevertheless strong enough to warrant mention.

Many state companies have been privatised and are now operating successfully as private companies. However, the privatisation programme has encountered its own difficulties. First, there is a resistance to privatisation, mostly from former Soviet officials. Second, there has been a tendency to overvalue companies for disposal. This has resulted in making it more difficult to dispose of former state enterprises.

Recent changes in policy have suggested that more realistic prices be put on state enterprises to be sold to the private sector. This is encouraging and may mean that such companies can be acquired at minimal rates, allowing the purchaser to invest more than was previously possible. This in turn may enable the company to become more profitable and so in the longer term generate more revenue. It should be noted that, for a cash starved government, such a policy is not easy to contemplate, let alone implement.

Summary

Opportunities for business in Azerbaijan abound. For those able to afford it, setting up an office in the country is possibly the best option to follow. For those who cannot justify such expense, local representation can be a very good entry into the market, allowing the option of further developing your presence later.

Friendship is the key to business; the trust and loyalty built through those friendships is not to be underestimated.

The right partner is more valuable by far than an office in a good position – in the retail industry, for example, the right partner can be invaluable in helping a business acquire a prominent location.

Do not be put off by any difficulties – after four years, I am still going back for more.

Part 2

Market Potential

2.1

Agriculture

I Abasov, First Deputy Minister of Agriculture

Introduction

Azerbaijan's agriculture is a major contributor to GDP, employment and trade. Since 1990, the sector accounted for 26–30 per cent of GDP, 34–38 per cent of employment and about 30 per cent of total exports generated by cotton, tobacco, fruit and vegetables.

In Azerbaijan there is an understanding that if the agricultural sector is not placed on a sound footing with appropriate incentives for investors and a comprehensive institutional framework, the expected large gains in oil revenues could result in a continued reliance on food imports.

The strategic goals of the national agricultural strategy are to stimulate growth by increasing productivity and exports. Productivity gains are expected to result from increased yields in cotton, wheat, fruits and vegetables, and a reduction in post-harvest and storage losses. Export gains are expected to come from cotton, where European markets have been established, and from fruit and vegetables, for which new markets need to be developed. This will require the transformation of the agricultural sector into a competitive market-oriented system involving changes in the structure of agricultural production, marketing and domestic consumption.

The magnitude and speed of these changes depends on the design and implementation of selective intervention in three strategic areas: privatisation, investments and supporting infrastructure.

Reform legislation and privatisation

Since the inception of a policy of privatisation and of reform in agriculture, the Azerbaijani government has obviously made a huge effort to draft and enact the legislation required to make a market-oriented system work properly.

The process is incomplete and important pieces of legislation have yet to be adopted or reviewed in the light of the new policies. The quality of the adopted legislation appears to vary, but the major pieces of required legislation are now in place.

The key question of land ownership has finally been resolved by means of the Law on Land Reform adopted by *Milli Majlis* (National Assembly) of the Republic on 16 July 1996. This law establishes the right to private ownership of land. Land is transferred to all rural inhabitants free of charge – it can be freely sold or exchanged, be transferred by right of succession, be leased and be used as mortgage. Before the adoption on this law on 18 April 1995 a number of other laws were adopted, and these laid the foundation for the realisation of agrarian reforms: the Law on Reform of State and Collective Farms and the Law on Principles of Agrarian Reform. The State Commission on Agrarian Reform was created by presidential decree; its regional and local bodies have been established, and more than 40 normative and legal documents regulating the realisation of reforms have been developed. In order to gain some practical experience in various districts of the country (Zagatala, Khizi, Masalli and Salyan), privatisation was begun in collective farms and state farms as an experiment before regulating normative and legal documents were adopted in 1996. At present, 14,730 private farms have been created and there are about 180,000 hectares of arable land in their ownership. By March 1997 there were 1,450 rural co-operative societies and 2,050 small enterprises with a total area of arable land of 295,000 hectares.

Before the adoption of the Law on Land Reform, more than 560 collective farms and state farms had ceased to exist and the rate of privatisation of collective farms and state farms was expected to increase sharply.

The urgency that marks the creation of private farms has been reinforced by the fact that on average, in a number of regions, the productivity of cereals is 1.5 to 2 times as high as that of former collective farms and state farms in the same regions, having only 10 per cent of the area under cereal crop. At present, while only 50 per cent of orchards (51,000 hectares) are in private ownership, 90 per cent of production is attributable to the private sector and average productivity reaches 50 centner per hectare, as against 10 centner per hectare in state farm orchards. Private sector productivity of potatoes and grapes is 2 to 4 times as high.

In the cattle-breeding sector privatisation has also had a positive effect, with 94 per cent of milk production and 82 per cent of meat production of the country attributable to the private sector. The livestock count has increased, as has the production of meat and milk. Furthermore, these products benefit from stable prices.

The government's opinion about the management and ownership of enterprises in agriculture, the trade in agricultural products and the agro-processing industry has apparently evolved over time, towards a considerably limited role for government.

The Law on Principles of Agrarian Reform of 18 February 1995, the Law on the Privatisation of Kolkhozes and Sovkhozes of the same date, and the Law on Land Reform of 16 July 1996, each mention a number of categories of enterprises and of land not to be privatised. According to the State Programme for State Property Privatisation, adopted by Parliament in 1995, state-owned cattle-breeding and seed farms, hybrid breeder centres, state-owned seed inspections, culture testing laboratories, stations and farms are not to be privatised. Agricultural enterprises, which can only be privatised upon a special decision by the Azerbaijan president, are enterprises for wine, sparkling wine and brandy manufacturing, cotton processing factories, tobacco factories, tobacco-fermentation factories, tea-processing and tea-packing factories, and fish processing plants. Enterprises that are to be subject to obligatory privatisation by decision of the State Property Committee (SPC) are enterprises of wholesale and retail trade, agricultural infrastructure and agri-product processing, poultry farms, agricultural service, food industry, bread and bakery production, and external trade associations.

A three-pronged approach to the privatisation process was to be applied: (i) auctioning and selling of small enterprises (1997); (ii) mass-privatisation of medium to large enterprises with privatisation shares and investment fund schemes (1997–1998); and (iii) combining mass privatisation techniques and a case-by-case approach for restructuring and selling large enterprises. Mass privatisation is crucial for creating competition and may also reduce the need for government-funded restructuring.

It was planned to privatise 130 enterprises of agro-industry, involving 37 small, 62 medium and 31 large enterprises. Of these, in 1997, 37 small and 45 medium-sized enterprises were to be privatised. The small enterprises were to be prepared for sale by auction. The medium-sized enterprises were to be transformed into open joint-stock companies and shares in these joint-stock companies were to be distributed by type of sale as follows:

- 15 per cent to be sold under allowance schemes (mainly offered among the working staff members);

- not less than 50 per cent to be sold in a voucher auction (investment tender or bidding);

- 10–20 per cent to be sold in a cash auction (investment tender or bidding);

- up to 25 per cent to be transferred to set up specialised industry and inter-industry investment funds, of which 15 per cent was to be transferred to the Guaranty Reserve Investment Funds, this being obligatory, and 10 per cent to be transferred to the Closed Investment

Funds, unless the stock market situation were unfavourable, in which case the latter could be sold at cash auctions.

According to the classification of enterprises by number of employees, there were one small and 15 medium enterprises in the tea industry, two small and four medium enterprises in the tobacco industry, 12 medium enterprises in the winemaking industry and 18 small and 21 medium enterprises in the canning industry.

Privatisation plans for 15 enterprises of the canning industry were being considered by the State Property Committee for approval and 25 canneries were being prepared for privatisation. There are plans to begin the privatisation of some of the 19 existing ginneries.

Encouraging foreign investment and credits

In collaboration with international financial organisations, the Azerbaijan government is involved in the implementation of the following projects:

Farm privatisation project

The farm privatisation project has been designed to assist the government in implementing the privatisation programme of representative state and collective farms in a systematic manner. The project will focus on: (a) the provision of the most important support services, namely land registration services, farm information and advisory services, and the rehabilitation of the most critical off-farm and on-farm infrastructure necessary to sustain privatised agriculture; (b) the development of suitable financing mechanisms for public infrastructure and private investments in agriculture; and (c) encouraging education and collaboration in support of land privatisation and farm restructuring.

This project was undertaken as a pilot operation, with the objective of drawing lessons from it, so that similar projects could be launched in other parts of the country. The estimated project cost is US$27 million, with International Development Association (IDA) financing of US$14.7 million, IFAD-US$9.3 million and the remaining US$3 million being financed by the government of Azerbaijan and participating privatised farms.

Regional Agricultural Reform Project (RARP)

The Regional Agricultural Reform Project (RARP) was set up by the European Union in early 1996 to assist with the disbursement of the Counterpart Funds (CPF), which were created in each of the three Caucasus countries, through the proceeds from the sales of EU wheat flour during the winter of 1995–1996. In the case of Azerbaijan these funds amounted to 68.5 billion manats (approximately US$16 million). The objectives of the credit scheme are to ensure that the money realised from the sale of food aid is used to enable Azerbaijan to achieve an increase in wheat output through greater efficiency. The project also aims to support the privatisation of the cereals sector by providing credit to private farmers and privatised traders and processors of grain. In addition, the EU and the government of Azerbaijan have agreed to set aside from the CPF, US$1 million to fund development in the agricultural sector in Fizuli, and another US$1 million to assist in the establishment of a grain market and the repair of grain storage facilities.

The principal beneficiaries of the credit scheme are expected to be private farmers (40 per cent of the fund), private traders and processors (32 per cent of the fund) and credit unions set up to help the smaller private farmers obtain credit (6 per cent of the fund). In addition, 10 per cent of the fund will be used for financing agricultural income generating projects for which up to US$100,000 may be advanced for each suitable project, repayable over three years.

Irrigation projects

The reconstruction and the transformation of the irrigation system in the country is a critical area related to increased crop productivity, because about 70 per cent of the total cropped area is under irrigation.

The country is incapable of financing this sector on its own and is seeking to attract foreign credits from international financial organisations.

The Islamic Bank for Development will give a credit of US$9.8 million for the project to reconstruct the Main Mil-Mugan collector.

Another project, the Irrigation and Drainage Project, focuses on the rehabilitation of the most critical irrigation and drainage infrastructure of the country to improve the reliability and efficiency of water use, develop and implement cost recovery mechanisms and user-based water management arrangements. The estimated project cost is US$75 million with World Bank financing of US$50 million.

New investment opportunities

Wine production and bottling

The reorganisation of the grape-growing and winemaking industry in Azerbaijan is based on the following factors.

The vineyards for wine production are concentrated in the Shamakhy-Devechi-Talish foothills (Djalilabad) area and the valleys to the west of Ganja. The Apsheron peninsula area also has good potential as a table-grape-producing area, especially as it is near Baku.

In 1996, the table-grape-producing area was 15,000 hectares and production was 100,000 tons, vineyard areas totalled 55,000 hectares and vine production was 200,000 tons. This does not account for the 40,000 hectares of vineyards that had been destroyed by philloxera. In this regard, it is important to undertake a replanting project and create, in the Shamakhy region, a national centre for the local supply of suitable virus-less rootstocks and grape scions, with annual capacity for grafting of 10 million. The estimated cost of this project is US$5 million.

Azerbaijan needs to diversify its range of grape-based products. The production of high-quality grape juice should be reactivated. The processing facilities at the winemaking plant in Baku, if supported by the installation of a Tetra-Pak filling line, could be a good solution. This type of product would be competitive on export markets in the Persian Gulf, Pakistan, etc, as well as, in the longer term, Russia.

The Ministry of Agriculture owns 117 factories for the primary processing of grapes with capacity of 1.25 million tons and 13 wine-making factories with a total capacity of 22.7 million decalitres (dcl). Azerbaijan could produce 1.5 million decalitres of wine, 0.5 million decalitres of vodka and 338,000 decalitres of champagne. To achieve such production levels, the industry needs 2 million decalitres of ethyl spirit and 1,000 tons of sugar powder and the construction of a factory for the manufacture of spirits.

The wineries and distilleries are in need of full renovation to remedy their enormous technological deficit. It is also vital to build new processing facilities, rather than try to install new systems on top of old ones, which would not be realistic from an economic point of view.

An autonomous bottle supply should be ensured by facilitating the installation of a bottle factory. There is a wine bottle factory in Ganja but this factory needs to modernise its equipment. Due to the shortage of glass bottles, 70 per cent of wines are sold as a semi-products, which greatly damages the country's economy. Foreign partners could be interested in investing in the construction of a bottle factory in Khachmas. Quartz sand deposit to a volume of 6 million m^3 has been prospected in the Kuba region, bordering Khachmas. A bottle factory should be able to manufacture 100 million 0.5 litre bottles per year.

Investments totalling US$105 million are required to rehabilitate the viniculture sector and wine industry: that is, US$85 million as capital investment and US$20 million as working capital.

Cotton sector

Twenty regions among the 55 constituting the Azerbaijani Republic are involved in cotton growing. The cotton growing area is 210,000 hectares and is generally well situated along the Kura and Arax rivers.

The country's potential cotton production is more than 1 million tons, which was realised in 1981. Since 1986, production has regularly decreased and the yield per hectare fell to 1.3 tons in 1996; production is now approximately 274,000 tons.

Pest control is not perfect and few insecticides are applied, with the result that the majority of the cotton fields have been under attack from aphids, stives and bollworms. The quality and price of the cotton has decreased. A further cause for the deteriorating quality of cotton is the picking process. In Azerbaijan, 34 per cent of the seed cotton is hand picked and 66 per cent is harvested with cotton pickers that are not always in good working condition (broken spinners). Products to remove the leaves from the plants are not always available and many neps remain in the lint after ginning. There are also financial reasons that cause delays in cotton production. Cotton growers are not paid immediately for their production and must wait until the lint has been sold before they can be paid. This delay can last for up to one year. A seasonal credit should therefore be set up to help farmers by providing the input and spare parts they need, in time before the cropping season. A specialised bank would be ideal for the cotton sector.

Azerbaijan has a comparative advantage in cotton production and has great potential to increase this considerably and for cotton to become an important foreign exchange earner. This advantage arises out of the low unit cost of production. Presently, the cotton yields are only about one-half of their full potential under similar ecological conditions. During 1995 the country earned about US$114 million from cotton exports and prospects look bright in the short term provided substantial improvements in the quality and quantity of cotton production can be made.

The proposed Cotton Development operation will (a) introduce high-yielding, medium, long and extra-long staple cotton; (b) promote private sector input supply services; (c) promote IPM technology; (d) promote the privatisation and modernisation of the existing 19 ginneries in order to improve the management and the cotton lint quality to meet international grade levels; (e) strengthen the seed-growing economies; and (f) develop and implement suitable private marketing channels.

For lack of present-day processing technologies, 70 per cent of cotton fibre is sold abroad as raw material and this gives rise to considerable financial and economic losses. About 90,000 tons of cotton fibre were manufactured in Azerbaijan in 1996. About 58,000 tons of cotton fibre should be exported and that would generate approximately US$64 million. Moreover, this amount of cotton fibre could be processed to 49,000 tons of yarn and US$108 million could be earned.

The country's total annual capacity for yarn production in five factories is 38,000 tons. The goverment in Azerbaijan is interested in attracting investors to build another two cotton-yarn factories with annual capacity of 5,000 tons in each of the centres for cotton production (Beilagan and Sabirabad (US$30 million)) and to modernise the existing 19 ginneries (US$40 million). Investment is also needed to pay for modern technologies for the manufacture of textile products in the country (US$15 million).

In total therefore, investment of at least US$160 million is required to develop the cotton sector: that is, US$85 million as capital investment and US$75 million as working capital.

Fruit and vegetables

In 1996, the production of vegetables, potatoes and fruit was as follows: vegetables – 586,000 tons (500,000 tons attributable to the private sector); potatoes – 209,000 tons (200,000 tons attributable to the private sector); and fruit – 321,000 tons (291,000 tons attributable to the private sector).

The main problem in the potato sector is the lack of high-quality seed, which results in a low yield of ten tons per hectare. It is important to increase production of this widely eaten food product.

As for fruits, these are very tasty and rich in vitamins and microelements. Sixty thousand tons of apples, 80,000 tons of pomegranates and 30,000 tons of khurma are considered as having good potential for export to the CIS countries and Europe. This would generate income of US$30 million. To achieve this, the sector needs to create grading, packing, storage and transport facilities by foreign companies in co-operation with the local private sector.

The fruit and vegetable production that is processed by existing canneries is about 45 per cent fruit and 50 per cent tomatoes; the canneries cannot undertake any more as they lack working capital to purchase raw material, spare parts, etc.

The country's canneries can be divided into three specialised groups that produce:

- tomato paste;

- natural fruit and pomegranate juices;

- apple concentrate.

Among the existing canneries, 12 could be considered as having good export potential, provided these factories could attract investment, especially for the modernisation of their equipment and the installation of modern packaging technologies.

The six canneries in Lenkoran, Masalli and Khachmas could form a first group producing tomato paste. The potential for annual production of these factories is 18,000 tons, which could generate US$15.3 million.

The requirements for capital investment (new packing equipment and reconstruction) and working capital are US$10.8 million and US$7.4 million respectively. Calculations show that by investing US$25 million in these factories over two years, the costs can be recovered and profits reach US$5 million, subsequently increasing in later years to US$8 million per year.

A second group of factories producing apple concentrate is made up of four factories in Kuba, Gusar and Khachmas. The requirements for capital investment and working capital in this group are US$5.2 million and US$2.8 million respectively. Investment of this nature would be recouped within four years and assuming an annual production of apple concentrate of 4,700 tons per year, US$5.6 million could be generated annually.

A third group of factories as potential exporters of fruit and pomegranate juices is situated in the Mil-Mugan Zone and the Kuba-Gusar Zone. Seven factories in this group could produce over 35,000 tons of natural fruit juices and US$17.5 million could be earned from exporting this production. The requirements for this group in terms of capital investment (new equipment and reconstruction) and working capital are US$7.8 million and US$12.8 million respectively. All costs could be covered within three years and annual profits thereafter for this group can be estimated at US$7 million.

Agricultural input and machinery supply

The supply of agricultural input and machinery in Azerbaijan is dependent on imports into the country of fertilizers, pesticides, machinery, spare parts, etc.

In 1985, the total of delivered fertilizers made up 0.31 million tons. In 1996, this figure made up just 4,500 tons. In 1996, deliveries of phosphoric, potash fertilizers and chemical fodder additives were completely halted.

Currently, the estimated demand is for 350,000 tons of nitrogen fertilizers and 250,000 tons of apatites for the production of phosphate fertilizers costing US$52 million and US$21 million respectively. Azerbaijan's agriculture also needs investment to subsidise the purchase of seeds (wheat, potato, etc) and of necessary herbicides and pesticides, amounting to US$10 million and US$18 million respectively.

The estimated cost of meeting the country's needs in terms of agricultural machinery and spare parts is US$100 million.

The total cost of meeting Azerbaijan's needs in agricultural inputs and machinery supply is about US$200 million.

It is imperative to create ventures for the manufacture of fertilizers and pesticides. The chemical industry of Azerbaijan is rather advanced, and there are large plants for the manufacture of phosphate fertilizers in

Sumgait. However, due to a halt in raw material (apatites) deliveries, mainly from Russia, these plants are not operational. Joint use of these factories could be profitable for both Azerbaijani and foreign partners.

The Karadag copper-porphyry deposit, located in Shamkir region, has been prospected. It could supply raw material for the manufacture of copper vitriol with an annual volume of up to one million tons, which would allow a sharp reduction in current losses of grapes and fruit–vegetable plantations.

Deposits of natural zeolite have been found in Azerbaijan, most of which is located in the Alidag deposit situated in Tovuz district. This mineral was successfully used in the agriculture and livestock-breeding sector. The industrial manufacture of this mineral could be attractive to foreign companies.

Also of interest could be the construction of a plant for the manufacture of nitric fertilisers in Ali-Bayramli. This industrial centre, rich in electric power and water resources, is located close to the main regions for the cultivation and processing of cotton.

As for agricultural machinery supply, it is imperative to create foreign and joint venture leasing companies, which would rent machinery and equipment to rural private leasing machinery stations, and who in turn could use them to serve the farming communities. It is very important to the development of this business that the government supports such initiatives with tax privileges. It would also be helpful if agricultural machinery (tractors) were to be assembled in Azerbaijan – this could be achieved through the co-operation of foreign companies with existing local plants.

Milk and meat

Back in 1996, the production of meat, milk and eggs was estimated at 151,000 tons, 842,000 tons and 476 million pieces respectively. Between 83 and 95 per cent of this production was attributable to the private sector, showing the deep crisis that state enterprises faced in those sectors. At present, more than one-third of food products consumed in Azerbaijan is imported. This figure includes one-third of all dairy products, one-quarter of all meat products and one-fifth of all eggs consumed in the country.

The main sources of supply for meat and milk products are through poorly organised private marketing channels that fail to meet hygiene requirements. The state farms are not able to supply the state milk and meat processing plants with enough raw material and these plants are operational at only 10–20 per cent of full capacity.

Previously, more than 20 per cent of the total volume of meat products was met by the poultry industry. At present, the poultry industry is practically unable to operate because of a halt in the supply of feed. Equipment in the poultry factories can easily be rehabilitated, but the equipment in the existing 17 meat processing and 33 milk processing plants is in need of serious modernisation.

The state Dairy and Meat Company has been liquidated and the existing factories are due to be privatised. The main objectives for the improvement of the meat and milk processing industry in light of forthcoming privatisation plans are:

- the improvement of the livestock-breeding sector to increase production of meat and milk;

- the organisation of suitable collection, primary storage and processing of meat and milk directly in the production area to meet necessary (technological, hygiene) requirements;

- the modernisation of milk and meat processing factories.

In order to realise this programme, the industry needs to attract foreign investors. The amount estimated to be needed in this respect is about US$120 million: US$70 million as capital investment and US$50 million as working capital.

MORRISON

MORRISON CASPIAN LIMITED

With over 25 years of international construction projects behind us, including six years in Azerbaijan, Morrison has the experience and technical capability to provide you with a cost-effective solution to your building or infrastructure requirements.

Whether your needs are for industrial or production facilities, office or even residential space, we will be pleased to assist.

We have the local knowledge to help you find a suitable site, and can provide you with a turn-key solution, including funding in appropriate cases.

With the resources of a US $600 million p.a. turnover, leading UK construction group behind us, you will have the peace of mind that standards of quality and service will be of the highest order.

To discuss your requirements, please contact Robbie Davidson at our Baku office.
Tel (99412) 92-94-18, 92-35-13 or 92-78-50 or fax 98-09-66

or

one of our Business Development Team at:

Shand House, Matlock, Derbyshire DE4 3AF UK

Tel +44(0)1629 734441 Fax +44(0)1629 734330

"Aiming to deliver world class customer service and value through our innovative, quality driven approach."

www.morrcon.co.uk

2.2

Construction

Abid Sharifov, Deputy Prime Minister for Construction

Introduction

For many years the construction industry has been one of the leading sectors in the Azerbaijani economy. This is not only because it has long been the foundation of many people's livelihoods and the focus of a large proportion of investment, but also because, in economic terms, it makes a large contribution to the nation's income and employment. As a result of the mobile nature of the construction industry's means of production, it automatically attracts growth where it is located, promoting regional development, and thus development in Azerbaijani society as a whole. The construction industry has therefore always earned due recognition and has been a benchmark for assessing the course of economic reform.

History

By the end of the 1980s the Azerbaijani Republic possessed a mighty proportion of the Soviet Union's construction capability. Virtually every aspect of construction was located in the Republic – from surveying and assembly to equipment installation – all within the capabilities of construction firms and organisations. The fabrication of all essential building materials and machinery, as well as the manufacture of domestic appliances, experienced widespread growth. Builders and planners were able to erect complex buildings and communication infrastructures. All this was made possible due to a specialised structure of government ministries and departments. In every city and region there were several construction-oriented organisations or firms with different levels of subordination. Through regimented integration it was possible to assign orders for any piece of equipment or technology or the production of non-standard components. A large proportion of this was financed through a centralised system of Soviet departments.

For some time after the break-up of the Soviet Union the construction capability of the Azerbaijani Republic suffered from an acute lack of investment. However, as the political and economic situation stabilised, the investment situation took an upward turn – especially from 1996 onwards. As a result of the policy of opening up the domestic economy – a key factor in de-monopolisation and integration – the markets experienced a significant surge in investment, which was a boon to the construction industry.

The way in which the construction industry is managed has also changed. The hand of the government no longer holds the same grip over the direction of the economy and the demands of market forces exclude the possibility of monopolisation and strict specialisation.

Structure of the industry

Today in Azerbaijan, alongside hundreds of private construction and building materials companies, repair and maintenance firms, there are only eight joint-stock construction companies. This has facilitated the development of private means of ownership and competitive market conditions, while preserving a necessary minimum of competitive joint-stock companies in this sector. All of these organisations were formed through privatisation and the restructuring of state-controlled companies. As well as these domestic companies, foreign-owned and joint-venture firms also operate in the market.

Construction companies and organisations with joint-stock status make up approximately 3 to 4 per cent of all the domestic construction companies operating in the Republic. Their impact on market activity is virtually imperceptible, giving this sector of the economy a genuine anti-monopolistic and competitive atmosphere.

During the changeover to the market economy, a whole host of construction companies were either liquidated, merged, downsized, or simply went bankrupt. This was an unavoidable consequence of the transitional period. Such a tendency is likely to continue, and in the future will ensure change and renewal in the corpus of the industry, as well as serve as a regulatory and democratising process.

The Azerbaijani construction industry has at its disposal sufficient technical prowess. Scrapers, bulldozers, excavators, tower cranes, wheel-mounted cranes, concrete mixers – stationary and wheel-mounted – heavy-load transporting gear, rock-cutting machinery and other similar equipment make up basic stock of the construction trade. Despite the joint-stock companies having accumulated only the minimum of such equipment, they are able, nevertheless, to mobilise them very rapidly in the event of national emergencies and natural disasters.

In comparison with previous times, the construction industry is experiencing an investment shortfall. In spite of this, construction still has a noticeable impact on the country's GDP. For example, it has made up, on average, 13 per cent of the national product. Approximately 2 to 3 per cent of the labour force is employed in construction. This is partly due to the work-intensive nature of the industry, together with the abundance of willing labour in the region, and is a result of the great demands made by reconstruction work and the work involved in creating favourable conditions for investment activities.

The construction industry is currently predominant over oil, petro-chemical, power, transport, and housing infrastructures, and is likely to continue to be so in the near future. In reconstructing the essential services and industrial and agricultural infrastructures, major construction work is expected to take place after the liberation of occupied Armenian territory (20 per cent of the Republic's territory).

The regulatory environment

In order to regulate the relationship between the participants in construction and related investment activities, and to create a legal basis for any relevant policy- and decision-making activity, a package of judicial acts has been passed. It takes into account a multitude of inter-national guidelines and regulations, as well as realistic and reasoned assumptions about the economic tendencies in the country's transitory market.

Legislation has already been passed in a multitude of areas, including investment activity, foreign investment protection, standardisation, consumer rights' protection, tenders, architectural activities, town planning, natural monopolies, author's rights, rent and leases, bonds and securities, valuation activities, private companies, joint-stock companies, limited companies, land reform and laws, and employment law. Regimes have been established covering contractually agreed prices and cost esti-mates for construction, the signing of contracts, the licensing of various spheres of construction activity, planning, project appraisal and restoration of historical monuments. Also adopted are new wage rates and skills schedules as well as new job descriptions for management, technical and engineering staff, clerical personnel and line-workers. This should serve to enable future certification and ensure the inclusion of individual, collective and trilateral bargaining and agreements. Moreover, the country has established codes for material and labour charges, stan-dards for projected profits, and also those that define suitability and other qualitative parameters of building materials.

The presence of this multi-faceted normative base allows swifter and more precise determination of the technical and economic effectiveness of various projects, realistic assessments of investors' and contractors' proposals, and prevents the manifestation of elements of unfair competition. It also provides measures for providing protection from the effects of seismological or man-made tremors and other undesirable occurrences. Such norms are also useful in prognoses of investment activity, not only on a country-wide scale, but also in the context of separate branches of industry and even other individual companies.

In the realisation of a specific construction programme, an investor should first and foremost receive a suitable part of land, which is allocated by the local competent authorities in accordance with the general planning regulations in any given territory. The project must undergo an expert appraisal, and in particular, seismic stability testing. During labour negotiations the parties' rights or obligations may not be infringed upon, and any disputes are to be settled with trilateral wage-bargaining. In short, the legislative framework in force in the Republic must be observed – a legislature that creates conditions conducive to serious investment.

All issues relating to the co-ordination of construction activities, purposeful investment and corresponding government technical and economic policy in that area are addressed by one organ of central power – the Government Committee for Construction and Architecture (*Gosstroi*), which is freed of economic activity. Matters relating to licensing, government expert opinion and state supervision of the observation of the rights of the industry's consumers are also entrusted to this committee. *Gosstroi* also implements a number of government building orders by organising the respective contracts.

Training, research and development

Azerbaijan has one university specialising in engineering and construction as well as several technical colleges and polytechnics, whose courses are designed to enhance the qualifications of the industry's professionals. There is also a trade union of construction workers and an industry newspaper, *Inschaatschi* ('Builder'). Surveying and exploratory organisations number 24 in all; several of these organisations are involved in normative research and two institutes deal with scientific research activities, one of which is dedicated to building materials, the other to general construction and planning issues. A new self-financing centre dedicated to pricing issues has been set up, engaging in marketing and consultancy activities. There is a great need for investment to build on the existing material and technical resources in the industry, for example, stone-dressing technology, cement, masonry materials and panelling, sanitation appliances, refractory brick and paints.

Business forums provide good opportunities for more detailed involvement in current projects and investment opportunities, not only in construction, but in other branches of the economy. Set up with the needs of investors in mind, forums and investors' groups exist across the country, enabling companies of all types to get involved in joint projects, industrial societies, partnerships and other ventures.

Conclusion

The principles of fair competition, transparency, and democratisation of the economy are considered paramount in the construction industry and the investment climate that surrounds it. Fundamental also are equal rights of all involved parties, protection in the contracts market from anti-competitive participants, as well as support for integration and entrepreneurial development.

In conclusion, then, we would note that the construction capability of the Azerbaijani Republic has been formed, for the most part, over the course of the last 30 years. A programme of reform has been put in place alongside the general economic reforms implemented by the president of the Azerbaijani Republic, Geidar Aliyev.

At present the state companies involved in the production of building materials have, on the whole, been privatised – a process that, in the construction industry, is on-going with the aim of consolidating the development of the private sector.

2.3

Environmental Issues

*Dr Heike Pflasterer, Azerbaijan Environment &
Technology Centre (AETC)*

There exists a general perception that countries of the former Soviet
Union, including Azerbaijan, have serious environmental problems and
lack effective institutional organisation and regulation. In reality,
however, Azerbaijan inherited a relatively well-developed command-and-
control system of environmental laws and regulations from the former
Soviet Union, including some standards that are more stringent than
equivalent western regulations.

This system was implemented through enforcement mechanisms that
were effectively weakened as a consequence of the setting of too stringent
standards and of the charging of state-run facilities with the responsibility
for monitoring their own operations. In particular, this led to the operators of the facilities either providing false monitoring data, making
regular payments of fines to the regulators for routine exceedence of the
standards or obtaining exemptions from the standards. This in turn led to
the widespread pollution and subsequent environmental degradation
observed today within Azerbaijan.

Since Azerbaijan became independent in 1991, the country has
initiated measures to improve its national environmental management
system. However as the National Environmental Action Plan, 1998 has
highlighted, fundamental institutional problems remain and are intensi-
fying due to a reduction in state expenditure on environmental
management, loss of competent staff and lack of equipment. There is a
clear need for institutional training and for the defining of the responsibilities of the individual regulatory agencies.

According to government statistics, Azerbaijan spent around US$13.5
million per year or less than 0.4 per cent of its GDP from 1992 to 1995 on
environmental management. The target for 2000 is 1 per cent of GDP. At
a national level, areas of environmental management requiring specific
urgent attention include wastewater treatment and waste management
infrastructure and the development of capabilities for clean-up of
contaminated land.

Regulatory framework

Legislation in Azerbaijan consists of laws, decrees, resolutions, regulations, codes, guidance and facility- and operations- specific technical standards. Former Soviet Union and Azerbaijani environmental regulations coexist creating a very complex system. In addition to this formal legislative framework, a discretionary approach towards an individual potential investor may be adopted by the relevant regulatory authorities. It is therefore recommended to obtain facility- development- or industry sector-specific advice on a case-by-case basis with the assistance of a consultant familiar with the regulatory structure. An outline of the applicable basic regulatory framework is presented below.

Institutions

There are several key environmental regulatory and enforcement authorities in Azerbaijan, encompassing national, regional and local levels of administration. They are:

- Azerbaijan State Committee of Ecology and Control of natural resources utilisation (ASCE);
- other environmentally related organisations, including the Ministry of Health (sanitary supervision authorities);
- State Committee of Mining and Technical Supervision;
- State Land Committee;
- local environmental committees (specific to the location of business);
- Azerbalyg (Azerbaijan Fisheries Agency);
- Azermescher (Azerbaijan Forestry Agency);
- State Hydrometeorological Committee;
- State Committee on Geology and Mineral Resources;
- Institute of Archaeology and Ethnography, Academy of Sciences.

Of these, the most important is the ASCE. This governmental body is ranked higher than all other ministerial departments and reports directly to the President rather than to the Prime Minister. There are plans to convert it into a Ministry in the future.

The administrative structure of the ASCE comprises a central administration department, based in Baku, and a series of regional, city and territorial (inter-regional) committees. Notably, the State Caspian

Inspectorate is the territorial committee responsible for the administration of the Azerbaijani sector of the Caspian Sea.

A key structural problem – the overlap of responsibilities of various government agencies – can lead to conflicting activities and/or duplication of work, sometimes with opposing scopes of work and cross purposes. Monitoring of the state of the environment is currently divided between the State Hydrometeorological Committee and the ASCE. Environmental management responsibilities are shared between the ASCE (overall environmental protection), Azermescher and Azerbalyg. However, there are proposals in the National Environmental Action Plan, 1998 to merge the authorities and their roles into one regulatory body in the future.

Key regulations

Since 1991 Azerbaijan has developed new environmental laws and regulations either replacing or amending (through a system of Republic decrees) those developed under the Former Soviet Union (FSU) system. Key legislation includes:

- Law on Environmental Protection (1999);

- Law on Ecological Safety (1999);

- Law on Protection of Historical and Cultural Monuments (1998);

- Law about joining the European Convention on Protection of Archaeological Heritage (1999);

- Water Code (Decree No 685, 1998);

- Law on Industrial and Utility Wastes (1998);

- Resolution of the Cabinet of Ministers No. 122 (1992);

- Law on Air Protection (1981, as amended);

- Administrative Codes (as amended).

Specific environmental operating standards are contained within a hierarchy of documents from framework documents to facility- or operation-specific documents. Key framework environmental standards include:

- resolution on standards of maximum allowed discharges of pollutants to the atmosphere and negative physical influences (1981, as amended);

- water protection regulations (1991);

- surface water protection standards (1988, as amended).

Guidelines

Guidelines in Azerbaijan are currently considered to have the same legal status as laws. The provisions of the guidelines will remain in force until a new law on the topic is passed by parliament. The key guidelines currently in force include the *Handbook for the Environmental Impact Assessment Process in Azerbaijan* (UNDP/ASCE, 1996).

Future trends

The development of national environmental legislation is continuing, with new laws recently brought into force and draft laws pending in several key areas. In particular:

- the new law of the Republic of Azerbaijan on Process and Everyday Wastes of 30 June 1998 and associated Decree of 26 October 1998 have recently been enacted. This law contains provisions for the control of waste collection, transport, recycling, reuse, and for the generation and management of waste associated with production processes;

- a new framework law on Environmental Protection of 8 June 1999 and associated Presidential Decree of 4 August 1999 has recently been enacted. This includes provisions defining: the powers and duties of particular government organisations and the public with respect to environmental matters; permitting requirements and constraints relating to the use of natural resources; and economic regulation with respect to environmental protection. Notably, in parallel with the development of this framework law, revisions of the maximum allowable concentrations (MACs) for air and water pollutants and charges for the use of natural resources and pollution are in preparation;

- a new framework law on Environmental Safety of 8 June 1999 has also been enacted. This includes provisions relating to the protection of human health and safety from use of the natural environment (ie protection associated with land use and operational discharges, emissions and wastes).

Key permit requirements

Environmental permits may be needed both for existing facilities and for new developments, and are issued under Azerbaijani law in the form of administrative decisions or resolutions from the relevant governmental body.

Existing facilities

For existing facilities, permits likely to be held include:

- water abstraction permit

- minerals extraction permit

- air emission permit

- wastewater permit/discharges to water permit

- waste disposal permit

- hazardous waste permit

- waste management permit

- material handling and storage permit

- land conversion, acquisition or allotment permit.

The relevant operational information may be summarised in a facility-specific EcoPassport.

New developments

For new developments, as part of the initial planning process for the proposed development, the developer should first approach the ASCE to determine whether or not there is a requirement to prepare and submit an Environmental Impact Assessment (EIA).

If an EIA is not required, the developer will have to submit an Application for Environmental Permission (the relevant application form is contained in the *Handbook for the Environmental Impact Assessment Process in Azerbaijan*). The requirement for an EIA is dependent on whether the development is considered by the ASCE to have significant potential impacts on the environment.

Both the Application for Environmental Permission and the EIA should provide details of the physical and ecological environment in the vicinity of the development, proposed operations and associated emissions discharges and wastes likely to be generated and materials to be used. Submitted information is required to be fairly specific.

The EIA process is more or less comparable to the European system. The *Handbook* states the minimum scope of an EIA. A table of contents and any additional permit requirements are usually agreed in a meeting between the investor and the ASCE.

The EIA report, including copies of the additional permits, has to be submitted to the ASCE for expert review and approval, which can take up to three months. Officially the EIA process includes public participation. The EIA should focus on the most significant potential impacts (both normal and abnormal conditions) of the project and the proposed mitigation measures.

Once approval is received, the EIA and Application for Approval are legally binding documents. The operator will operate in accordance with the regime described in these documents during the initial verification period. After this period, performance will be reviewed and the administration of the operation of the facility may be required to transfer to the EcoPassport system.

For both new and existing facilities, proposed changes in technology or forecasted volumes may require a supplementary approval from the permitting authority.

Liabilities

Pre-development issues

Environmental liabilities can arise from both past and present operations. Currently there is limited existing reliable information on the status of the environment and past land use readily available. It may therefore be prudent for potential investors to commission an independent study of the status of the environment at their subject sites to assess and document the level and type of potential existing pollution prior to commencing any development activities and to protect themselves from future potential liability.

For a new development an investor is required to submit in the EIA or Application for Approval a description of the existing status of the environment within the vicinity of the proposed development. Further, the information obtained on existing conditions will be of particular use for investors who would be subject to the requirement to establish ongoing monitoring programmes during their proposed operations.

Such a study normally takes the form of a phased environmental audit process. The first phase (the so-called Phase I audit) consists of a desk study relating to site history and former land use (coupled with site visits and discussions with site personnel), process, operation and documentation review. This study identifies visible pollution, environmental risks associated with identified pollution pathways and, if required, potential investment needs. If the results indicate contamination or if existing data is insufficient, then a Phase II audit involving site-specific intrusive ground investigation and, if required, a monitoring programme (air quality and ground water) with subsequent analysis and interpretation may be recommended.

To date, legislation does not ascribe liability in connection with past pollution and there are no indemnity provisions. Investors are therefore advised to establish a clause for exclusion from liability for past pollution in their contractual agreements prior to a transaction. Further, as there are no existing clean-up standards for contaminated land, it may be advisable to include provisions setting agreed standards for future potential clean-up requirements associated with investors' own operations.

Operational issues

Enforcement of standards and pollution regulation for all operations is the responsibility of the ASCE. A 'polluter pays' principle is applied. Under the provisions of the Nature Protection Law, 1992, a fee system for the use of the natural environment, and a fine system for breach of permit standards and conditions have been established. Specific procedures for the fee system are contained in the Resolution of the Cabinet of Ministers No. 122 (1992), and the procedures for the fine system are contained within a system of administrative codes. The fee system is administered directly by the ASCE. However, responsibility for the administration of the fine system is principally shared between the local executive powers of the city, regional and territorial committees.

The foreign investor

The foreign investor needs to seriously consider environmental management requirements as these can have a direct or indirect impact on project timing and finances. For example, failure to do so may result in your company having to pay direct clean-up costs, costs associated with project delays incurred as a result of failing to obtain the required permits, operating costs associated with employing appropriate equipment and practices to ensure compliance with standards, and fines associated with failure to comply with the standards.

The principal environmental management issues identified for each of the three stages of the investment process, namely site development, acquisition and merger, and operation, are outlined below.

Site development

An environmental permit is an essential prerequisite for obtaining a site allotment licence and for obtaining acceptance of the basis for design of a proposed development. The investor will need to establish the scope of the environmental studies required to ensure satisfactory completion of the Application for Environmental Permission or EIA (as required) in order to ensure confidence in obtaining the required environmental permit. At a preliminary level, the investor should ensure that there are no potential 'show-stopper' issues and identify any issues that may lead to the requirement for pre-development site remediation works or special operating procedures during construction works. The investor should also investigate supporting infrastructure serving the site such as vehicle access, sewage discharge, electricity and other utilities.

Acquisition and merger

There is currently no comprehensive regulation concerning environmental liability in the privatisation process. Any costs assessed are therefore either to be deducted from the purchase price or covered/shared by the seller (the government) and the purchaser as agreed. Due diligence environmental audits prior to a purchase may be carried out to assess the potential liability.

The requirement to address the environmental liability issues has been identified. It is envisaged that a regulation will be set up in the near future under the framework of the National Environmental Action Plan, 1998 to attract further foreign investment.

Operation

The investor will be required to pay fees for use of the natural environment and will be subject to fines for any breaches of the standards set within the environmental permit/EcoPassport or within the administration codes or relevant regulations. For new developments, the operation will be subject to a verification period during which the actual emissions, discharges and wastes will be monitored against those forecast in the environmental permit.

Conclusions

Despite the need to restructure the regulatory agencies, define their responsibilities and improve the environmental laws and regulations, there is an established system of environmental management in Azerbaijan.

For a potential investor, the assessment of environmental issues prior to undertaking any significant investment is crucial as these issues can have a severe impact on finances and on the scheduling of a potential development, operation and acquisition/merger. Environmental audits can be used in a risk reduction strategy to document existing pollution and to establish ways of off-setting some of the environmental risk.

Environmental permits are essential prior approvals for site allotment and a review of the basis for design will need to take into account environmental issues.

Environmental issues, therefore, should be considered at the early stages of negotiations and the establishment of a good working relationship with the environmental regulator will help to establish a successful operation in Azerbaijan.

"Our people move heaven and earth for you. That's why we look after them."

First in Projects Expertise
First rate Trained Personnel
First class Safety Record

Air Freight	**Ocean Freight**	**Module Movements**
Road Freight	**River Barges**	**Air/Sea Charters**
Rail Freight	**Heavy Loads**	

London Tel: + 44 181 900 2060   **Houston** Tel: + 1 281 7742300   **Baku** Tel: + 99 412 984 061

Bertling

2.4

Shipping and Freight Forwarding*

Martin Burt, Managing Director, Murphy Shipping and Commercial Services

Azerbaijan's Minister of the Economy, Namiq Nasrullayev, has been quoted as saying: 'We are a small country, strategically positioned between Europe and Asia, and we are blessed with good energy and other natural resources.' This simple statement, however, does not do justice to the importance of Azerbaijan within the region, as Mr Nasrullayev was well aware, when he added that: 'Our geographical position is the next vital resource.'

The TRACECA Programme (Transport Corridor Europe, Caucasus and Asia; informally known as the Great Silk Road) was launched at a European Union (EU) conference in 1993. It encourages the development of a transport corridor to be built on an east–west axis from Central Asia, through the Caucasus, and across the Black Sea to Europe. The programme clearly demonstrates the importance of Azerbaijan both as a gateway and as an international transportation hub. The existing transport facilities and the planned development of pipelines, road, sea, rail and air links underline this sector as a serious driver of economic development in Azerbaijan. The country is being greatly assisted by the EU, the European Bank for Reconstruction and Development and by global financial and development institutions.

In September 1998, 12 nations (including Azerbaijan, Bulgaria, Kazakhstan, Romania, Turkey and Uzbekistan) signed a multilateral agreement known as the Baku Declaration. The Declaration was designed to develop the transport corridor through closer economic integration between the signatory countries and to rehabilitate and develop a new transportation infrastructure by fostering stability and trust in the region. The corridor will include all forms of transport: air, automobile, pipeline, rail and sea, as well as serve as a telecommunications pathway. Baku,

---

* The information provided in this chapter changes frequently. For current shipping and transportation criteria, contact Murphy Shipping.

Azerbaijan's largest city and port, is poised to become a major regional transportation and communications hub for the trans-Caucasus and central Asian republics.

Azerbaijan accounted for 1.5–2 per cent of the capital stock and output of the former Soviet Union. Although the country faces the same formidable problems as the other former Soviet republics in terms of making the transition from a command to a market economy, its considerable energy sources brighten its long-term prospects.

The total value of Azerbaijan's exports in 1996 was US$789 million (1996 free on board (fob) estimate) in commodities, oil and gas, chemicals, oil-field equipment, textiles and cotton; the total value of imports was US$1.3 billion (1996 customs, insurance, freight (CIF) estimate) in commodities, machinery and parts, consumer durables, foodstuffs and textiles. The most prominent products of Azerbaijan's economy are oil, cotton and gas. Production from the Caspian oil and gas fields has been in decline for several years, but the November 1994 ratification of the US$7.5 billion oil deal with a consortium of western companies should have generated the funds needed to spur future industrial development.

Foreign direct investment (FDI) has steadily increased from US$15 million in 1993 to US$546 million in 1996, to US$1.3 billion in 1997 and to US$1.6 billion in 1998, which is equivalent to about 40 per cent of Azerbaijan's gross domestic product (GDP). Azerbaijan's Ministry of the Economy has projected that foreign investment could reach US$2 billion in 1999. More significantly, total investment in the oil and gas sector may reach US$23 billion by 2010. These figures show how business has increased in Azerbaijan, and how key support services in the oil and gas sector, such as freight forwarding and financial services, will play an important role in the foreseeable future.

Freight forwarding

Baku is served by air, sea, road and rail freight.

Air

Air freight companies include British Mediterranean Airways, Coyne Airways, Lufthansa, Emirates, Swissair, Azerbaijan Airlines (AZAL) and Turkish Airlines. British Mediterranean Airways operate directly, while AZAL has a fuel stop in Istanbul, and the other carriers transit via their main operational hubs, whether in Europe, Dubai or Istanbul. All carriers operate wide-bodied aircraft, except AZAL, which has severe size and weight restrictions on its Boeing 727s.

Shipping

The main shipping route from the west is via Poti or Batumi, both located in Georgia on the Black Sea. Coming from the east, it is cheaper and quicker to transit through Bandar Abbas in Iran. Routing through either Poti or Bandar Abbas is perfectly suitable for containerised and break bulk cargo; large shipments (often aid cargo) are typically routed through Poti or Batumi, where they connect with rail or truck for final delivery. The main shipping lines are CMBT, Maersk, MSL, and CMN.

In addition to air and sea freight to Baku, some specialist companies are expert in groupage and full-load trailer road freight service, while others are experts in the rail freight business. During the summer months there is also scope for utilising sea-river vessels which operate on the River Volga from St Petersburg or from the Black Sea, via the Rivers Don and Volga, before entering the Caspian Sea at Astrakhan. These vessels are regularly used for discharging large equipment and bulk supplies for the energy industries, calling at Baku and all the main ports in the Caspian Sea.

Rail

Rail freight provides the most cost-effective option for on-carriage of goods from Batumi and Poti and can be useful when carriage is across many frontiers, right up to the Russian Far East, including Turkmenistan, Uzbekistan, Tajikistan, Kyrgyzstan and Kazakhstan. Rail cargo is also a viable option for carriage directly from western Europe, where International Service Order containers may be loaded in an identical way to ocean freight. These are then simply loaded onto the railways and transported all the way to Baku, usually changing wagon chassis in Poland, as the CIS Railway has a different wheel gauge to that in western Europe. The transit time is usually between three and five weeks depending on the time of year and volumes of cargo.

Road

Road services provide both dedicated and complementary services in the marketplace. In addition to supporting the on-carriage of containers to and from ports, transport operators (including Murphy Shipping) have been providing direct truck services from Europe to Baku using their own trucks, with British and Azerbaijani drivers and fully equipped with GPS systems or satellite telephones. A full load typically takes 12–14 days and groupage services for smaller shipments are very well supported, as they offer considerable savings over air freight.

According to Murphy's figures for 1998, 75 per cent of all the freight business handled was imported by surface means, and a further 14 per cent was trans-shipment cargo, using Azerbaijan as a gateway to other areas.

Transport facilities

Road

Growth in road transport is to be expected, given its greater flexibility and ability to satisfy the diversity of customer requirements. Around 60 per cent of Azerbaijan's 24,000 km of road are in poor or bad condition, causing excessive vehicle wear and tear and fuel consumption. The rising level of the Caspian Sea also means major roadworks are required on coastal highways.

In 1990 there were 36,700 km of roads of which 31,800 km were paved or gravelled and 4,900 km were unpaved or earth tracks. In 1995 there were 57,770 km of roads of which 54,188 km were paved and 3,582 km unpaved.

Rail

The 2,000-km rail network is the most important mode of transport for freight, accounting for 78 per cent of the 392 billion tons per km of total traffic in 1991. The total volume of goods carried by rail is greater than in Turkey and Iran combined. Locomotives are 49 per cent diesel run, and 51 per cent electrically run (though more than half of the latter have exceeded their service life). Due to damage caused by the war with Armenia, 700 km of rail lines are being rebuilt.

Seaports

The Caspian fleet also plays a very important role in transport, with Baku being one of the most strategically placed ports on the Caspian Sea. As projects to develop the energy resources in Azerbaijan, Kazakhstan and Turkmenistan advance, there will be a substantial increase in seafaring activities and travel. Cargo handling at Baku Port and its ferry terminal requires major improvements and expansion to meet these demands. Furthermore, the rise in the level of the Caspian Sea is flooding or seriously damaging existing facilities, often irreparably, and these will also require investment in order to counter the situation.

Baku Port

The oil harbour is situated 40 km from the city on the Absheron Peninsula, and comprises four oil quays each capable of berthing two tankers simultaneously. There are three terminals for dry cargoes consisting of 8 specialised berths and 24 gantry cranes of between 5 and 40 tonne capacity.

Airports

Baku Airport has only a medium level of service ability. In order to function efficiently as an international airport, permanent fuel availability, upgrading of traffic control, improved cargo handling facilities and a better geographical infrastructure must be implemented to provide adequate servicing of passengers and airlines.

Routing to Baku

The main road freight routing to Baku is through eastern Europe, Turkey and Georgia. Rail freight is mostly via Poland, though sometimes via the ports of St Petersburg and Riga, and occasionally Helsinki. Sea freight via Poti in Georgia is the most general routing, with on-carriage to Azerbaijan by rail or truck. Heavy equipment and out-of-gauge shipments are operated via the Volga/Don, via Mersin in Turkey or via Bandar Abbas in Iran.

Sea to river movements via the Volga/Don must be arranged periodically due to icy conditions and service difficulties on locks all the way through to Astrakhan in the north of the Caspian Sea. This service is only available between May and September, but despite the limitation in usage, it remains a highly cost-effective service when compared to others. The service through Iran via Bandar Abbas to Azerbaijan is also another well-utilised option. This, however, is tempered by the fact that any cargo originating in the USA is prohibited by US law from transiting Iran. The out-of-gauge port for all seasons is definitely Mersin, with sufficient heavy lifting equipment and great expertise in handling and onward delivery of such goods. At this moment, there is unfortunately no rail service to the Commonwealth of Independent States (CIS) from Mersin.

Customs formalities

All shipments arriving into Azerbaijan require customs' clearance. The freight company is usually able to complete the customs' declaration on the customer's behalf, but will nevertheless require a commercial invoice showing the cost, insurance and freight (CIF) value, a packing list, a certificate of origin and a certificate of quality. Furthermore, depending on the status of the importer and the type of commodity, a Tax Exemption Certificate, copy of company registration and other documents may well be required by the Azerbaijan customs.

Some importers may prefer to temporarily import goods and equipment, particularly if their contract is for a relatively short term. There is provision within the customs' mandate that allows for temporary importation (though a fee equivalent to 3 per cent of the CIF value is charged each month) of up to a maximum equivalent to the total value of the duty/tax rates of usually 38 per cent of the value of the goods. This amount is then reimbursed to source after export of the goods has been completed. Temporary import of goods may be extended for a further year, subject to the discretionary approval of customs, with no additional charge being levied. If, however, the goods are not exported within the allotted time frame, then penalties ranging from 50 per cent to 300 per cent of the CIF value may be imposed.

At present, there is also a customs' levy which is either 0.15 per cent or 0.3 per cent of the CIF value, depending on who the consignee is and what concession the consignee may benefit from (0.15 per cent is a concessionaire rate of levy). Additionally, VAT is applicable at a rate of 20 per cent of the CIF value, plus customs levy plus customs duty.

New import duty rates vary from 0.5 per cent to 15 per cent of the declared 'landed' customs' value. Some cargo is exempt from duty, such as assets imported into Azerbaijan by a foreign investor as contributions to a joint venture's charter fund, or for the establishment of a 100 per cent foreign-owned enterprise.

Expatriates' personal effects are also exempt, as are goods in transit and temporary imports, as detailed above. Import of goods under a production sharing agreement (PSA) may also be exempt, providing a Tax Exemption Certificate has been issued.

There are no import restrictions to Azerbaijan. However, permission from the relevant ministry is required if imports include pesticides, medicines or weapons and ammunition.

2.5

Infrastructure

Abid Sharifov, Deputy Prime Minister for Construction

Introduction

Bordering Asia and Europe, Azerbaijan is ideally located for the organisation of a high level of commercial goods transit – as is demonstrated by its historic 'Silk Route' connection. In ancient times, this highly populated area played an active and successful part in the transit and exchange of goods. The restoration of this commercial activity in present times could pave the way for a more rational system of trade between the east and the west.

As well as having such a valuable strategic position, Azerbaijan also has one of the oldest and largest geological hydrocarbon deposits in the world as well as various other valuable mineral reserves. All this gives the region great potential for thriving economic activity. In light of this, business interests are paying considerable attention both to the state of the region's infrastructure and to business possibilities that could promote the development and modernisation of this infrastructure.

The existing infrastructure cannot meet all of the requirements stipulated by international standards as it was largely developed during the Soviet era and was therefore built to meet the needs of that time. Nevertheless, as a result of the government's investment policies, much of the infrastructure and communications network has been brought in line with current international standards.

Transport

The transport infrastructure consists mainly of four types: rail, sea, air and road. As well as these four, pipeline transport has also undergone significant development.

Rail transport

Rail transport has a 120-year history in Azerbaijan and embraces all the industrial regions of the country, at times reaching even poorly accessible mountainous zones. The Republic's branch line offers direct access to Russia, Georgia, Armenia, Iran, central Asia, and across the Caspian Sea by train-ferry links to Turkmenistan and further. Some 60 per cent of track has been electrified and is controlled by automated signalling. Significant stretches are dual-track; the remainder is controlled by semi-automatic systems and a centralised control system.

A well-established network of railway terminals, stations and services deals with matters such as passenger and train services, carriage arrangement, train marshalling, cargo loading and unloading, and carriage and locomotive maintenance. The rolling stock consists of covered and semi-covered carriages, platforms, cisterns and refrigerator units.

Due to the actions of Armenian occupying forces, some 110km of track in the south-west and in the Nagorno–Karabakh region are out of service. Despite this, and thanks to the increased volume of cargo traffic and the growth of imports and exports, there has been a steady increase in the volume of cargo handled by Azerbaijan's rail network.

Passenger transport is also being targeted for improvement, with 28 trains already in service that are in line with international standards. Ticketing, including season tickets, is now handled by an automated system. A new passenger information system has also been introduced.

The government department responsible for the railway infrastructure is the State Department for Railways. Its various divisions include a special division for health and education, with representation from various schools, pre-school institutions and technical colleges. This department also runs a centre for the prevention of epidemics and infectious diseases.

However, there is still the need for further modernisation and reform of the country's rail infrastructure. The European Union (EU), recognising the important geo-strategic position held by the Azerbaijani rail system in the context of an integral Eurasian transport corridor, has for the past few years been investing in modernising and expanding Azerbaijan's infrastructure through the Tacis TRACECA Programme.

One of the EU'S major projects has been the restructuring of Azerbaijan's railways. This project will cost a total of approximately US$40 million and will be financed by various sources, including domestic resources, funds from the European Bank for Reconstruction and Development (EBRD), and resources from the Tacis Programme.

Should conditions deteriorate, the participation of other investors and specialised companies would be necessary for the completion of these projects. Furthermore, it is extremely important that the creation of a transport corridor such as TRACECA has the full support of the president, cabinet ministers and Azerbaijani business.

Shipping

Shipping in the Caspian Sea is the realm of the Azerbaijani fleet, which is represented by the government-held company, Caspian Sea Line. The company, having no other domestic competitors, has the monopoly on cargo and passenger sea transport. The fleet consists of 69 trading vessels of various classes, among them eight cargo and passenger train-ferries, 34 tankers and 27 sea-faring dry cargo ships. More than half of the fleet's ships operate in the Caspian Sea. Approximately 60 per cent of the remainder operate in various other seas and oceans.

The country's shipping industry is currently adjusting to the new economic climate and to the world market for sea freight, and is seeking out profitable links with established shipping companies for the transport of both liquid and dry cargo. As part of the concept of the Eurasian transport corridor under the auspices of the EU's Tacis Programme, a complex development programme for the major shipping routes of the Caspian and Black Seas is being developed through which two similar ferry crossings will be operational by 2010. This plan, when complete, will lead to further increase in the volume of sea freight, which almost quadrupled from 1996 to 1999.

It must also be noted that Caspian Sea Line possesses robust maintenance and repair facilities (though these deteriorated somewhat following the collapse of the Soviet Union). The three specialist graving-docks used for reconstructing and re-equipping the fleet are still very much in demand. Furthermore, in light of the government's policy of de-monopolisation, the time is ripe for the establishment of private enterprises involved in shipping in the Azerbaijani-owned parts of the Caspian Sea. The plans for the international corridor in the Azerbaijani and Turkmen stretches of the Caspian, together with the growing influence of cargo ports in Kazakhstan, Turkmenistan and Azerbaijan are likely to lead to a steady increase in both shipping and marine oil and gas production.

The fisheries of the Caspian, the exciting possibilities for further development of tourist resorts, the extraction of minerals and other marine products, the scientific potential of untapped natural resources of the sea and all the attendant possibilities for further development and specialisation are hoped to attract investment in the coastal regions of Azerbaijan and the Caspian Sea.

Air transport

Air transport in Azerbaijan was traditionally – and still is – state-owned and takes the form of the Azerbaijan Hava Yollari state concern (AZAL). This is a relatively small-scale enterprise in global terms, with a fleet of aircraft and a network of provincial airports as well as an academy for staff training, various security outfits and other services.

Since Azerbaijan's newly gained independence and its transition to a market economy it has actively involved itself in global economic activity that has in turn led to increasing demands on the country's transport infrastructure. Nowhere was this impact more profound than on air transport, where urgent measures had to be taken in order to bolster the industry's resources. In response to increased demands on the air transport system, work was completed on the largest airport in the country, Baku International Airport (BINA), in 1999. This was built on the same site as the capital city's existing airport.

Both passenger flights and cargo air-traffic at BINA were increasing steadily, but development was limited by the lack of an individual, modern freight terminal. In response to this increasing pressure, a new runway dedicated to cargo flights was added to the airport and plans are now in the pipeline for a special cargo terminal for handling high-capacity jets such as the Boeing 747. This will complete the modernisation of Baku International Airport, which, by dint of its technical capabilities and its future potential, will put it on a level with the world's major airports.

The country's provincial airports will also need modernising and reconstructing, with a view to improving their technical capabilities and comfort. For this reason, investors could examine the possibilities of their involvement in this area and, in the spirit of mutual benefit, consider possible ventures to be undertaken.

Road transport

Road transport is the most popular sector of the economy owing to its 'connecting' role between other forms of transport. Mostly privately-owned, road transport companies are either local or foreign, with various forms of transport and varying levels of comfort. Sufficient bus and truck depots, a service and maintenance infrastructure, and cargo-handling facilities already exist. New filling stations have been built to cope with increasing demand. Besides independent specialist road haulage companies, the fleets of leading companies and concerns can also fulfil transportation orders. In addition, the Baku International Coach Station is in the final stages of completion.

Both national and foreign road transport companies operate under licence from Azeravtonegliyat, the state concern, which also decides on matters relating to standardisation and certification. Local haulage companies operate under licence from local government bodies.

The law governing transport motor vehicles and their loads require these to carry appropriate insurance cover. Furthermore, in accordance with current international agreements and treaties, the means of trans-portation, and transport workers, have the right to free movement on Europe's highways.

With the resources available to road haulage companies in Azerbaijan, it is now possible to transport loads of any type and size. Azerbaijan has an extensive road network of approximately 23,000km, ensuring a smooth flow of road traffic throughout the country. Of these roads, 21,500km are hard-surfaced (made with gravel, bitumen, asphalt, concrete). More than 6,000km of road has 'primary-road' status, of which 1,000km is classified as motorway. While the Azerbaijani road network falls short of European standards, it is coping with the demands imposed on it by the volume of traffic. Bridges – the length of which amount to over 4,000km – have been built to take Azerbaijan's roads over water or other obstacles. In the main, the roads are also well provided for with roadside services. Principal roads, motorways and bridges are the responsibility of the state-owned company, Azerovtoyol, which also runs a research and development institute and other services relating to the operation and monitoring of the roads.

With the aim of regulating road transport in the Republic, the government has adopted laws on road traffic and set up a state fund for roadways. Parliament has also approved a white paper relating to highway regulations.

If the Government's 'Silk Route' programme – which aims to create a trans-caucasian motor corridor – is to generate integration on a global level and encourage mutual trade, the main arterial route though Azerbaijan will require serious reform and modernisation. Considering the possibilities which would be opened up by the introduction of toll charges on certain stretches of road, and the expansion of roadside services, it is surprising that investor interest surrounding such plans has not been more enthusiastic. At present, work being carried out in this sphere by foreign companies is having some impact and Azerbaijan has sufficient material resources for road construction and development projects.

Pipeline transportation

Pipeline transportation for the transit of liquid and gaseous compounds consists of oil and gas pipelines, internal pipelines for the supply of water and domestic gas for heating, and an external sewerage system connecting populated areas.

The country's main oil pipelines are managed by the State Petroleum Company while the main gas pipelines and services are controlled by the joint-stock company, Azerigaz, and the water supply by the Russian joint-stock company, Alsheronsu. Local water supply networks and drainage systems are operated by the local authorities. To ensure regular operation of the country's pipeline networks, a vast system of terminals, compressor stations, pumping plants, purifying plants and distribution regulators are in place.

Azerbaijan needs more investment to help increase the levels of oil and gas production in the Caspian Sea. Capital is also required for laying new pipelines and funding other associated services and operations. The existing infrastructure requires modernising and reforming, and outdated and defunct structures need replacing. Therefore, for this sector to fulfil its global potential the country needs dozens of specific projects. These could cover areas such as the construction of new terminal and storage units and environmental impact studies, the installation of automated monitoring and regulation systems, the construction of purifying plants, and the building of new stretches of pipeline. At the same time, existing systems require reconstruction and maintenance to meet the requisite technical and legal standards.

Communications

Radio and telecommunications have long been essential to daily activity in Azerbaijan. Almost all the population has access to telephones, and radio links can be established in case of emergency. Certain major companies have their own telecommunications networks, which are connected to the national network, but can be used on a stand-alone basis if necessary. Under Azerbaijani law, telephone tapping is forbidden.

Over the last few years the old mechanical telephone exchange has been replaced by a fully digital system. Mobile telephones are now also in widespread use, and work is being carried out on the construction of a highway of fibre-optic cable to connect to European networks.

Current telecommunications policy has at its core the aims of ensuring efficiency, discouraging monopoly and promoting competition. A government commission has been set up for the allocation of radio frequency bands. Non state-owned telecommunications companies and information services are flourishing alongside the state-owned companies. Regions also have their own TV and radio broadcasting centres. Programmes are, on the whole, broadcast in Azeri, but those in Russian, Georgian, Armenian, Lezghin, Talish and other languages are also available. In addition, Turkish, Russian and other radio stations are transmitted through the Azerbaijani airwaves.

Communications legislation has been adopted, under which much work is being carried out in the areas of certification and standardisation of the telecommunication networks. Internet access as well as audio and visual satellite reception is available. Companies wishing to get involved in this area of activity must apply for the relevant licences.

There is much scope for business opportunities in the telecommunications industry, particularly in the development of cable TV and in the production and distribution of decoder sets for cable and satellite reception. This is true not only for Azerbaijan, but also for other countries in the region.

Tourist infrastructure and health resorts

The tourist infrastructure in Azerbaijan still lags behind that of other countries, and is not keeping pace with other developments in Azerbaijan's infrastructure.

Of the 11 climatic zones in the world, nine exist in Azerbaijan. The country has numerous natural sources of mineral and thermal waters. For many years some of these have been used commercially in the treatment and prevention of diseases of the stomach, joints, kidneys and skin, as well as diseases of the liver and the gall bladder. A particularly special property of the water is its naphthalene content, which is useful in the treatment of inflammatory diseases, radiculitis and depressive illnesses.

Mud spas have always been popular amongst the population of Azerbaijan because of their healing properties. The salt-mines of Nakhichevan also give excellent results in the treatment of bronchial and pulmonary illnesses.

The high iodine and bromine content of the sea waters and, on warm, sunny days the temperate breezes and comfortable humidity make for excellent conditions for those recuperating from cardiovascular ailments and diseases of the nervous system.

The development of tourism has been assisted by the variety of land-marks, sights, nature reserves and historical monuments in the country.

In order to ensure effective and controlled usage of the country's water resources, a number of reservoirs and artesian wells have been constructed. Those also help to ensure the quality and safety of the water supply.

During Soviet times, the region's health resorts were in constant use by citizens from every corner of the USSR. There was even a special development programme devoted to the resorts of the Caspian Sea – unfortunately this remains incomplete due to lack of investment. Sanatoria and health resorts in the country are in serious need of redevelopment and outfitting with modern medical and fitness equipment. At present, there are great opportunities for establishing world-class health resorts, sanatoria and spas. The country has sufficient labour with the necessary qualifications to staff such new developments.

Despite the fact that every town in the country has some sort of hotel industry, there is clearly a shortfall in quantity. In addition, the standards of service and facilities are not as high as they could be. Already much of the country's hotel industry has been privatised; the remainder is in the process of being privatised. While this tendency is likely to continue, monopolies still exist in most cities due to the lack of competition. Baku is an exception; here the country's hotel industry has experienced more profound growth. Today hotel guests can stay in one of the many hotel complexes that provide comfort and good quality facilities including suites of world-class standard. On the whole, however, there is still insufficient investment and much potential for further development of Azerbaijan's hotel industry.

As a result of Azerbaijan's territorial compactness, there are plenty of opportunities to develop the hotel industry, even in peripheral areas. The joint-stock company, Azerkurort, which operates in conjunction with the Azerbaijani tourist board, is currently in charge of the task of promoting and monitoring growth in this area.

Energy

Energy, and electric power in particular, has a large role to play in the functioning of all of the aforementioned types of infrastructure, as well as many other aspects of everyday life in the country.

Azerbaijan's energy comes under the sole authority of the joint-stock company, Azerenergy. The major source of the country's energy output comes from fossil fuel power stations.

Electric power cables are designed to carry voltages of 500, 300, 220 and 110 kilovolts. This allows the system to be linked with the electric power systems of neighbouring countries Russia and Georgia. Because of the conflict with Armenia, some of the power supply in that area of Azerbaijan has been disrupted, which has necessitated the re-routing of energy supplies from Turkey and Iran.

The country's various regions have their own individual bodies that are responsible for power output. The existing electric power network in Azerbaijan ensures reliable supply of energy to the whole of the country. As well as providing for its own consumption, the network can – when necessary – handle the import and export of electric power.

In 1991 the accumulative power output of the country's electric power stations was more than 23 million kilowatt-hours. However, because of the high rate of amortisation the resultant power output tends to be lower.

In light of the above, and considering the possibilities of the export of the country's electric power, the development of the country's production capabilities features high on the agenda. With the assistance of long-term credit from foreign investors, a project to build a hydroelectric dam on the river Kura is making good progress. Once operational, this power station should prove to be a significant addition to the country's electric power base.

However, the great potential in this area is not being fulfilled. New power stations must be built, and modernisation and reconstruction work must be carried out on existing plants and technology in order to increase energy output.

This investment must not only be pumped into the large power plants – indeed, the majority of regional sub-stations are also in need of modification and expansion. In all, billions of dollars will be needed to implement all of the desired developments.

A number of private investors and financial institutions from various countries are currently engaged in discussions with Azerbaijani specialists on the implementation of specific development projects. In the future there is to be a clear divide between energy production and its sale.

A legislative framework has been established for the various operations in this industry. Laws on electric power and a series of other acts and statutes reflecting the current requirements have been passed to regulate the activities of those involved in the power industry.

2.6

Insurance

Akif Kerimov, President, Union of Insurance Companies of Azerbaijan, and Chairman, Aon Azeri Insurance and Reinsurance Brokers Company

The insurance profession in Azerbaijan has passed through many stages in its development, from the late 19th- and early 20th-century pre-Russian Revolution era to the equally momentous post-revolutionary period.

The first signs of development in the insurance business appeared by the beginning of the 20th century, with the establishment of the first petroleum and shipping companies, and with the influx of foreign investors in the petroleum sector of Azerbaijan. The main form of insurance during the pre-revolutionary period was voluntary insurance, usually carried out by joint-stock companies or societies of mutual insurance. There were several insurers present in Azerbaijan during this period. Lloyd's of London had offices specialising in marine hull insurance and there was a Russian equivalent to Lloyd's. The Anglo-German company, Northland-German Lloyd's, was represented by the trading house Repman and Rust, which was engaged mainly in cargo insurance from and to Russia and Iran, and the German Levant Line, devoted to the insurance of vessels and cargoes within Azerbaijan, was also present. A large sector of the insurance industry was under the control of Russian insurance companies. In 1912, 30 insurance societies and agencies already operated in Azerbaijan.

In the post-revolutionary period, insurance in Azerbaijan has passed from operating in the Soviet system of a state-controlled monopoly, to the present conditions of operating in a developing market economy. Under the Soviet Union's monopolistic insurance regime, insurance offered to the population was limited in terms of available services and only the system of state social security was effective.

Development of the insurance market

The development of a market economy has meant the growth of private business, the formation of a market infrastructure and a sharp decrease in state influence, thus providing the freedom to develop industrial relations and to distribute consumer goods. This, in turn, has encouraged the establishment of an indigenous insurance market, completely changing the previous structure and the way in which business had been conducted, and much improving the range of insurance services provided.

In the early 1990s, with the transition to a market economy, a State Insurance Supervision Office was created. It is responsible to the Cabinet of Ministers and its basic duties are to regulate the development of insurance services, to protect policyholder, underwriter and state interests, to police insurance activities and to prepare the appropriate guidelines and regulations that affect the insurance industry.

In January 1993 the first law of the Azerbaijani Republic on insurance was adopted. It outlined the concept of a national insurance market and its development, and included documents regulating the insurance market.

The creation of a domestic insurance market, operating in open market conditions, began when the monopolistic system was disbanded and, as a consequence, when the rapid growth in the number of alternative insurance organisations became evident. As of 1998, and despite a difficult financial situation, 62 insurance companies, of which 9 were joint ventures with foreign capital, and 4 branches of international broker companies were operating in Azerbaijan. Only one insurance company is state-owned.

The total capitalisation of the insurance market is over 25 billion manats, or about US$6.5 million.

As a rule, insurance is carried out on the basis of a voluntary agreement between parties, but insurance can also be obligatory when required by the appropriate laws of Azerbaijan.

The market results for 1998 show a total collected insurance premium of 56 billion manats (US$14.4 million), which exceeded the 1997 figure by 4.8 per cent. The amount of claims paid in 1998 was 10.5 billion manats (US$2.7 million), which exceeded the 1997 figure by 28.7 per cent. In 1998, insurance companies contributed 2.3 billion manats to the state budget and invested 34 billion manats (US$8.5 million) in the economy.

A positive factor in the present insurance market is the growth across the board of all classes of insurance, with 74 per cent of business now accounted for by voluntary policyholders and obligatory policies accounting for 26 per cent. The number of policies issued on a voluntary basis in 1998 was 67.8 per cent of the total number issued, with the balance of 32.2 per cent coming from obligatory policies.

The Azerbaijan insurance market has a large potential for development. The fact that the total volume of insurance premiums in the Republic represents less than 0.4 per cent of annual gross domestic product (GDP), shows that there is plenty of room for growth (insurance accounts for 8 to 10 per cent of annual GDP in western countries).

Future developments

Developments to date show that the foundations for an indigenous insurance market have already been established, that the market is financially adequate and that it is capable of providing insurance services and of further expansion. However, the ability of local insurance companies to cover catastrophic losses remains low, and there is no incentive or mechanism available to encourage enterprises and organisations to seek insurance cover for their property interests.

A precondition for the further development of the insurance market in the Republic is not only the revival of the economy, but also the enhancement of resources within its revival. Strengthening of the private sector, the growth in private property ownership, developing the real estate market, the privatisation of state enterprises, including the selling off of residential properties, and the reduction and downsizing of existing state subsidies are all expected to provide opportunities for the insurance sector.

The adoption of the Law 'On Obligatory Liability Insurance for Vehicle Owners in 1996 was an important step towards the further development of the insurance market. In 1997 the following Laws were enacted: On an Obligatory Personal Accident Insurance Program for Military Servicemen, About Courts and Judges, On Fire Safety, On Public Health, About Communication and The Code for Customs and Excise. All these contain special clauses relating to the requirements of insurance.

In 1993 the Union of Insurance Companies of the Azerbaijan Republic was established. The purpose of the Union is to represent and unite insurance organisations and coordinate their activities. The Union also aims to assist in the formation and development of the insurance market and to consider and protect the interests of members in their dealings with the state, with international contacts and with other sectors of the economy. The Union draws up recommendations to enhance the development of insurance legislation, participates in expert studies and considers other proposals regarding the insurance industry.

The Union of Insurers, working hand in hand with the State Insurance Supervision Office, seeks to improve insurance legislation and regulations on insurance activities.

Insurance legislation

The Law on Insurance, adopted in 1993, played a key role in establishing a foundation for the insurance business in Azerbaijan, especially during the period of transition from socialism to a market economy. However, further developments within the insurance market, the development of reinsurance and the integration of countries into the European Union (EU) have forced Azerbaijan to enact a new Law.

On 25 June 1999 the Milli Majlis (National Assembly) of the Azerbaijan Republic accepted a new Law on Insurance, which meets world and European standards. At the time of writing the new Law awaits ratification by the President of the Azerbaijan Republic.

The new Law comprises six sections:

1. General provisions;

2. Organisation of insurance business;

3. Insurance contracts;

4. Basis of insurance activity and its financial stability;

5. State supervision of insurance activities;

6. Conclusion.

Overall, it:

- Provides for the development of operating standards in the practice and conduct of the insurance business and for the protection of the rights and interests of insured parties.

- Provides for the establishment of solvency margins to ensure the financial stability of insurers and for the professional regulation of those wishing to be involved in insurance (eg consultants, actuaries, agents, brokers and others).

- Regulates the contractual rights of parties under insurance contracts and defines obligations and liabilities of the state in the insurance sector.

- Details the possible forms of establishment and structure of insurance organisations and the procedures for the professional conduct of consultants, actuaries, agents and brokers. Insurance involvement by foreign companies and individuals is also defined.

- Expands on the coverage provided by insurance contracts, the duties of insured and insurer, the insurance rates and claims. In order to ensure financial stability of an insurance organisation, there are clauses in the law concerning insurance guarantees and the establishment of insurance reserves.

- Enables the State supervision of insurance. The duties and rights of the state supervisory body are enshrined in the Law, as is its responsibility to ensure the financial stability of insurers.

- Defines accounting and reporting procedures and what penalties may apply for any infringements of the insurance law.

A full package of regulations and guidelines on insurance activities will come into force simultaneously with the enactment of the law.

The reforms carried out within the insurance industry will encourage insurance organisations to take advantage of opportunities to increase the volume of business being underwritten.

According to our conservative projections, insurance premiums will reach an estimated US$35 million in 2001, US$140 million in 2006 and US$310 million by 2009. Investments in the insurance sector will be profitable in the relatively short term, which should encourage the large European, American, Turkish and Russian insurance, reinsurance and brokerage companies to become more active in Azerbaijan.

2.7

Minerals and Mining

I Tagiyev, First Deputy Chairman and Y Zamanov, Deputy Chairman, The State Committee on Geology and Natural Resources

Introduction

Azerbaijan is located in the eastern part of the Caucasus. In the north, the country borders the Dagestan Republic of the Russian Federation; in the west, Georgia; in the south-east, Armenia, and in the south, Turkey and Iran. Part of the Caspian Sea coast belongs to Azerbaijan. The country's area is 86,600 km^2.

Among the major industrial sectors are oil, gas, chemical, metallurgical, machine-building, power generation, electricity, food, construction and other industries. The basic agricultural products are cotton, grape, grain, vegetables, tobacco, tea, cattle and others.

The mining sector is a large and increasingly important sector of Azerbaijan's economy, and benefits from well-developed regulations governing the use of land and its resources, thus making it an attractive sector to foreign investment.

The climate for foreign investment

Ownership

Ownership issues are regulated by the Constitution, the Law on Ownership, the Land Code and the Law on Natural Resources of the Azerbaijan Republic.

Pursuant to the Constitution, there exist three forms of ownership: state, private and municipal. All of these are inviolable and protected by the state. The Law on Ownership states that international bodies as well as local and foreign physical and legal entities may own land in Azerbaijan.

Land may be owned by the state, by individuals and by municipal authorities. All issues pertaining to land use are regulated by the Land Code. Natural and mineral resources belong to the state and may be offered for use to physical and legal entities, foreigners included. The Code establishes the principle of separate use of land and mineral resources.

Natural resources may be used for exploration, mining and other purposes given special permission (licence). The entities pay for the use of natural resources, the terms for which are fixed. There are also a number of payment exceptions and incentives for certain land-users, designed to stimulate activity in certain areas.

Legal and economic regulation of the relations between the land-owner (the state) and the land-user (investor) is based on the Law of Natural Resources.

Licences

Licences for exploration and recovery of minerals are given in line with the procedure fixed by the Law on Natural Resources and relevant by-laws of Azerbaijan.

The president's decree specifies the types of activity in the sphere of use of natural resources and also the state body that issues the licences. The government governs the procedure for issuing licences for the exploration of natural resources, the survey and recovery of underground waters, commercial mining of non-metallic building materials and gem minerals.

The rights to explore and recover minerals are given to foreign investors in the form of contracts concluded by the government (Cabinet of Ministers) and approved by the Majlis (National Assembly).

Taxation and fees

The issues of taxation and payment for the use of natural resources are specified by the Law on Natural Resources, the Law on Royalty, the Land Code, the Law on Land Tax and other relevant by-laws.

The following payments are effected for the use of natural resources: royalty, payment for the use of land, payment for the use of the water bed, deductions for renewal of mineral resources and licence fees. It is also envisaged to charge for the provision of geological and other pertinent data.

There exist tax rates for the different types of minerals, and procedures for the calculation of these, as for the amount at which licence fees should be set. The normative documents concerning other types of taxation are being elaborated.

The relationship with foreign investors is regulated by the Law for the Protection of Foreign Investments and the Law on Investment Activity. The laws are intended to regulate the extraction and efficient use of foreign material and technical resources, advanced technologies and state of the art equipment. They guarantee the protection of investments and investors' rights.

Foreign investors may take part in privatisation of state and municipal property, transfer of profits abroad (after payment of taxes and compulsory duties), and transfer abroad of foreign currency. The profits made by investors in Azerbaijan may of course be re-invested in the same monetary unit.

The procedure for export–import operations and the customs duties payable on goods required for the conduct of investors' economic activity have been fixed.

Exploration and development of mineral deposits

The territory of Azerbaijan is one of the most promising regions of the Mediterranean Alpine belt of Eurasia. It includes geologically complex beds of minerals, the folded systems of the Big and Small Caucasus and the Kuryn depression separating them, the Nakychevan folded area and the Gorny Talysh area, rich in different mineral resources. Azerbaijan's mineral resources are the most important part of the country's natural wealth.

In addition to oil and gas, the Republic boasts some 350 explored deposits of ferrous (iron), non-ferrous and rare (aluminium, copper, lead, zinc, antimony, molybdenum, cobalt, etc.) and precious (silver and gold) metals. These deposits also include non-metallic minerals (bentonite clays, zeolite, china stone, minerals for glass, chemical and cement industry), construction materials (facing and gang-sawn stones), bromide-iodide, underground fresh, thermal and mineral waters.

The total cost of explored reserves of 38 basic minerals (excluding oil and gas) as per the value of final products amounts to US$36.3 billion. About 48 per cent of explored deposits are developed and operated by mining companies.

In the Big and Small Caucasus and in the Nakychevan areas, there exist a number of explored and operating deposits. These areas are quite promising for the exploration of new deposits.

In the southern slope of the Big Caucasus are situated the commercial reserves of the large Filizchaisky deposit and the medium-sized Katsdagsky and Katekhsky deposits of polymetallic ores. Also found there are the reserves of the Sagatorsky copper-zinc deposit, the Mazymchaisky copper pyrites and the Karabchaisky pyrites-polymetallic deposits, which are located close to each other and form the Filizchaisky group of deposits. The Filizchaisky deposit is one of the largest in Europe.

The development of this group of deposits will help each year to produce 25,400 tons of copper, 32,600 tons of lead, 79,600 tons of zinc, 1,050 tons of gold, 85,000 tons of silver and other valuable materials (sulphur, bismuth, cobalt, cadmium, tellurium and indium). The mining metallurgical complex, functioning on the basis of these deposits, will provide the raw materials for a period of 50 years. The manifestations of gold in black shales have been found in this area as well.

In the Small Caucasus and Gazakhsky ore region there exists the unique (in respect to quality and reserves – 120 million tons) Dashsapakhlynsky deposit of bentonite clays for use in making finely ground iron ore concentrates and bentonite powder, used in drilling fluid. The residual reserves of this deposit are 99 million tons. Ball clay is supplied to the ore-dressing works in Russia, the Ukraine and Kazakhstan. The optimal output is 950,000 tons of ball clay per year, but the output of this deposit is considerably lower as a result of economic difficulties.

Gold reserves in the Dagkesamansky gold-polymetallic deposit have been evaluated. The deposits of cement aterials, zeolite, cladding and sawed stones are being developed.

In the Kedabeksky mining region the Goshinsk gold-sulphide, Kedabeksk copper pyrites and Karadagsk group (Karadag, Kharkhar, Khoshyal) of copper-porphyry deposits, quartz, gold and ore traces have been explored and evaluated. The same is true of the Karadagsk deposit of copper and porphyry ores (318,700 tons of copper). The potential reserves of this deposit are 910,000 tons of copper, which will be used in the production of blue vitriol and copper.

The gold reserves of the Kedabeksky and Goshinsk deposits are being evaluated, as is the potential of other promising areas for copper-porphyry mineralisation. There exist good prospects for the discovery of new deposits in this region.

In the Dashkesansky mining region there exists a group of deposits (Dashkesansky, Southern Dashkesansky, Damirovsk) of cobalt-bearing iron and magnetite ores whose reserves make up 234 million tons. The deposit is developed by the Azerbaijan ore-dressing works (the annual optimal output is 1.8 million tons of raw ore), which has permission to use the minerals in this deposit for 90 years. There also exists a cobalt deposit at Northern Dashkesansky that had been developed in the past, but is now in dead storage.

The Zaglinsky deposit of alunite ores is under development. Its residual reserves (130.2 million tons) provide the Gyandzhin aluminium plant with raw materials for a period of 40 years. The optimal output here is of 3 million tons of alunite ore.

The deposits of white marble and building materials are also being developed. Large reserves of china stone for the Gyandzhin china and earthenware plant have been explored and approved.

The Alabashlynsk deposit of hematite ores for the oil industry has been found in the northern part of this region.

There has also been much activity in the Karabakh mining region. The Kyzylbalagsky copper gold ore and Mekhmaninsky polymetallic deposits with commercial reserves of gold, copper, lead, zinc and selenium have been explored and prepared for development. The copper reserves in the Damyrlynsky deposit of porphyry ores have also been evaluated.

The Zangelansky mining region is home to the Vezhnalinsk quartz and gold deposit with proven reserves of gold, silver and copper, and to the Zangepansk deposit with proven unique reserves (130 million tons) of chemically pure limestones for the chemical industry.

The Kelbadjarsky and Lachynsky mining region contains six mercury deposits, the Agduzgagsky gold deposit, a group of gold and chromite manifestations, unique reserves of mineral waters called Isti-Su (similar to the famous Czech mineral water Karlovy Vary), facing materials and decorative stones. Over 70 per cent of the commercial reserves of the Zodsky gold deposit, which is now extensively developed by Armenia, are located in the Kelbadjarsky region of Azerbaijan.

The Nakychevan Autonomous Republic's Ordybadsk and Shakhbuz mining regions are home to all the deposits of molybdenum (Paragachai), copper (Diakhchey, Goidog, Misdeg, Gyzyldja), polymetals (Agdara, Nasirvaz), gold (Agyurt, Shakardara, etc), cobalt (Kylyt, Krtam), mineral water (Badampy, Syrab) and facing travertines. Deposits of antimony, gold, copper and complex ores are being explored and evaluated here.

In the Shakhbuz region, the unique reserves and quality of the Shakhtakhtynsky deposit of travertines have been developed. Also explored have been the large reserves of travertines in the Karabaglyar and Buzgovsky deposits, and teshenites in the Karadashky deposit that are used for the manufacturing of facing materials.

The Gyumushligsky mining region is home to the development of small zinc and lead deposits, to a large deposit of rock salt (736 million tons), to large reserves of dolomites for the glass industry (9.9 million tons), for the production of soda ash and metallurgical magnesium (140 million tons).

In the south-east of the country five deposits of large reserves of bromide-iodide waters have been explored. The Novo-Neftechalynsk bromide-iodide and Baku iodine plants use water from two deposits in this region.

More than 250 deposits of non-metallic and building materials, 32 deposits of mineral water (daily output of 20,000m^3) and thermal water (12,500m^3) have been explored in Azerbaijan.

Privatisation in the mining industry

The privatisation of state-owned enterprises (SOEs) began in Azerbaijan following the passing of the Law on Privatisation and the state's programme of privatisation of state property, begun in 1995.

SOEs are classified as small, medium and large. There are different groups of SOEs and enterprises, including those subject to compulsory privatisation, not subject to privatisation and those subject to privatisation by presidential decree only.

The first stage of the state privatisation programme concentrated on the privatisation of small SOEs and the second stage of the programme saw the privatisation of medium and large SOEs, followed by their transformation into joint-stock companies.

Natural resources and geological establishments are state property and are not subject to privatisation. Mining companies and non-ferrous and ferrous metallurgy works can be privatised, but only by presidential decree at the second stage of privatisation.

In December 1997 the president decreed to dissolve the state concern 'Industrial Building Materials' and its divisions and enterprises have been transformed into joint-stock companies.

At present, over 13,000 small SOEs have been privatised, and the process of privatisation of large SOEs has begun.

Proposals for the development and efficient use of mineral resources

It is hoped that Azerbaijan's investment and business activities in the mining sector will develop sufficiently to see the realisation of the following projects:

- the establishment of a mining and metallurgical complex based on the Filizchaisky group of polymetal deposits;

- the establishment of a company for the processing of cobalt-bearing iron-magnetite ores and the extraction of cobalt from tailings based on the Dashkesansky group of deposits;

- the production of iron ore pellets based on the reserves of iron-magnetite ores of the Dashkesansky group and bentonite clays of the Dashsalakhlynsky deposits;

- the construction of a plant for the production of bentonite powder for ferrous metallurgy based on the reserves of the Dashsalakhlynsky deposit;

- the development of the Karadagsk deposit of copper-porphyry ores and the establishment of a company for the production of copper and blue vitriol;

- the establishment of a joint venture for the mining of copper in the Mazymchaisky deposit of copper pyrites ores;

- the production of glass based on the Negramsky deposit of dolomites in the Nakychevan Autonomous Republic;

- the establishment of a plant for production of soda ash based on the reserves of rock salt and dolomites in Nakychevan;

- the development of deposits of quartz sand and construction of glass manufacturing plants;

- the joint development of the Aidagsky deposit of zeolites and construction, and possible works for the manufacturing of different products;

- comprehensive treatment of bromide-iodide water and the production and sale of the finished products;

- the development of the technology for the extraction of rare elements from industrial water, and the establishment of a plant based on this technology;

- the construction of a company for the recovery and production of tiles based on the deposits of facing and decorative materials;

- the establishment of a joint venture with modern stonecutting and processing equipment for the production of the articles made of semi-precious and decorative stones;

- the construction of a mineral water bottling plant;

- the construction of a resort and health complex based on the reserves of thermal and mineral waters.

An agency for investors

The forms of investment activity that these projects require in order to be realised can be determined by negotiation and these proposals can be viewed as opportunities for investors in the mining sector of Azerbaijan.

An Agency for Investments has been set up in Azerbaijan, which answers to the Cabinet of Ministers and the Ministry of the Economy.

Thus, rich mineral resources in the Republic, good prospects for their development, adequate legislation for the regulation of ownership issues and land use are all factors that combine to offer broad opportunities for participation by foreign investors in such developments. Importantly, they also provide equal conditions for all categories of users of natural resources in Azerbaijan.

2.8

South Caspian Oil

Tim Eggar

Introduction

In recent times there has been much negative reporting in the media regarding the current state of Baku's oil boom. Serious doubts are being expressed as to whether or not underlying fundamentals are now seriously flawed. These doubts coincided with, and were perhaps caused by, more global concerns. The dramatic collapse of the economies of East Asia with the anticipated domino effect that would engulf Russia, South America and Europe, all fed an increasing sense of pessimism. This economic pessimism escalated with the coeval collapse in global oil prices, with downside scenarios predicting that US$5 per barrel oil would become a reality.

But the focus of concern in Baku rapidly centred on the failure of two large consortia to find material oil reserves in the first phase of new exploration drilling. The decision to exit their production sharing contracts was seen to be a major disaster for ongoing western upstream investment in the Caspian.

So, how real is the general concern that Baku oil potential had been seriously over-hyped? Perhaps these events were simply another temporary dislocation, with which the upstream oil industry is familiar?

Oil reserves

There has been continued speculation as to the realities surrounding Caspian oil reserves predictions. Nevertheless, the enthusiasm with which western oil companies have competed for new contract areas in both the south and north Caspian, reflects their firm belief that these Caspian basins held substantial and accessible upstream reserve potential. And this was clearly done not with emotion but after considerable technical due diligence.

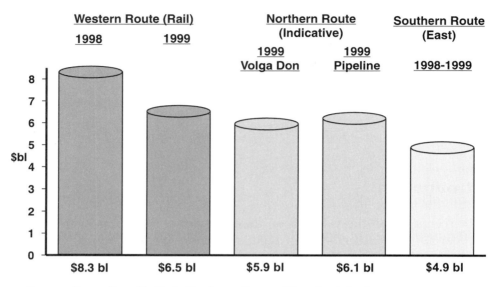

Figure 2.8.1 South Caspian Transportation Costs (ex Cheleken)

Consequently, the attraction of the Caspian focused on proven oil fairways: Plio-Pleistocene palaeodelta systems to the south, and Palaeozoic reef complexes to the north. Both oil provinces had extensive databases, developed over a considerable period of time. The petroleum geology and basin architecture of the Caspian is particularly well under-stood. More importantly, the area included many proven super-giant fields and there were a large number of known untested virgin structures of a similar dimension. These were favourably located within the hydro-carbon fairways and were available for licensing. This fact drove the early oil boom.

But the question must be asked, how did this opportunity arise? Up until the collapse of the former Soviet Union, the Caspian was inaccessible to western investors, so the answer to the question is twofold. First, Soviet technology imposed operating water depth constraints that had already been breached in the West; Soviet technology could not access structures in deeper water structures for conventional field development. Hence, for example, the Azerbaijan International Operating Company (AIOC) investment in the Azeri Chirag Deepwater Gunashli Field in offshore Azerbaijan. Discovered many years previously, SOCAR (the State Oil Company) successfully developed Shallow Water Gunashli and fully appreciated the merits of the extended structural trend. In 1994, this field became the centrepiece of the 'Contract of the Century', which opened up Azerbaijan to the West. Second, in the mid-1970s, a strategic policy decision was taken in Moscow to redirect oil investments from the Caspian to West Siberia. Oil developments in the Caspian declined, with many world-class prospects remaining untested as a consequence.

Detailed analysis of available databases confirmed that some 17.5 billion barrels of oil had already been found within the South Caspian. It remains a realistic expectation that a further 20 billion barrels could be found in Azerbaijan and Turkmenistan, in already well-defined untested traps. To put this into context, this Yet To Find (YTF) is a North Sea equivalent reserve level, which is replicated for similar geological reasons in the North Caspian Basin also. In the north, numerous untested Palaeozoic reefs have been identified on seismic and are true Tengiz Oil Field look-alikes. Tengiz itself holds a proven oil reserve in excess of eight billion barrels. Thus, it would again be surprising if a further 20 billion barrels YTF were not found in that prolific oil trend. Two critical exploration wells will test these fairways soon: Shak Deniz is now testing offshore Azerbaijan and Kashegan is soon to drill in offshore Kazakhstan. But these are exploration wells and they carry geological risk. Nevertheless, there is every confidence that the Caspian will provide a further YTF of 40 billion barrels, with an upside of perhaps 65 billion barrels. This projection is geologically sound and reflects a common understanding in the industry.

But these numbers are too modest in comparison with much of what has been published in the media. There, a YTF reserve in excess of 200 billion barrels still persists as a favoured number. This would place the Caspian on a par with much of the Middle East. It is equivalent to the reserve potential of Kuwait and the United Arab Emirates combined, and close to Saudi Arabia itself. Clearly this YTF prediction is flawed and is not technically supportable. Essentially, it arose in early 1995, from a Reserves Review commissioned by the US State Department, now held by the Department of Energy. It was compiled at a time of considerable geopolitical repositioning of the USA within the Transcaucasus. The number so derived reflects the concept of an Ultimate Reserve, in which oil would fill every conceivable trap, with no exploration risk. This is commercially meaningless.

But such is the misuse of technical concepts that they have become embedded in the myths of contemporary journalism. More realistic reserves projections, such as those identified above, have been promoted since the inception of the Baku oil boom in 1995. They remain unchanged and present a more modest but important message. With a YTF reserve potential of some 40 billion barrels, by 2010 an oil production potential of between three and five mmbd for the Caspian can be projected with some confidence. It will be a North Sea equivalent for the coming decades: an important player in global oil supply, but not a future swing producer. That privilege remains safely entrenched within the Middle East.

Failed exploration drilling

So, what of the two failed offshore exploration ventures in Azerbaijan? The Karabakh Contract Area (CIPCO) of Pennzoil, and the Ashrafi Dan Ulduzu Contract Area (NAOC) of BP Amoco, were both priority targets in an early drilling campaign. Located close to, but not on trend with AIOC, how could they have failed? They failed for sound technical reasons. The geology and geophysics of the Apsheron Sill is particularly well known. Plio-Pleistocene oil fields trend along the flank of this emerging basement ridge, where giant structural traps are ideally located to entrap oil migrating northwards from a deep basin centre to the south.

SOCAR geologists knew only too well that explorers should beware if they went too far north of this critical edge. Thus it was predicted well in advance of any new drilling that significant hydrocarbons were not likely to migrate up dip to the north of AIOC. This was the consistent view held by Azeri experts – a view shared by many western experts also. But the structures were large and needed to be tested. Operationally they were simple to access. Consequently, it was always known by CIPCO and NAOC that these were high-risk exploration ventures. Subsequent events have proved that the original technical predictions were sound. Therefore, the outcomes from these two wells have reinforced the understanding of the South Caspian geological model, not undermined it. It was a commercial failure for the investors who took the risk. But this is the nature of upstream exploration and therefore came as no surprise.

Thus, rather than diminishing the offshore oil potential of Azerbaijan, these results from early drilling have reinforced the exploration under-standing that underpins reserve predictions. But this is a different message to the one being portrayed in the media.

Commitment, work programmes and seismic support demand

So, what does all this mean for continued work commitments in Baku and Ashgabad? Of the 19 Contract Areas now agreed in Azerbaijan, all but one (AIOC) are Exploration Production Sharing Agreements.

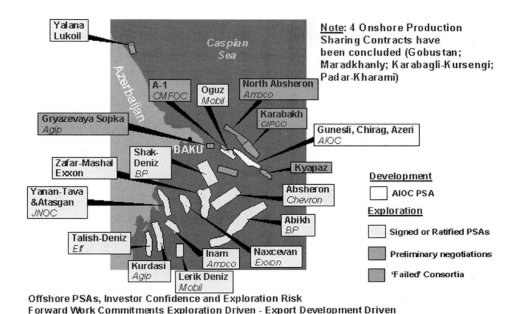

Figure 2.8.2 1999 Offshore Azerbaijan Exploration and Production Contract Areas: The Baku Oil Boom – 'Flag Follows Trade'

This means that some 29 investing upstream companies have now made contractually binding work commitments for the next few years. This will not be abandoned. Most, if not all, of these contracts carry the requirement to do 3D seismic and a minimum of two exploration wells. Several carry far greater commitments. Consequently, drilling, oil field services, logistics and social infrastructure, etc will continue to be needed in Baku, and the current work momentum will not disappear.

However, financial prudence imposed by recent oil price pressures will now dictate a greater cost challenge than perhaps has been seen to date. The reductions in Baku work activity so vividly described in recent news reports are not failure-driven, but simply good business practice. AIOC and its current approach to development planning is an excellent example of this newly imposed discipline. The exceptional results in reservoir performance experienced at Chirag 1 bodes well for future plans. Well productivities and flow sustainabilities have far exceeded original expectations. Regional infrastructure has worked well. The 'Contract of the Century' is delivering!

Therefore, with only a modest success from what is an extensive early exploration programme, some will inevitably result in new oil developments. This must mean that the essential fundamentals that underpin the Baku oil boom remain well in place. The US$30 billion plus development

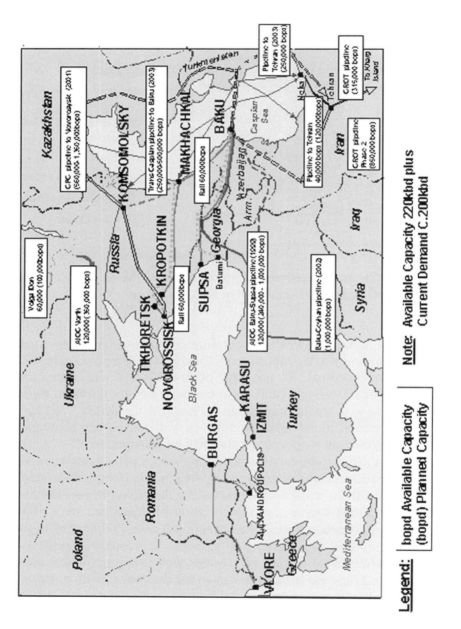

Figure 2.8.3 South Caspian Oil Transportation Options 1999

plans envisaged in existing contracts will ensure the longevity of Baku oil, albeit at a more prudent pace.

Turkmenistan has come relatively late to this upstream game, but already it too has some US$400 million of work commitments in place for contracts in its western region. But more importantly, the enormous gas deposits already found in eastern Turkmenistan will have a far greater impact on its future economic growth.

South Caspian oil transportation

To reinforce this positive message, recent developments in regional oil transportation are perhaps the most understated successes to date. AIOC and SOCAR have been moving Azerbaijan oil from Baku northwards through their pipeline to Russia, onwards to Novorosysk, since the end of 1997. They have commissioned their second pipeline along the western route through Georgia and this is already working at full capacity, and AIOC oil has already been exported from the new Black Sea terminal at Supsa.

Likewise, for over three years East Caspian oil has been successfully shipped by rail by Caspian Transco from Baku to Batumi. Other Turkmen oil produced by Monument and others from the Burun Field has been successfully transferred to the Tehran Refinery via Neka, for profitable oil swaps for sale in the Asian markets of the East. Some additional options are also open for South Caspian oil transportation: through the Volga Don Canal system (for summer operations) and by rail from Makhachkala to Novorosysk.

So, at this point in time there is already an excess of export capacity options available to third parties from the South Caspian. The pipeline market has responded to commercial demand and Caspian oil is moving internationally. In 1995, the media focused on a land-locked Caspian, where export risk was seen to be the primary obstacle. By 2000 events have proven otherwise and will continue to do so.

For the longer term, the future is equally bright. There is an emerging strong demand for regional pipeline development to the north (CPC), to the west (Baku Supsa – Baku Ceyhan), and to the south (NIOC). It is no longer a matter of *if* but rather *when* these pipelines will be built. The clear message is that once new oil is found, expansion plans and new pipelines will follow to respond to market forces.

Thus, once more the fundamentals for a sustainable South Caspian oil boom are falling into place. Periodic dislocations will inevitably occur, but with multiple export options and the opportunities for choice, the Caspian producers can clearly hedge their risks. Multiple pipeline strategies are the only viable option for the prudent development of their Caspian resources.

South Caspian transportation costs

As a direct consequence of early competition for export crude, there has been a market response in reducing transportation costs. For strategic reasons Monument uses two export routes to move its Turkmen crude to market. It moves westwards across the Caspian to Dubendi (Baku) and then by rail with Caspian Transco to Batumi. It also moves oil south to Neka and Iran, for pipeline transfer to the Tehran Refinery. Monument then receives a corresponding swap of equivalent export oil from NIOC at Kharg.

For 1998, the Iranian route gave the most favourable tariff of the two options. However, in 1999, rail transportation costs were materially reduced from Dubendi to Batumi, in response to increased competition. With a new competitive option becoming available for third parties with the AIOC–SOCAR pipeline to Novorosysk, even greater downward market pressure results. For the Volga Don, a viable summer export system is in place. Therefore, with excess export capacity being available, we can realistically expect further reductions in tariffs to be made. Existing tariffs are clearly set above true cost and are at a level that the market will currently bear. These tariffs will fall progressively.

Oil price

But what has surely reinforced investment confidence in the Caspian is the return of an improved oil price. Oil, in the same way as any other commodity, is subject to the laws of supply and demand. It is also a commodity whose supply can be controlled by one or only a few swing producers, and this role falls to OPEC. The key oil producers in the Gulf are all facing material budget deficits. Consequently, it is in their fundamental interest to maintain an oil price of around US$15 per barrel or better. It is not in their interest to drive oil prices down. With an immediate cash-driven need to service short-term debt, the Organization of Petroleum Exporting Countries (OPEC) has responded positively to the oil price challenge. Material cutbacks in production have been made for the benefit of all, and oil price again sits happily in a higher price bracket.

With a breakeven development cost of between US$12 and US$13 per barrel, at US$15 per barrel the Caspian becomes commercial. However, profitability is further reinforced by falling transportation costs, and with financial prudence (cost savings) and new technologies, all factors will combine to reduce development cost also. The economic fundamentals are all in place for the Caspian to become a significant oil producer in the coming decades, albeit to supply niche markets in the Black Sea and Mediterranean.

1994	1999
• Collapsed Soviet Economy, Hyperinflation, Negative Economic Growth	• Emerging Free Market, Stable Currency, Low National Debt, Low Inflation, Controlled Budget, Low Economic Growth, IMF approval
• Political Chaos, weak Central Government	• Political Stability, strong Central Government, Emerging Democracy and political Opposition with vocal free Press
• Regional Confrontation	• Regional Co-operation
• International Isolation	• Geopolitical Status
• An untested business environment	• An effective business environment with proven track record
• Literate People, Low Expectations	• Literate People, High Expectations
• Unresolved Karabakh War, one million IDPs	• Unresolved Karabakh War, one million IDPs

Figure 2.8.4 Azerbaijan 1994–1999

Political and business risk

The dramatic political changes that have occurred in Azerbaijan since 1994 reinforce the positives and not the negatives. They encourage and support long-term investment rather than the contrary. Collective memories can be short. Baku in 1994 was a very different city to the one we see today. Azerbaijan was a country in economic collapse, enduring political chaos, weak central government, an unstable currency, regional confrontation and international isolation. In any scenario, it was a country that held out exceptionally high pre-investment risk.

Today we see strong central government, a country with international status and broad-based geopolitical support, enjoying an emerging free market, with a developing democracy and a vocal and viable political opposition. More importantly, despite the serious effects of the recent collapse in world oil price, the country's debt position remains sound, the currency has not collapsed and the economy remains stable (albeit at a low level). Clearly, investor risk in the South Caspian has in a very short time improved beyond all original expectations. But some fundamental problems do remain. Although regional conflicts in Chechnya and Karabakh are currently passive, they remain unresolved. The issue of political succession both in Baku and elsewhere continues to provide cause for concern. Political volatility in Moscow, Ankara and Tehran promotes uncertainty. Nonetheless, regional political stability is more secure now than at any other time since the break-up of the Soviet Union. The direct support of the USA and European Union will ensure that any dislocations will be controlled. The progress and political change we currently see will inevitably continue into the foreseeable future.

Conclusion

Caspian resource predictions remain unchanged and recent exploration drilling has reinforced our understanding of South Caspian reserves potential, not undermined it.

Regional export systems are working well, are cost effective and are improving.

A modest rise in oil price, together with a general reduction in both development and transportation costs, makes upstream investment in the South Caspian increasingly more commercial.

With commitments that already exist within existing production sharing contracts, work programmes will ensure that current investment activities will not diminish over the next five years.

Fundamental changes in the political environment at all levels have materially reduced investment risk. They reinforce security of upstream contracts as a whole.

Although some political dislocations will inevitably occur, these will be temporary, and the forward positive momentum seen to date will continue.

With a production forecast of perhaps three to five mmbd by 2010, the Caspian as a whole will supply some 5 per cent of potential world demand. The Caspian is not, and never will be, a global swing producer. With YTF reserves of some 40 billion barrels, the Caspian will be a new North Sea, but never a strategic alternative to the Middle East.

With low-cost transportation being a material economic issue, Caspian crude will focus on proximal markets rather than global. The bulk of Caspian crude will inevitably go west to the Black Sea and the Mediterranean, where it will displace other regional oils. Perhaps up to 10 per cent or more of Caspian crude will go south, to service the commercially attractive market of northern Iran.

In all scenarios, the Caspian is clearly an important niche player for international oil supply. The fundamentals for its longevity are clearly in place. There are still many problems to be solved and great challenges to be overcome. No one would have predicted that the future for the Caspian would be easy. The South Caspian oil boom of 1996–1998 has clearly lost some of its initial energy and gloss, but what we will now see is a more measured approach to continuing investment that will be sustainable in the long run. Despite what we read in the media, at this point in time the Caspian is still a 'half-full' cup, and not a 'half-empty' one.

ABBOT GROUP plc

Minto Drive, Altens, Aberdeen, AB12 3LW
Telephone: 01224 299600
Facsimile: 01224 230400

OIS International
Inspection plc
Silverburn Place,
Bridge of Don

Aberdeen, AB23 8EG
Telephone: 01224 226700
Facsimile: 01224 226701

Worldwide Inspection, Testing &
Corrosion Engineering

100%

KCA Drilling Limited
Minto Drive, Altens
Aberdeen, AB12 3LW
Telephone: 01224 299600
Facsimile: 01224 895813

International Drilling & Workover
Contractors, Drilling Facilities
Engineering, Well Engineering &
Project Management

100%

B.W. Group plc
Abbotswell Road, West Tullos
Aberdeen, AB12 3AD
Telephone: 01224 879013
Facsimile: 01224 890265

Drilling Muds & Completion Fluids,
Fluids Engineering & Chemistry

100%

PowerGen Renewables Ltd
Westwood Business Park,
Westwood Way,
Coventry, CV4 8LG
Telephone: 01203 424000
Facsimile: 01203 425432

Developers, Owners & Operators of
Wind Power Electricity Projects in the
UK and Ireland

50%

2.9

Oil and Gas

SOCAR

A brief history

Azerbaijan and oil – these two words have been linked for over 2,500 years. Interest in Azerbaijani oil is not a derivative of its quantity, but of its historical roots. The area around Baku has long been known to be rich in oil reserves. Marco Polo visited the region in the 13th century and wrote of a great fountain of oil and hand-dug pits that produced oil which was used for lighting, medical treatment and military purposes. Historians have irrefutable evidence proving that it has been exported for the past 2,500 years from the Absheron Peninsula to Iran, Iraq and other countries by camel caravans loaded with skins filled with oil. Records indicate that in 1594, a local citizen had dug an oil pit to a depth of 35 metres. By 1806 there were 50 oil wells on Absheron, by 1821 there were 120 and by the middle of the 1860s there were 218.

The first oil well in the world was drilled in Azerbaijan, in the Bibi-Heybat field by V Semyenov in 1844, 11–12 years earlier than those drilled in the USA (Pennsylvania in 1859). The hand-dug wells were in continuous use in Absheron until 1872. The wells were constructed like a stepped inverse pyramid. The oil produced from the wells was placed into stone-lined pits (ambars). After settling and cleaning, it was transferred to ambars in town. In 1870 Baku had 14 ambars. One of the wells drilled in 1871 produced 70 barrels of oil per day. The first gusher occurred on the Bibi-Heybat field on 13 June 1872. During the first three months, the field yielded over 90 million poods (1,474,000 tons). A second and more powerful gusher occurred in Balakhanli on 14 October 1875 from a well 95.85m deep. That well flowed for some months at a rate of 2,457–3,276 tons per day, resulting in the formation of four large lakes. In 1859, the Nobel Brothers built the first paraffin factory in Surakhani, next to the Temple of Fire Worshippers. By the beginning of the 1870s, there were 47 small, simply equipped paraffin factories in Baku. Oil production increased with subsequent technological innovations. It reached 538,900 poods (8,620 tons) in 1864, and 1.658 million poods (26,700 tons) in 1869. The modern factories were built between 1876 and 1881 for the production of lubricant oils.

The first oil tanker in the world, the *Zoroaster*, built with a metal hull, was put into operation for the transportation of kerosene used for heating. Oil was transported by rail tank cars for the first time in 1881. Several oil pipelines were constructed between 1878 and 1884, connecting the Balakhani industrial region with the oil-refining enterprises in the city. By 1896, 26 pipelines for transporting oil from the fields to factories were already in existence. A total of 230km of oil pipeline had been laid in Baku by the end of 1898, with a total annual flow of 1 million tons. From 1897 to 1906 an 850km oil pipeline was built, which extended from Baku across the Caucasus to Batumi on the Black Sea.

In 1884 percussion drilling was applied and became known as the 'Baku method'. The very first attempts to produce oil from the offshore area took place as early as the beginning of the 19th century, and were initiated by a Baku entrepreneur Kasim-Bey. He dug two wells 30–40m from shore in Bibi-Heybat Bay. His idea of holding back the sea with a framework of tightly fitting planks was the forerunner of modern offshore facilities and fixed platforms. Efforts to create the landfill of previous offshore land areas in Bibi-Heybat started in 1911. After the completion of this landfill in 1924, large-scale offshore production commenced. By 1913 there were 3,500 wells in Baku.

In 1901, 11 million tons of oil were produced in Azerbaijan. This was a worldwide production record for the time and accounted for more than half of that year's global production of crude. The first oil industry machine building plant, now known as the Sattarkhan Plant, was founded in Azerbaijan in 1922. Between 1923 and 1925 it manufactured down hole pumps, rotary drilling rigs and Christmas trees. The large-scale production of pumping rods began in 1925.

A sharp reduction occurred in 1918 when production dropped to 3,425 million tons as a result of the political reverberations in Russia and Azerbaijan, as well as the nationalisation of oil and formation of the Soviet Union. Since 1923 stability has been re-established. The drilling of 'super-deep' wells began in the Baku oilfields in 1940. The following year the deepest wells in the entire Soviet Union were being drilled in the Husani region, at depths of 3,200–3,400m. Oil production reached a record level of 23,482 million tons in the 1940s. Between 1941 and 1945 Azerbaijan produced 63.2 per cent of all the oil in the Soviet Union; in fact it is often said that the Soviet Union's victory over Germany in the Second World War was won on Azerbaijani oil.

In 1949 the Neft Dashlari (Oily Rocks) offshore oilfield was discovered. Since 1950 offshore production has increased in the Republic simultaneously with the development and exploitation of new onshore oil and gas fields. By 1963, 800 self-contained constructions were built in the Caspian Sea. Around 1,300 fixed platforms and over 450km of piers have been constructed in the Caspian Sea. In the period from 1969 to 1988 oil fields such as Sangachal, Duvannyi-Kharazirya, Bahar, Bula Daniz, Gunashli, Alyaty Daniz and March 8 were developed.

The industry now

Thanks to the economic policies of the President of the Azerbaijani Republic, Heydar Aliyev, and as a result of new regulations and governmental guarantees for investors, Azerbaijan has attracted foreign investment for the development of its natural resources since the 1990s. International recognition by the world oil and gas sector came after the decision by President Aliyev to host an annual oil exhibition, which would heighten awareness and interest in the hydrocarbon potential in the Republic. From 24 to 28 May 1994 the first international exhibition took place. It was devoted to all aspects of oil and gas exploration and of production in the southern Caspian Basin. For the first time, many leading international companies participated.

On 20 September 1994 the first contract was signed for the joint development of the Azeri, Chirag and deep-water portion on the Gunashli field in the Azerbaijani sector of the Caspian. Contracting companies included Amoco Caspian Sea Petroleum Limited, BP Exploration (Caspian Sea) Limited, Statoil, LUKOIL Joint Stock Company, Pennzoil Caspian Corporation, Ramco Khazar Energy Limited, Turkish Petroleum and Unocal Khazar Limited. Exxon Azerbaijan Limited joined the consortium in 1995, and ITOCHU joined in 1996. The oil reserves of these fields are estimated at 500 million tons. In the 'Contract of the Century', Azerbaijan is carried with 90 per cent of the investment required for development provided by contracting parties of the consortium. Azerbaijan retains the right of control and management of the field development.

The critical issue for oil development in Azerbaijan relates to logistics – limited and complicated access to international markets. Because of the complexity of political and economic issues, President Aliyev personally visited Moscow for the signing ceremony of the agreement for transit of Azerbaijani oil through the Russian Federation to the Novorossiysk port on the Black Sea. This agreement was signed with Russia on 18 February 1996.

A few weeks later, on 8 March 1996, Aliyev visited Tbilisi for the signing of the agreement with Georgia on transit of crude oil from Azerbaijani offshore fields on the Caspian Sea by means of a new pipeline connecting Baku and Supsa – the Georgian port on the Black Sea.

Another important event in the history of the oil industry of Azerbaijan took place on 25 October 1997. On this day the first portion of SOCAR's crude oil crossed the state border of Azerbaijan and was transported through the Russian territory to the port of Novorossiysk. The first tanker cargo of SOCAR's oil was lifted from Novorossiysk on 26 December 1997. Almost 5.2 million tons of crude oil has been exported from Azerbaijan through Novorossiysk port since 26 December 1997 to the present day.

On 17 April 1999, the Azerbaijan International Operating Company and SOCAR along with the Georgian Pipeline Company, and the Georgian International Oil Corporation, celebrated the completion of the Western Route Export Pipeline (WREP). The ceremony took place in Suspa, where heads of state including Azerbaijan's President Heydar Aliyev, Georgian's President Eduarde Shevarnadze and Ukraine's President Leonid Kuchma officially inaugurated the WREP and the new modern oil terminal in Supsa.

Transportation cost through the Georgian territory is considerably lower than through Russia. The line is 530mm with three pump stations in Azerbaijan and three in Georgia. Planned rate from commencement is 100,000 barrels per day, the line is rated as 115,000 barrels per day with existing boosters pumps, but this could be increased to 250,000 barrels per day if additional pumping capacity is installed. Vessel size is in the range of 80,000–140,000 tons and lowered by three pumps each rated at 1900 metric tons per hour. The Motor Tanker 'Agip Piemonte' lifted the first cargo of ACG crude oil from Supsa terminal on 8 April 1999. Its destination was a refinery in Castellan, Spain. This marked the first time that Azerbaijan's crude oil was originally delivered to the world market. Since that day more than 7.3 million tons of Azeri Light – a new trademark of Azerbaijan offshore crude oil – has been exported from Supsa.

Along with two existing export pipelines Azerbaijan is looking to widen its export routes. On 29 October 1998, in Ankara, the Presidents of Azerbaijan, Turkey, Kazakhstan, Uzbekistan, Kirghizistan and Georgia signed a joint declaration announcing their political support to the Baku–Ceyhan Crude Oil Pipeline Project. On 18 November 1999, in Istanbul, the Presidents of Azerbaijan, Georgia and Turkey signed the Agreement for transportation of crude oil through territories of these three neighbour countries by means of main transport pipeline Baku–Tbilisi–Ceyhan. On the same date, the Presidents of Azerbaijan, Georgia, Kazakhstan and Turkey signed the 'Istanbul Declaration' and the 'Agreement between the Republic of Azerbaijan, Georgia and the Republic of Turkey, regarding crude oil transportation through territories of the Republic of Azerbaijan, Georgia and the Republic of Turkey'.

The length of new pipeline will be 1730km: Azerbaijan 468km, Georgia 225km and Turkey 1,037km. Basic engineering work on the

Baku–Ceyhan pipeline should start on 15 June 2000. Construction is scheduled to start in December 2001 and should be completed in the third quarter of 2004. The new pipeline will diversify export routes and give Azerbaijan ability to export large quantities of crude oil in years to come.

In conclusion, it is most relevant to quote President Aliyev speaking during the signing ceremony of the Azerbaijan first international oil contract, which has since become known as the 'Contract of the Century'. He said:

By signing this agreement we have once again demonstrated to the world the restoration of the sovereign rights of the Azerbaijan Republic as an independent state whose natural resources belong to our people. Through this cooperative effort, relationships have been formed between the developed countries of the world and international companies and we have created the basis for establishing a market economy. By signing this agreement, we have once more demonstrated to the whole world that the Azerbaijan Republic is a democratic and legal state.

2.10

Pharmaceuticals

Charles W Simpson, Country Manager,
GlaxoWellcome

In this chapter, the practicalities of operating a pharmaceutical business in Azerbaijan are addressed. Our experience and knowledge of Azerbaijan have been synthesised over a four-month period, since our arrival here. During this time we have registered and established the GlaxoWellcome office in Baku.

The focus will be on four key areas, providing a structure for this chapter as follows:

- Product registration
- Product distribution
- Marketing
- Sales.

At the time of writing, there seems to be no adequate manufacturing facilities that could perform to the worldwide standards (GMP) required by a global pharmaceutical company. That is not to say that Azerbaijani people lack the skills or know-how, but that there is currently no infrastructure to provide such a function. GlaxoWellcome is optimistic that there remains an opportunity for a western pharmaceutical company to invest in local manufacturing, if it made geographic and commercial sense. Due to the short nature of this chapter and to the strategic questions surrounding local manufacturing, addressing manufacturing opportunities any further in this chapter would not be appropriate.

The healthcare environment

Before getting into the specifics of the pharmaceutical business, an overview of the healthcare environment that a pharmaceutical company operating in Azerbaijan will encounter may be useful.

Disease prevalence

The health status indicators for Azerbaijan are surprisingly good considering the country's per capita income. The population is young, however, with more than 40 per cent of the population under the age of 18. The leading causes of death in Azerbaijan are mostly non-communicable diseases (see Table 2.10.1).

Table 2.10.1 Leading causes of death

Disease	*Rank (mortality rate)*
Cardiovascular	1
Respiratory	2
Cancer	3
Trauma	4
Intestinal	5
Infections	6
Birth Defects	7

Infectious diseases are not yet a large contributor to the mortality rates; however, there are indicators that suggest change, with a recent rise in cases of diphtheria, tuberculosis and other infectious disease. Human immunodeficiency virus (HIV) reports are minimal, but this may be largely to do with the huge social stigma attached to all sexually transmitted diseases in the Muslim Republic of Azerbaijan.

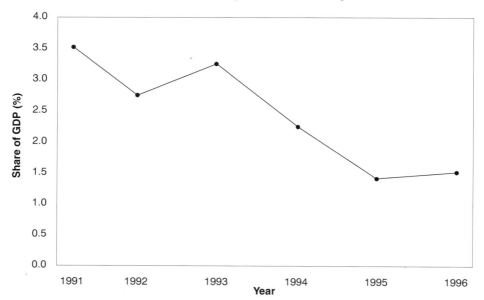

Figure 2.10.1 Public health expenditure 1991–1996

Generally, there is a lack of funds available for adequate state provision of healthcare. Unfortunately, this problem has grown progressively worse as the per capita spend on healthcare has declined significantly in the years following Azerbaijan's independence from the former Soviet Union (see Figure 2.10.1).

The healthcare system

Conceptually, there is a social network that provides free healthcare for all. The reality, however, is that Azerbaijan has developed into a 'fee for service' system, where patients pay for every item associated with their healthcare intervention. This ranges from the provision of pharmaceuticals to the sterile gloves and scalpels used in the procedure itself. It is also common for most families, due to the expense of hospital stays, to cook meals on-site for the duration of the patient's treatment. The fees for services are based on the procedure itself, plus the credentials and reputation of the doctor performing the procedure.

This system is currently not affordable to the masses, hence hospitals are running half-empty. There are plenty of doctors though. This has created an added problem in that greater numbers of women are opting to have their children delivered at home. A study conducted by a joint national health survey in 1996 (Centers for Disease Control and Prevention/UNICEF/World Health Organisation), showed that one-third of children are born at home. Besides the medical concerns associated with this, these children have no formal state identity or papers to prove their national origin, as it is currently against the law to have home births.

The majority of medical facilities in Azerbaijan are state-owned, and the health personnel are state employees. Doctors are paid minimal salaries by the state, hence the fees charged to the patient. There is a formal medical referral system from primary care to secondary care, but it is fair to say that primary care is underdeveloped and uncoordinated. Developing the power of individuals and communities to share responsibility for the improvement of their own health, along with providing cost-effective primary care will be essential to delivering improved healthcare in Azerbaijan and making the country's health situation better.

Reimbursement of medicines

There is an essential medicine list that makes medication conceptually free of charge for the patient through reimbursement by the government. The reality is that there are currently no funds available for reimbursement and this benefit is therefore not available.

There are four ministries in Azerbaijan that are supposed to offer their employees free medical and pharmaceutical provision. Unfortunately, none of the ministries have been given the financing that they need in order to provide this benefit, so once again, in practice, this is not done (see Figure 2.10.2).

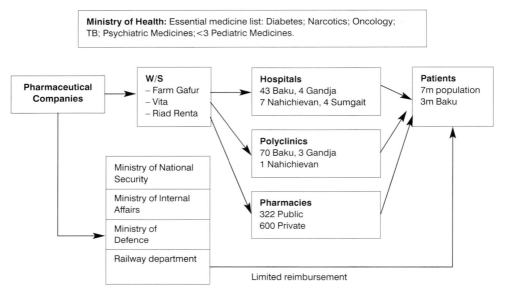

Figure 2.10.2: Healthcare delivery

Many modern medicines were not available in this part of the world during the Soviet years. Only since the mid-1990s have these medicines begun to trickle into the country, some legally, and some illegally, smuggled across borders. In consequence, a patient's expectation of pharmaceutical intervention is drastically outdated and different from that experienced in the West. This is important, as it becomes paramount not only to make doctors aware of new therapies but also to help them educate their patients. It is not an exaggeration to say that intravenous vitamin C is a common request of Azerbaijani patients. There is a common perception by patients that if something is not stuck in their arm they do not get better. This proves particularly challenging for pharmaceutical companies promoting oral and/or inhaled products.

The current perception will take some time to change as there seems to be a more symbolic, rather than substantive, approach taken by doctors. Giving patients what they want to make them feel immediately, but only temporarily better, rather than giving a fully effective drug is not uncommon. The cynical view says that treating patients' symptoms as opposed to their disease brings them back for further therapy, and hence further fees. This attitude is clearly in direct conflict with the goals of the more innovative pharmaceutical companies, which preach and have proven that focusing on the most effective treatments can reduce secondary care costs significantly, therefore reducing the overall healthcare budget.

Pharmaceutical operations

Product registration

Product registration in Azerbaijan is relatively straightforward and affordable. The process requires that a pharmaceutical company submit two sets of dossiers for each product submission. The dossiers should include the following: pre-clinical data, clinical data and chemical, pharmaceutical and biological data. In addition, five registration samples are required for the submission. These samples should be identical to the product to be sold on the market in Azerbaijan. These items, along with a letter of request should be submitted to: Akif Magerramov, Chief of Registration, Ministry of Healthcare, Baku 370014, Azerbaijan Republic.

While the process itself is relatively straightforward, the length of the process can vary significantly. As the process is a relatively new one for Azerbaijan, the resources and attention given to this area are minimal. It is advisable to solicit the support of a local wholesaler (see 'Product distribution' below) with good relationships in the Ministry of Health who can help speed up the process and even manage the submission process on behalf of a company. The average time from submission to registration approval varies from three to six months, with the average being closer to three months when using the effective contacts of a local wholesaler.

Product distribution

The World Bank surveyed 91 population points in 1995 and found that 60 per cent of rural points reported a lack of availability of essential medicines. The figure has improved in recent years, caused by the snowball effect of private pharmacies.

Pharmacies are supplied by various local and regional pharmaceutical wholesalers. There are three principal privately run pharmaceutical wholesalers, all based in Baku. They are listed below in size and importance. Like all successful local business in Azerbaijan, there is political sponsorship at various levels within these organisations – this can be a help and a hindrance. (See Figure 2.10.2.)

Farm Gafur
The largest of the three main wholesalers, carries more than 1,700 lines of pharmaceutical products. Farm Gafur works with over 38 foreign firms

and has had significant experience working collaboratively in a consignment stock arrangement. It is fair to say that in addition to foreign firms' products, all wholesalers carry the older former Soviet pharmaceutical brands. Farm Gafur has a relatively impressive data system for monitoring prices in the market on a daily basis.

Vita

The second largest pharmaceutical wholesaler in Azerbaijan, Vita also has many foreign partners that it works closely with. This organisation has close ties with Gideon Richter from Hungary and it has recently been rumoured that it has changed its name to Vita Richter. Depending on your product range, such close ties with this major generic player may be prohibitive.

Riad Renta

The third and smallest of the major pharmaceutical wholesalers prides itself on delivering the lowest price to its customers. However, it does not currently employ the same degree of information systems that the others do.

It cannot be overstressed how extremely important it is to seek out a good pharmaceutical wholesaler in Azerbaijan. Signing a consignment stock agreement will allow you to get a full product portfolio available on the market and the penetration needed to be successful.

In addition to the legitimate pharmaceutical distribution methods mentioned above, there is a significant amount of parallel trade coming in from Russia in the north. This business is scornfully referred to as the 'suitcase business', because entrepreneurial citizens take advantage of the deflated regional currencies and loose pharmaceutical company pricing strategies by buying products in a lower priced market and carrying the product illegally across the border in suitcases. It is therefore advisable for companies to have tight product pricing strategies to stop this illegitimate flow and to maximise the true potential in this market.

Marketing

There are many local printers and advertising companies that can help produce everything from promotional literature to television advertisements. There are various views on what quality marketing literature looks like. Shop around, ask for references from other foreign firms and check them out. Above all, only sign contracts with companies that are prepared to accept payment after the delivery of goods. It sounds straightforward, but many companies will ask for prepayment or partial prepayment prior to starting a job.

Doctors and patients alike are happy to receive Russian literature, which means that the costs of translating product information into

Azerbaijani can be saved. There is a growing patriotism towards Azerbaijani, which may mean that further translation of promotional material may eventually be required.

Pharmaceutical advertising is allowed for over the counter (OTC) products. Various media are available including TV, radio and several Azerbaijani and English language newspapers. In addition, there are local courier companies that can support mass mailing campaigns to business and even to individuals. Prices vary for all of the above-mentioned options, but they are extremely affordable by western standards.

Sales

As previously mentioned, there is an abundance of doctors in Azerbaijan and as a consequence the availability of qualified medical representatives is high. A word of caution however, as qualification can sometimes be deceiving in Azerbaijan. It is advisable to hire staff with a three-month probation period in order to assess their diligence, commitment and acumen. Training of medical representatives is required, not so much for their medical knowledge, but for the business and sales skills required for them to become effective medical representatives.

The size of the sales force required to cover Azerbaijan will vary according to your company's product mix and entry strategy. It is safe to say that with almost half the population of Azerbaijan living in Baku, the majority of one's focus will be in Baku and the surrounding areas including Sumgait.

Public transport in Baku is quite good so a company car is not necessary for medical representatives, nor advised due to the punitive import tax on automobiles at the current time. The relatively low cost of labour in Azerbaijan also allows the affordable employment of a driver who, with his own car, is able to transport two to three medical representatives around Baku.

Summary

So far, our experience in Azerbaijan has been both exciting and frustrating. In business terms, GlaxoWellcome has tremendous optimism over the future of this oil-rich nation. Differing oil reserve evaluations show varying economic projections for the country. However, the strategic position of Azerbaijan, at the crossroads of East and West, means that the country will always have its place at the world table and therefore its fair share of economic attention.

The business environment is tough and full of potential traps for western businesses. Healthcare is currently in a state of disarray and needs much help, not only in terms of investment but also in terms of education in western medicines. There is a tremendous opportunity for the pharmaceutical industry in Azerbaijan. Moreover, there is tremendous opportunity for Azerbaijan with the pharmaceutical industry.

2.11

Small- and Medium-sized Enterprises (SMEs)

Dr Alekper Mammadov, President, Azerbaijan Entrepreneurs' (Employers) Confederation

Investment stimulation in the SME sector and the role of the Azerbaijan Entrepreneurs' (Employers) Confederation

In a period of transition to a market economy, one of the most important factors in promoting the prosperity of a country is the development of the private sector and of entrepreneurial activities. From this point of view, the development of the private sector in Azerbaijan is of vital importance.

Since 1996 more than 22,000 small- and 1,000 medium-sized enterprises have been privatised in Azerbaijan and, as a result, about 200,000 people have become entrepreneurs and shareholders.

As in other former Soviet Republics, the development of the private sector in Azerbaijan began in the 1990s. Since 1994, the production of consumer goods in the private sector has increased 11.2 times, and productivity in agriculture 1.7 times. The development of the private sector has also resulted in the creation of new jobs; today, 33 per cent of the population is involved in the private sector.

The development of the private sector is directly related to foreign investment and the activity of foreign companies. Today, about 70,000 private companies are operational and more than 3,500 companies with foreign investment have been registered in Azerbaijan. Of these, 36.6 per cent are joint ventures, 43.9 per cent are fully foreign-owned, and 19.7 per cent are representative offices.

The rate of development in the private sector is determined by the volume of foreign investment. One of the main aims of Azerbaijan's foreign economic policy is to attract foreign investment to the priority areas of the economy. Thus, approaching sources of foreign investment and directing these to the priority areas has become paramount.

The SME sector plays a very important role in determining the country's investment policy. In order to stimulate investment in the SME sector, recognised as a priority area of the economy, the special 'Programme on State Support of Small and Medium Enterprises in Azerbaijan Republic (for 1997–2000)' was approved by order of the President.

This programme made it clear that investment could originate from both foreign and domestic sources and that investment should be directed towards the production of food, medicine and other consumer goods. Investment assistance in the SME sector covers the following areas of priority:

- the production of goods, using local and foreign raw materials, to substitute for imports;

- the production of goods for export, using new technologies;

- projects to update production facilities and support technological innovation;

- the development of traditional folk art.

The main precondition for attracting foreign investors is to create the right legal environment to guarantee the safety of their investments. Over the last few years, over 100 laws covering different areas of the economy and industry and relating to foreign investment activity were adopted. Furthermore, the Law of the Azerbaijan Republic, About the Protection of Foreign Investment, has been in force since 1992.

The country's economic, industrial and human potential, its geographical position and natural resources, its integration in the global community and the world economy and its development of a market economy provide many opportunities for the attraction of foreign investment to the country.

Another important measure ensuring normal conditions for foreign investments is the creation of an institution with extensive authority. From this point of view, the establishment of an Investment Assistance Centre in Azerbaijan was a very important step. The main aims of the Centre are to improve the general business environment, to improve conditions for foreign investors in the Azerbaijan economy and to increase the volume of foreign investment in non-oil sectors. To achieve these aims, the Centre will concentrate mainly on international marketing, research, mediation, lobbying and investor support.

The Azerbaijan Entrepreneurs' (Employers) Confederation ('the Confederation') a private sector organisation, can also play an important role in the development of the SME sector. The principal aim of the Confederation is to coordinate the activity of businesses and business persons involved in entrepreneurial activities, to protect their legal and economic interests and to promote the development of entrepreneurship in Azerbaijan. The Confederation acts in close coordination with entrepreneurial bodies and organisations, national and international financial/credit organisations and related state executive organs.

In accordance with its objectives, the Confederation undertakes the following responsibilities:

- to ensure the protection of the legal and economic interests of entrepreneurial entities before the corresponding executive organs of state;

- to foster the establishment of a sound entrepreneurial environment through financing investment and innovation and through initiating projects by way of competition;

- to prepare draft laws and other legislative acts, and to study other proposed legislation related to the development of entrepreneurship;

- to assist local entrepreneurs in their search for business counterparts in Azerbaijan and abroad;

- to contribute to the collection and dissemination of information related to entrepreneurship.

Today, the Confederation works closely and actively with the country's entrepreneurs. It benefits from great support from the European Union's Technical Assistance for the Commonwealth of Independent States (TACIS), an organisation that has always held the support of SMEs as a key objective of its work.

Though it only obtained full legal status in April 1999, the Confederation already has over 250 active members, 80 per cent of which are SMEs. It works with the government in the development of modern commercial legislation, particularly in the areas of insurance, leasing, taxation and transport.

The Confederation is keen to act as a focal point for trade between local SMEs and the West, and offers communication and data bank facilities to its members.

2.12

Telecommunications

The Commercial Section, British Embassy, Baku

Long before the implementation of a three-year International Monetary Fund (IMF) programme in Azerbaijan, Turkish telecommunications companies such as Netash and Alcatel Teletash first came to Azerbaijan. The Turkish companies began to upgrade the existing exchanges based on the analogue system. After the implementation of a successful fiscal policy by the government, financial institutions such as the World Bank began operating in the country, placing emphasis on infrastructure development projects. The Ministry of Telecommunications of Azerbaijan (MoT) received support from the government in setting up joint ventures, a step which constituted the initial phase in restructuring the telecommunications system in Azerbaijan. The revenue generated as the result of business activity by these joint ventures enabled the MoT to upgrade the exchanges inherited from the former Soviet Union.

Present conditions

Domestic and international communication network

Until 1991, Azerbaijan was only connected by direct communication cable with several cities of the former Soviet Union and Iran. A satellite system of communications also existed between Baku and Moscow. In 1991, by creating an international switch centre (DMS-100/200 Netash-Turkey production), Azerbaijan was given a line by the Union of International Telecommunications and its own international access code, +994. This has provided access to international automatic connections via Turkey with more than 150 countries in the world.

Developing access to the international system of communications has raised some difficulties for Azerbaijan. For example, approximately 92 per cent of switching equipment now being used in cities, regional centres and villages is outdated and some villages continue to use manual exchanges.

In 1993, telephone penetration was increased to 500 lines in Sumgait and, in 1995, to 2,500 lines in Ganja, with new telephone exchanges using System-12 in which a local loop is connected to the intercity circuit. The capacity of these stations has now been increased to 3,000 and 10,000 lines respectively. In 1996, a 60-channel satellite communications link, supported by the Turkish satellite Turksat, was set up between Baku and Nakhchivan.

Telephone growth

The need for a central administrative organ for long distance and international telephone services has been recognised by the government. Aztelecom Industrial Association (IA), established by the Ministry of Communications in 1992, aimed to provide companies, organisations and the population with long distance and international telephone services, but is not able to fully satisfy their needs.

Simultaneously, IA carries out technical operation works on cable structures and turnpikes, some of which is on optical-fibrous cable. The organisation consists of 60 subdivisions (municipal and regional telecommunications hubs and technical cable turnpike service centres) and has telephone stations covering a total subscriber capacity of 382,000 channels, of which 7,000 are electronic-digital type.

Telephone network in regions

The Azerbaijan telephone network is located and operated in the three main largest economic zones – Baku, Ganja and the Autonomous Republic of Nakhchivan.

By the end of 1999, 735,000 lines for companies and individuals were connected to the regional telephone network. On average, there are 9.6 telephones per 100 persons, covering 14.2 per cent of the urban population and 3.32 per cent in rural areas. This can be compared to a telephone density of 68.1 per cent in Switzerland, 62.6 per cent in the USA, 59 per cent in Canada, 15.3 per cent in Armenia and 14.6 per cent in Moldova.

Telephone network in Baku

After the installation of a manually operated exchange station in 1886, the number of Baku Municipal Telephone Network (BMTN) subscribers had reached 40 by 1915.

The development of the Baku telephone network accelerated during the period 1970–1982, when the number of subscribers increased by 2.6 times, to 179,000. Today, over 320,000 companies and individuals are connected to the Baku telephone network, a density of telephony of 17 per 100 persons.

In 1994, and for the first time in Baku, an analogue-digital telephone system operated by the BakCell joint venture was put into commission. A British electronic-digital system, Simmons-X, introduced in 1995 by the AzEurotel joint venture and invested in by parent company Lukoil, has enabled the upgrading and doubling of the capacity of telephone exchanges in the centre of the city. The main and only competitor to BakCell, the joint venture AzerCell, came to market in 1996, providing a GSM-type of mobile communications system, through which communications with 45 countries around the world (roaming) has become possible.

Radio and TV broadcasting

In Azerbaijan, TV and radio programmes are transmitted on telephone exchanges by means of radio-relay lines, satellite and cables. The acting radio-relay lines are used mainly for transmissions of TV programmes. The total length of these lines, covering 61 radio-relay stations across the Republic, is 2,500 kilometres. The programmes of only six channels – AzTV 1, AzTV 2, TRT 1, RTR, ORT and NTV – are broadcast by high-power gauges (1–5kW); all the other channels operate on low-power repeaters. It should be mentioned that the programmes of TRT1, STV and TGRT channels are retransmitted through KOMSAT analogue receiving stations from the Turksat satellite.

In 1997, the B&B TV joint venture, set up with participation from the Ministry of Communication, began providing cable television services. Today, the number of cable television subscribers, based on the MMDS multi-channel television system, has reached 3,000.

The communications industry

The communications industrial complex mainly produces equipment and accessories for telecommunication companies and is represented by three organisations – the joint-stock company Azerrabitasanaye and the joint ventures Ultel and Aztel. Azerrabitasanaye has the highest production volume of the three. With capital assets of AZM366.6 million annual output represents AZM2316.3 million and the balance of profit is equal to AZM120.5 million. AZM5 million are required to restructure this enterprise to enable the production of telephone sets and mini ATS.

Ultel and Aztel specialise mainly in the production of low-capacity electronic ATS (DRX-4) and their spare parts for use in settlements and villages. Annual output of each of these enterprises does not satisfy the needs of the various regions of the Republic. In order to increase the productive capacity of Ultel and to restructure Aztel for the production of various types of telephone cables, each enterprise would require investment of US$10 million.

Investments of US$25 million in industrial communication enterprises for high technology equipment implementation will be completed in three years time.

Table 2.12.1 Investment needed for development and modernisation of telephone networks (US$million)

	1998	*1999*	*2000*	*2001*	*2002*	*2003*	*Total*
Investment in telephone network by communication companies and enterprises	25	32.5	37.5	45	57.5	63.9	261.4
Investment in telephone network by creditors	8.9	26.1	29.3	44.2	11.4	6	125.4
Of which: Telephone network	7.4	24.1	26.3	40.2	6.4	0	104.4
TV and radio broadcasting	1.5	2	3	4	5	6	21.5
By foreign investors	40.5	88.4	74.9	83.4	93.9	1402.4	1783.5
Total amount of investments for development and modernisation	74.4	147	141.7	172.6	162.8	172.3	840.8

Government plans

The government has worked out a special programme for the modernisation and development of the telecommunications sector, covering a six-year (1998–2003) period. During the three stages of the proposed programme's implementation, a total investment of US$870.8 million will be necessary. Of this, US$467.8 million is required for the upgrading and development of the telephone network and US$21.5 million for radio and TV broadcasting. The remaining investment earmarked by the programme will cover the development of the cellular, wireless and satellite networks, as well as cable television, videotelephone and Internet services by foreign capital formation.

The main concern of the programme is to increase the density of telephones per 100 persons, aiming to reach 11.4 per cent in 2001 and 14.5 per cent in 2003. The programme also aims to increase the number of telephone numbers in the Republic, including the cellular network, to 1.079 million by the end of the first stage (1998–9), up to 1.534 million by the end of the second stage (2000–1) and up to 2.103 million by the end of the third stage (2002–3). It should be mentioned that the AzerCell and BakCell joint ventures were planning to increase the number of exploited numbers by the end of 1999 to 60,000 and 40,000 respectively, and also to introduce 13,500 new numbers to the modern wireless telephone network.

The rapid growth in the number of local telephone network users and the introduction of new services increases the need for international and long-distance telephone services. Taking into consideration the important role of the long-distance network, its development and modernisation is necessary for further progress of the telecommunications sector. In 1999, the industrial association Aztelecom should have received AZM252 billion (US$64.6 million) for rendered services and in so doing increased its profits by 48.2 per cent or by AZM82 billion over 1998. A total of US$45 million is needed for the reconstruction of the whole subscriber network, excluding 7,000 electronic-digital-type channels, where the cost of each number is US$120. It is assumed that this programme will be implemented before 2004. At the same time, US$130 million will be required for the reconstruction of trunk lines, particularly the transition to fibre optic cables and radio link.

Table 2.12.2 Ownership structure of joint ventures in telecommunications

Name of joint venture	Authorised capital	Share of Ministry of Communication	Share of foreign partner	Third party founder
ULTEL	US$8,087 million	US$0.223 million (cash) – 2.8%	US$4.294 million – 53.1%	Ulduz $3.57 million – 44.1%
AzTel	US$5 million	US$5million – 10%	US$2 million – 40%	Ulduz US$2.5million – 50%
ARTEL	US$1.7 million	US$0.68 million – 40%	US$1.02 million – 60%	–
BakCell	US$4.857 million	US$2.477 million – 51%	US$2.38 million – 49%	–

Table 2.12.2 continued

Name of joint venture	Authorised capital	Share of Ministry of Communication	Share of foreign partner	Third party founder
B&B Commun- ication	US$5,400	US$2,700 – 50%	US$2,700 – 50%	–
AzerCell	US$43.47 million	US$22.17 million – 51%	US$21.30 million – 49%	–
EMS	750,000 roubles	150,000 roubles – 20%	300,000 roubles – 40%	Commun- ication Centre 1.3 million roubles – 40%
Dex Ltd	US$5m	–	2.45 million manats – 49%	Central Post Office 2.55 million manats – 51%
AzEurotel	US$100,000	US$50,000 – 50%	US$50,000 – 50%	–

The telecommunications development programme included the accelerated improvement of the long-distance network by transition to satellite data links. The appropriate works have already been carried out in several areas. Baku now has direct satellite communication channels connecting by means of the INTELSAT satellite to Rome, London, New York (two channels through AT&T and MCI), Frankfurt (Germany), by means of TURKSAT to Ankara, and by means of STATIONAR to New York (through World-Com and Tele-E-Star) and Moscow. Construction of one more ground (earth) satellite station is planned in order to improve the direct satellite telephone network in Baku.

With regard to the modernisation of TV and radio broadcasting, a partial transition to the analogue mode of operation is planned from the year 2000, focusing primarily on the retransmission of AzTV1 programmes through the Turkish satellite TURKSAT. Works on upgrading the quality and extension of coverage will be carried out simultaneously. Modernisation of TV stations by the year 2000 should enable 99.6 per cent of the population to receive the programmes of one (AzTV1) channel, 96 per cent to receive two channels, and 75 per cent to receive three channels.

There are plans to build and put into commission 25 satellite receiving stations in order to enable the satellite transition of TV programmes in the analogue mode of operation. The cost of the rent required for this satellite segment is approximately US$2.5 million to US$3 million. The extension of a cable-transition TV net is also planned. In the first stage of the government plans, the appropriate re-transmitter was to be installed in Sumgait, Ganja and other areas, while the number of TV programmes was to be increased. In addition to the US$21 million investment required for the upgrading of TV and radio broadcasting in Azerbaijan, annual maintenance and reconstruction of technical equipment is estimated to come to US$8 million.

Conclusions

Further rapid development of the telecommunications sector is expected due to the multi-million dollar investments being made. Although national communication enterprises could rely on their own sufficient and stable earnings to fund their operations, real progress would be hindered without investment.

For telecommunications to be an economically rational and profitable industry, large investments are required. This is less to meet current expenses as to upgrade facilities and to promote rapid development, essential to furthering technical progress and to the evolution of technologies in this sphere. The solution to the problem rests on direct foreign investment involvement and on the privatisation of state communication enterprises. However, even this presents some difficulties.

Foreign investors showing interest in the Azerbaijan market sometimes lose hope in the face of difficulties presented by the state structure. Large telecommunication companies such as the US General Electric and the Japanese Sumitomo Corporation have repeatedly approached the government with offers of co-operation but have yet to receive an answer. The Ministry of Telecommunications is preventing all encroachment on its 'diplomatic' monopoly by hindering any powerful corporation that attempts to enter the national market.

Almost all enterprises with a foreign capital shareholding come under the control of the ministry that holds the controlling share of those enterprises. Licensing of telecommunications activity is probably not considered to provide enough control for the state over the telecommunications industry. The Ministry of Telecommunications intends to keep a controlling stake (51 per cent) of privatised enterprises until the year 2004, and this is reflected in its development programme for 1998–2003. This is explained as retaining control of a sector that is of both state and security importance.

In these conditions, the telecommunications sector will be unable to develop. As it is a sector closely connected to technological progress and changes in world market conditions, the sector will not be able to react to technological development as fast as private companies working under the pressure of severe competition.

The Ministry of Telecommunications is the only government ministry that does not have any financial problems such as wage and inter-enterprise arrears. There are 60 exchanges in Azerbaijan, of which eight have already been modernised. The telecommunications market has become one of the leading sectors in Azerbaijan, and its share of gross domestic product (GDP) is approximately 8 per cent. The outlook for the sector is therefore healthy and prospects are good.

Market opportunities

Several direct investment opportunities exist in the modernisation and expansion of Baku's telecommunications network. This sector has already attracted foreign participation and the successful establishment and operation of several joint ventures in the areas of traditional, cellular and radio network. The government has initiated a National Programme for the Development of Telecommunications for 1997–2010. As part of this programme, the focus of attention is being placed on upgrading exchanges to absorb a doubling of penetration rate to some 30 per cent in the Absheron Peninsula area by 2010. Estimates show that the programme requires an investment of some US$200 million.

However, the general views about the upgrading of the old exchanges in Azerbaijan are different. All the exchanges date from the age of the former Soviet Union. Modern and reliable telephone links are urgently required by the rapid development of the oil sector, and the decision of the Azerbaijan government to achieve an initial modernisation of the telecommunications system can be explained by the desire to replace, as rapidly as possible, an old system by a new one. The technology introduced is not fully up to date, but is sufficient for the present moment. The second round of upgrading of exchanges in Azerbaijan to a more advanced system will take place in due course, once revenue from 'big oil' has been received.

Ongoing projects

The largest ongoing project in Azerbaijan is the upgrade of local exchanges. The Ministry of Telecommunications decided to have a closed tender for that project. As a result of the closed tender, the Alcatel Teletash is the project executor for the upgrading of exchanges. Between 70 and 80 per cent of the upgrading work is being carried out by Alcatel. Since 1991, the total investment by Alcatel in Azerbaijan has been in the region of US$20 million.

Quite recently British Telecom has reached the MOU with the Ministry of Telecommunications about setting up a private circuit in Azerbaijan. This project will increase the number of clients both in the United Kingdom and Azerbaijan with reliable international access. The current providers of international access are international companies such as MCI WorldCom and BT. The MCI capacity is one and two mgps and BT has two 2 mgps access.

Additional information

Ministry of Telecommunications
33 Azerbaijan Avenue
Baku
Tel: 93 00 04
Fax: 93 44 80
Minister: Nadir Ahmedov

Legislation on telecommunications

The Law on Communication of 20 June 1997 regulates telecommunications. This law covers the postal service, telecommunications, radio and the printing of stamps. The Cabinet of Ministers enacted the law in compliance with a presidential decree dated 25 July 1997 that envisaged the identification of responsibility and authority of the different government ministries. There are other laws that relate to the telecommunications sector such as Protection of Foreign Investment and On Information Protection. The Laws are not perfect and different interpretations of these sometimes lead to confusion. Moreover, systemic changes mean continual amendments to the existing laws.

Cabinet of Ministers
Lermontov Street 68
Baku
Tel: 98 97 86
Prime Minister: Artur Rasi-zade
Tel: 98 00 08
Deputy Prime Minister: Abid Sharifov (Construction and Communications)

Supervisory bodies

The Ministry of Telecommunications is officially in charge of any development in this sector. It acts as both regulator and operator at the same time. The Ministry of Telecommunications issues licences for operations in Azerbaijan. Once a licence is issued, a company is obliged to pay a monthly fee of US$500. To obtain an operational radio frequency, the applicant should submit the required papers to the department in the Cabinet of Ministers. After authorisation by the Ministry of Defence, the Ministry of National Security and the prime minister, a frequency is issued. Kismet Ibrahimov, the head of the International Department at the Ministry of Telecommunications, is responsible for the collection and processing of all applications.

Ministry of Telecommunications
Tel: 39 46 07
Fax: 39 41 89
Kismet Ibrahimov

Setting up a company

The normal procedure for company registration is to apply to the Ministry of Justice. A number of international and local advisory companies are available to help with company registration in Azerbaijan. Normally an applicant should receive the decision of the Ministry of Justice within one month.

Ministry of Justice
13 Bul Bul Avenue
Baku
Tel: 93 97 85
Minister: Sudaba Hasanova

Telecommunications companies in Baku

Akhuundoff
Apt. 14a
3/6 S Rustamova Street
Baku
Tel: 92 12 42
Fax: 97 22 42

Alcatel Teletash
Apt. 30
6 R. Rza Street
Baku
Tel: 98 85 60/98 97 04
Fax: 98 85 61

ARTEL
41 Azerbaijan Avenue
Baku 370000
Tel: 98 28 00
Fax: 98 08 78

AzerCell
41 Azerbaijan Avenue
Baku 370000
Tel: 93 70 07/98 30 07
Fax: 93 37 28/98 30 17

AzEurotel
1 B. Sardarov Street
Baku 370001
Tel: 92 65 00/92 33 99/97 07 07
Fax: 97 01 01

AzInternet Services
19 Safaraliyeva Street
Baku 370017
Tel: 93 93 07
Fax: 98 38 16
Email: ais@azeri.com.
Website: http: //www.azeri.com

AzTel
Tbilisi Avenue
3166 District
Baku 370602
Tel: 93 19 62
Fax: 98 23 30

Aztrank
6 Efendiev Street
Baku
Tel: 92 22 27
Fax: 97 11 01

BakCell
24 U Hajibeyov Street
Baku
Tel: 98 94 44
Fax: 98 92 55

Baku & Boston TV Communication
(B&B TV)
2 Inshaatchilar Avenue
Baku
Tel: 97 52 32
Fax: 97 52 39
Mobile: 850 210 52 70
Email: jim@ bbvcom.baku.az

Caspian Net
82/23 Alekperov Street
Baku
Tel/Fax: 97 17 97

Complex
28 Telnov Street
Baku
Tel: 67 88 37
Fax: 67 88 63
Email: kmoplex@azeri.com

EMIL-S
105 Neftchilar Avenue
Baku 370004
Tel/Fax: 97 03 03/97 06 06
Fax: 98 10 01
Operator: 98 90 90

Ericsson Telecommunications A.S.
Tbilisi Avenue
3166 District
Baku
Tel: 98 28 24
Fax: 98 28 25

Five Continent (5C)
19 Safaraliyev Street
Baku 370017
Tel: 98 93 29
Fax: 98 38 16
Email: 5C@azeri.com
Website: http: //www.5c.azeri.com

GSM
Nizami Street
Baku
Tel/Fax: 92 93 68/92 60 22

Hazar Trade Inc
20 Beyuk Gala Street
Baku
Tel: 97 50 89/97 51 14
Fax: 98 18 20

IIG Group Limited
8 Istigaliyat Street
Baku
Tel: 92 92 89
Fax: 93 30 66

NAB-Group Co. Limited
40 Ataturk Avenue
Baku
Tel: 98 20 69/76
Fax: 98 82 78

Neptun LDT
143/2 Neftchilar Avenue
Baku 370010
Tel: 98 21 10
Fax: 98 21 11
Email: neptun@ans-dx.com

Nessco Caspian Limited
4 Sabail Street
Baku
Tel: 93 42 04/97 45 65
Fax: 97 45 02

Netash
41 Azerbaijan Avenue
Baku
Tel: 98 20 20/98 20 02/98 64 64
Fax: 98 48 36

On line
58 Nizami Street
Baku
Tel: 98 66 23/62 66 07

Siemens
Apt. 77
5 28th May Street
Baku
Tel: 98 23 70/98 23 72

Sinam – Invest
9 F. Agayev, 370141
Tel: 39 22 14/39 49 67

Ultel
41 Azerbaijan Avenue
Baku
Tel: 98 20 20/98 02 02
Fax: 98 48 36

URAN
14, 28 May Street
Baku
Tel/Fax: 98 35 79

URNAK
14 28th May Street
Baku
Tel: 93 11 39/92 83 94
Fax: 98 21 11/98 05 89

World Com
2 Abbaszade Street (TV Tower)
Baku
Mobile: 850 212 23 83
Email: bburns iekars@mci.com

Xazar Electronicasi
4 M. Shafi Street
Baku
Tel: 98 18 22/97 10 26
Fax: 92 05 91

2.13

Tourism

Improtex Travel

Azerbaijan has great potential for tourism, but unfortunately has not yet been discovered as a major tourist destination. In order to remedy this, the government and private sector in Azerbaijan aim to realise the country's tourism potential and in so doing, turn tourism into a major contributor to the economy. Azerbaijan has all the conditions necessary for the realisation of this ambition, including:

- varied natural resources;

- a pleasant climate that enables tourists to visit Azerbaijan at any time of the year;

- unique sites of interest and a rich and long history;

- great scientific, technical and cultural potential; and

- new socio-economic conditions that enable state-owned and private companies as well as foreign investors to take part in the development of tourism.

At present, there is an official governing body, the Council of International Tourism (CIT), that plays a significant role in the development of tourism. The CIT is a member of the Organisation of Black Sea Economic Collaboration (OBSEC), comprised of 11 countries, and is also a member of the international tourism organisation, EuroAsia, which has a membership of over 100 tour operators from different countries of the Commonwealth of Independent States (CIS). The main aim of the CIT is the development and strengthening of Azerbaijan's international tourism connections on the base of intergovernmental agreements in the tourism industry, as well as other agreements of tourism exchange. It has already made around 40 such agreements with Great Britain, France, Greece, Turkey, Egypt, Morocco, Iran, Pakistan, China, and members of the CIS.

There are over 200 national and international organisations, such as travel agents, tour operators, hotels, transport companies etc, working in tourism in Azerbaijan. The market is still in its formative stage, but is improving every year. The main factors for the development of tourism are the stabilisation of the political and economic situation, the cessation of the war in the Nagorno–Karabakh region and other significant improvements made in the process of transforming Azerbaijan into an independent democratic country. Another important factor is the activation of business contacts with foreign partners, for instance the signing of the oil contracts between Azerbaijan and leading oil companies in the USA, the UK, Norway, Turkey, Russia and Saudi Arabia. In addition, another important aspect was the signing of the agreement to develop the trans-Caucasus route, Europe–Caucasus–Asia in 1998; also in June 2000, Azerbaijan became a member of the Council of Europe.

Interest in Azerbaijan has significantly increased around the world. The country falls on the transcontinental route formerly known as the 'Silk Road', which is being developed under the supervision of the World Tourism Organisation and UNESCO. Independent Azerbaijan has become one of the main stop-off points on the Silk Road, as it was during the Road's golden age in the 15th and 16th centuries.

In Azerbaijan there is no separate classification for 'tourism' as an economic sector. Hotels, restaurants, travel agencies and shops patronised by tourists are all classified under retail and wholesale trade, while income generated by tourists is also classified under transportation, when international airfares are taken into account. Thus, the expansion of the tourism sector will increase the contribution of the trade and transportation sectors to Azerbaijan's economy in the future.

Azerbaijani businesses are seeking new overseas partners that would be interested in taking part in the development of the tourism industry. Mutual co-operation between both Azerbaijani and overseas businesses would allow for the increase of incoming and outgoing tourism in Azerbaijan, thereby further encouraging the development of the tourism industry.

The countryside

Azerbaijan has all the resources needed for the development of tourism – the most important factor being its geographical location. The country is at the geographical crossroads of central Asia, Europe and the Middle East, in the centre of the trans-Caucasian route, and has all the necessary infrastructure. All transport options are fully developed. In 1999 a newly built airport opened its doors and Baku's seaport, the largest port on the Caspian Sea, is under reconstruction. Other essential parts of the country's infrastructure are its motorways and railways, which link most of the countries of the Caucasus and central Asia with Europe.

The territory of Azerbaijan measures 86,600sq km and the country has a population of approximately 7.3 million. Within its borders, Azerbaijan enjoys nine of the 11 climate zones. Its climate varies from subtropical and dry in central and eastern Azerbaijan to subtropical and humid in the south-east, temperate along the shores of the Caspian Sea, and cold at the higher mountain elevations. Baku, on the Caspian Sea coast, enjoys mild weather, averaging 4°C in January and 30°C+ in July. Because most of Azerbaijan receives scant rainfall – on average 152–254mm annually – agricultural areas require irrigation. Heaviest precipitation occurs in the highest elevations of the Caucasus and in the Lenkoran' Lowlands in the far south-east, where the yearly average exceeds 1,000mm.

Azerbaijan also offers the stunning natural beauty of a diverse landscape that includes seashore, forest, mountain and plain, and a climate so diverse that, in various parts of the country, one can experience the four seasons in one day.

Vegetation in Azerbaijan is full of contrast and colour. Here people can find almost every type of Caucasian flora. There are also some very rare plants that grow only in Azerbaijan such as the Elder pine, which has survived climatic and relief changes for over 13 million years.

Azerbaijan also has a very rich animal kingdom. There are more than 12,000 vertebrate and non-vertebrate animals such as the spotted deer, chamois, moufflon, Caucasian goat, leopard, bear etc. There are also a significant number of birds of different kinds and the Caspian Sea is full of exotic kinds of fish such as sturgeon, stellate sturgeon, Caspian Sea trout etc. In addition there are around 13 natural and heritage parks, 17 reserves and a number of centres for hunting and fishing have been created in the country.

There are around 1,200 rivers, both small and large and many mountain rivers turn into great and noisy waterfalls. The most beautiful natural places in Azerbaijan are mountain and lowland lakes such as Gey Gel and Moralgel.

Other attractions are the mineral waters of Badamli, Tursh su and Isti su. Natural mud, especially Naftalan, has been used for the treatment of skin ailments, gynaecological complaints, nervous system disorders and other illnesses for about 100 years.

Recreational activities

Azerbaijan is a sunny country, with as many sunny days as countries such as Italy, Spain and Greece. The Azerbaijani Caspian Sea coast is about 825km long and has the potential to become a major holiday destination. The sandy beaches of the Absheron Peninsula, as well as the Yalama beaches of Hachmass, are very popular with tourists visiting Azerbaijan.

The bathing season in Azerbaijan runs from the middle of May to the end of September. The clear waters of the Caspian Sea contain iodine, bromine and fluorine, and are reknowned for their curative properties. The country as a whole has a reputation as being one of the healthiest places in the world, which is probably why a significant number of senior citizens visit it. Azerbaijan is also famous for its cuisine. Gourmets from different parts of the world, who travel to Azerbaijan to try Azerbaijani food, are fascinated by its taste. However, the most important factor that plays a significant role in the tourism industry is the hospitality of the natives; wherever you are in Azerbaijan, you will receive the warmest welcome from the Azerbaijani people.

Sites

Azerbaijan is a country with an ancient history and culture. Remains of a neanderthal man, found in the Azikh cave, prove that people lived there in the palaeolithic period over 250,000 years ago.

Some 6,000 historical monuments, dating back thousands of years, and built by a myriad of cultures, beckon travellers to this new nation of the Caucasus. Ancient cities and towns, palaces, mausoleums, churches and mosques, chapels, caravanserais and watchtowers are just some of the monuments that remain to fascinate visitors.

Ancient drawings in the caves of Gobustan (60km from Baku), ruins of ancient cities, cultic sites of pre-Muslim times such as Zoroastrian temples of fire, towers, and Christian churches abound, as do buildings of the Muslim period.

Architectural sites of Azerbaijan have been included in the 'golden' foundation of the world heritage listing. Icheri Sheher (The Internal Town of the 12th century) surrounded by a high fortress wall, is home to 44 unique sites from the Middle Ages spread over 22 hectares. The Internal Town includes the Shirvanshahs' Palace complex (15th century), the Sinik-kala minaret (11th century), The Maiden Tower (12th century) and the Juma-Mosque minaret (15th century). These sites stun visitors with their beautiful architecture. Near Icheri Sheher is situated the only museum of Azerbaijani carpets in the world. The museum is full of exhibits that characterise the rich variety in the artistic heritage of the Azerbaijani people.

The most beautiful building in Icheri Sheher is the Shirvanshahs' Palace — the ancient residence of the Shahs of Shirvan. Azerbaijani historians have called it 'Baku's Acropolis'. The palace houses a number of different buildings: the Divan-hane with its beautiful portal; the prayer's hall with its magnificent dome; the burial vault; the mosque and its incredible minaret; the mausoleum of the ancient mathematician and astronomer, Seyid Ahiya Bakuvi; the Eastern Gate; and the baths. It is worth travelling thousands of miles to see such a beautiful palace.

Another very popular palace in Azerbaijan is the palace of Sheki's khans, which is located in one of the oldest cities of the country – Sheki. The two-tiered walls of the palace are covered with colourful murals and frescos. The painting on the palace ceiling reflects the pattern of the giant carpets that once covered the floor.

Approximately 18km from Baku is the temple of fire worshippers, Ateshgyah (18th century), a Zoroastrian site that symbolises the cult of fire. According to ancient text, there were many such sites in Azerbaijan, but most were destroyed in the 7th and 8th centuries by the Islamic Arab conquerors. Some ten centuries later, merchants – fire worshippers from India – built Ateshgyah in the settlement Surakhani, a place where natural gas can be found. Today, the temple houses a museum of the history of fire worshippers.

The historical sites already mentioned are only a small part of what people can visit in such tourist centres as Baku, Sheki, Shemakha, Lenkoran, Gyandja and Kuba.

National heritage and nature are the main touristic advantages to Azerbaijan, and the ones with which the country integrated into the world tourism market. In March 1999 Improtex Travel, one of the leading tour operators in the country, presented Azerbaijan as a tourist destination for the fourth time on the ITB in Berlin. The company offered its own tours of Baku and other cities in Azerbaijan. The types of holiday offered were sports, theme, ethnographical and religious tours, deer hunting in the mountains of the Caucasus, recreation on the Caspian coast and a bus tour called 'Along the Silk Road'. The tour takes in various destinations along the ancient Silk Road (Baku, Shemakha, Sheki, Belokani, Georgia), crossing the country from east to west.

The Silk Road

For the last few years, Improtex Travel has played a significant role in the expansion of co-operation with other countries that are part of the famous Silk Road. Improtex Travel has created special 'carpet tours' that link the ancient centres of carpet makers in Azerbaijan, Turkmenistan and Iran. The itinerary of these tours are: Baku–Kuba, Baku–Ashkhabat–Mari, Baku–Tehran–Tebris. These tours are very interesting as they involve visiting different historic sites, carpet museums and factories. 'Along the Silk Road' tours take in visits to cities that were along this ancient route, and include:

- Baku–Sheki–Telavi–Tbilisi–Erevan–Kishinev;

- Baku–Ashkhabat;

- Baku–Tashkent–Bukhara–Samarkand;

- Baku–Tehran–Kerman–Shiraz–Isfagan–Tehran;

- Baku–Istanbul.

All kinds of hotels are available in Azerbaijan; three- to four- star hotels include the Absheron, the Azerbaijan, the Gyandjlik and the Intourist. Luxury five-star hotels include the Radisson SAS Plaza Hotel; the Grand Hotel Europe; the Hyatt Hotels, Baku; The Crescent Beach Hotel; the Oasis Hotel and the Yukhari Karvansaray Hotel, Sheki (built in the 18th century). It is also possible to organise professional guides and interpreters for tourists, as well as the more routine services, such as car rental and the like.

Tour operators in Azerbaijan are flexible and will happily satisfy tourists' requirements, creating any tour according to the customers' wishes and providing any accommodation required.

Future developments

The most important resource for Azerbaijan's tourism industry is the Caspian Sea coast, with its various landscapes and sandy beaches. This resource needs further development and the creation of a high quality tourist complex on the Absheron coast is one of the main objectives of both the government and the private sector. The creation of such a complex would make a significant impact on the economy of Azerbaijan in terms of generating up-market tourism, earning much-needed foreign currency, creating new jobs within the industry, and so on.

Another major benefit to tourism would be the creation of a national park in Azerbaijan. The country's natural resources are conducive to this and such a park would have both tourist and other uses. The development of new tourism products and services, however, requires major investment, as well as the establishment of contacts with major tourism and financial organisations.

As Azerbaijan's connections with other countries grow, the number of people that are interested in visiting the country also grows. Azerbaijan offers all the incentives that motivate people to travel – historic sites, an ancient culture, natural resources, centuries-old traditions, recreational activities, real eastern hospitality and so on. All these create an environment rich in possibilities for all types of tourism.

Despite all the problems Azerbaijan faces today, it still has huge potential for tourism. With the help of foreign investments and the profit made from oil, Azerbaijan will be able to improve infrastructure and the service sector. Many plans have been made, and the firm line taken by the government, aimed at increasing the socio-political stability in the Republic and continuing market transformation processes, has achieved noticeable results. The confidence of large international tourist institutions and the opening of Azerbaijan's economy are strong evidence that the government and private sector will get the country's tourist industry on track.

All the information you need - for doing business all over the globe

• Compiled and edited by leading experts, these are essential sources of information and advice for anyone considering export, investment, joint venture or expansion in a new market.

• Covers economic and political environments, legal, banking and accounting systems, business opportunities and support for overseas investors, cultural and social issues, useful contacts and case studies.

£40.00
ISBN 0 7494 3168 7

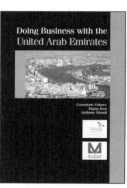

£40.00
ISBN 0 7494 3171 7

£24.95
ISBN 0 7494 2951 8

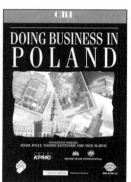

£40.00
ISBN 0 7494 3153 9

Also available in the Doing Business series:
Azerbaijan, China, Croatia, France, India, Saudi Arabia, South Africa, Spain and Turkey.

10% off any of these titles if you buy direct -
simply call our credit card hotline on **01903 828800** or e-mail **orders@lbsltd.co.uk**
and quote EXB1 (these titles are also available from all good bookshops)

KOGAN PAGE
120 Pentonville Rd, London, N1 9JN, UK   www.kogan-page.co.uk

All the information you need – for doing business all over the globe

10% off

- Compiled and edited by leading experts – from PricewaterhouseCoopers, the DTI, Confederation of Indian Industry, MOFTEC, Istanbul Stock Exchange, Saudi Chamber of Commerce and Industry and more
- Essential source of information and advice for anyone considering export, investment, joint venture or expansion in a new market.
- Covers economic and political environments, legal, banking and accounting systems, business opportunities and support for overseas investors, cultural and social issues, useful contacts and case studies.

£80 • ISBN 0 7494 3152 0   £47.50 • ISBN 0 7494 2924 0   £65.00 • ISBN 0 7494 3374 4   £40.00 • ISBN 0 7494 2554 7   £40.00 • ISBN 0 7494 2954 2

10% off any of these titles if you buy direct - simply call our credit card hotline on 01903 828800 or e-mail orders@lbsltd.co.uk and quote PLC (these titles are also available from all good bookshops)

 KOGAN PAGE   120 Pentonville Rd, London, N1 9JN, UK

www.kogan-page.co.uk

2.14

TRACECA (Transport Corridor Europe–Caucasus–Asia)

Compiled from documents provided by the Azerbaijan Embassy, London

Note

On 11 April 1998 the European Commission held a conference of delegates from the eight Republics of Transcaucasus and central Asia to elaborate a programme of EU assistance and to stimulate international financial interest in the development of transport infrastructure along an east–west axis. American senator Brown Bek tabled a suggestion for the consideration of a draft law about 'the strategy of the Silk Road' that foresaw US economic support for the countries situated along the 'Ancient Silk Road'.

The President of the Azerbaijani Republic suggested that an international conference be held in Baku and in September 1998 the suggestion was taken up by the EU with a conference on the restoration of the historic silk route. This conference saw the participation of the heads-of-state of 40 countries. The adoption of the 'Principal multilateral agreement on international transport and on the development of the corridor, 'Europe–the Caucasus–Asia' and its technical appendices on international railway and motor car transport, international trade navigation, custom procedures and documentation processes were covered during the conference. The documents adopted at the conference will promote the effective use of the international transport corridor Europe–the Caucasus–Asia that has great historical, economic and strategic importance.

Introduction

It is impossible to imagine the development of the modern world economy without either international programmes for energy resources or solutions to global ecological problems. One of the principal conditions of this must, therefore, be the availability and effective functioning of transport and communication hubs in keeping with the increasing demands of international economic co-operation. The possibility of the opening, or rather of the revival, of the famous Eurasia transport corridor is especially attractive within the framework of a programme of maximum rapprochement between the west and the east. This highway has a profound historical and economic background dating from the creation of the Great Silk Road, which connected many countries of Europe and Asia by the shortest route.

In antiquity and the Middle Ages, some of the most active lines of the Great Silk Road crossed the territory of Azerbaijan from east to west and from north to south. This made Azerbaijan an active participant in the exchange of trade and information with many countries throughout the world. It is symbolic that even in periods of antiquity, petroleum – known world-wide as 'the Midian oil' – was exported from Azerbaijan alongside other goods.

The revival of the Great Silk Road (the shortest and most economic route from Europe to Asia) and its information technology content, have made it one of the major projects for the development of integration processes within the international community at the start of the 21st century. Because of its geographical and geopolitical situation, Azerbaijan naturally has great interest in the prompt realisation of the TRACECA project.

The Great Silk Road

In the first instance, the Great Silk Road was a system of ways, direct live contacts, trade and exchange of cultural achievements between China and the Mediterranean. It was named after silk – an expensive, light and firm material that was very popular among the wealthier consumers in ancient trading days, the manufacture of which was then only known in the Far East.

Of course, silk was not the only commodity transported along the Great Silk Road. Caravans going to China were also loaded with gold and other noble metals, woollen cloth and flax, ivory, coral, amber, jewels, asbestos and glass. From China caravans took out furs, ceramics, iron products, glaze and cinnamon, ginger, weapons of bronze and mirrors. At its height, (2BC–4AD) the Great Silk Road connected the Khan dynasty of China and the Kushan and Parphan realms, with the Roman Empire. From Roman domains in the eastern Mediterranean, Roman merchants travelled through Iran and Kushan to the Khan dynasty, while Persian and Indian merchants settled in Egyptian Alexandria. The trade on the southern seas between Egypt, then a Roman province, and India was regular as was the contact between the Roman Empire and China and other states of Indochina.

In times of antiquity, one of the most popular routes of the Great Silk Road went from China and India to Middle Asia, and then via the Uzboy river to the Caspian Sea and further across the territory of Albania (the ancient state on the territory of the modern Azerbaijani Republic) by the Kur river. From there the road continued to Iberia and Kolkhida (the territory of modern Georgia), to the Black Sea area and Asia Minor, where a number of Greek city-states were situated. There was also a steppe branch of the Road, leading through the Volga region to the southern Russian steppes and further to the Crimea and eastern Europe.

After the collapse of the ancient empires, and during the great migration of peoples, the steppe routes began to play an important role in the links between west and east. Sasanid Iran, and later the Arabian Caliphate, fighting and competing with Byzantium, directed the main lines of the Great Silk Road to circumvent Byzantium domains. In this period, along with China, India and Khorezm, the ancient Turks began to trade with Byzantium and Sasanid Iran. One of the most active lines in the third and fourth centuries passed through the whole of Transcaucasus, Derbent, the Northern Caucasus and further to the west, to the countries of eastern Europe and Byzantium.

Beyond the traditional partners – China, India, Indochina, countries of Asia Minor, Transcaucasus, the Near and Middle East and Byzantium – trade within the Great Silk Road included a part of the Volga region, Ancient Russia and countries of central, southern and western Europe. It was not until the great geographical discoveries at the end of the 15th and beginning of the 16th centuries that the intercontinental overland trade lines gradually began to decline. The main trade between Europe and Asia, as well as between the Old and the New Worlds, was carried out over oceans and seas.

From the very beginning of the functioning of the Great Silk Road, Azerbaijan was always an important part of the trade line. One of the most active routes of the ancient way led through Azerbaijan in the first and second centuries BC. This route was frequently called the 'Strabon Way', named after the great geographer who was the first to describe it in his works. This route went from China and India through Middle Asia, reached the Caspian sea via the Uzboy river, and then proceeded through the territory of Azerbaijan. Here it divided into two branches: one led upstream of the Kur river towards Kolkhida and Iberia, the second one turned to the north along the western Caspian coast through Derbent and the Caucasian steppes and ended in the Greek city-colonies. Many of Azerbaijan's oldest cities have risen and functioned just along these two branches of the Strabon Way.

During the period of the early Middle Ages, Azerbaijan continued to play an active part in the functioning of the Great Silk Road and was an important transit point. In this period, its cities served as terminals or stores for Far Eastern and Middle Asian goods due to be transported to Byzantium and the north. Barda, which had been the capital of Azerbaijan since the fifth century, became the largest world trade centre on one of the branches of the Great Silk Road. Located on an active line, Barda became one of the largest trade craft centres of the Near East and in the Transcaucasus from the eighth century to the tenth.

The importance of Azerbaijani cities situated on the lines of the Great Silk Road significantly increased from the 14th to the 17th century. This was due to the developing of the Volga–Caspian highway by Russian and English merchants. In this period, Shamakha, Derbent, Baku, Ardebil, Tabris, Maraga, Gandja and Nakhchivan (cities of Azerbaijan) became transit centres, where goods from the east and Europe accumulated. Merchants from Russia, Europe, Turkey, Middle Asia and the Far East assembled here. Several caravanserais were built in all the cities that were involved in international trade, many of which remain to this day.

The Great Silk Road had an immense influence on the development of the economy and culture of Azerbaijan. The extensive relations over several centuries with many peoples of the east and the west served for the mutual enrichment of these peoples. These relations were also one of the most important lever of the development of world civilisation.

The modern geographical and geopolitical situation, as well as the natural resources of Azerbaijan (known as the 'Land of Fire' due to its oil and gas resources), present the perfect opportunities for development of the Eurasian economic and cultural communications at a new level. The Azerbaijani Republic is located on a joint of the south-western Europe and central Asian frontiers, bordered in the south by Iran and Turkey, in the north by Russia, in the north-west by Georgia, and in the south-west by Armenia. In the east, across the Caspian Sea, it borders Turkmenistan and Kazakhstan.

Its location also makes Azerbaijan a very important transit unit that connects Europe with the Middle and Near East (through Iran) by means of railway, as well as with central Asia by means of the Caspian ferry-boat. Azerbaijan also provides transit ties for the Transcaucasian states with Russia and the countries of central Asia. These routes have outputs to the Persian Gulf, and the Black and Mediterranean Seas, as well as to European countries.

The variety of geographical and climatic conditions in Azerbaijan has stimulated the development of a diverse economy for the country – from oil and gas production to cotton, wheat, and vegetable farming. Potentially, there are also great opportunities for the development of international tourism.

Among Azerbaijan's many mineral-rich natural resources, a special place is held by those derived from oil and gas. There are abundant natural resources for development of the chemical industry and the minerals base of the Azerbaijani Republic opens real and wide prospects for foreign investment and mutually advantageous co-operation with foreign partners. Since the beginning of production of the early oil and 'the big oil' contacts, the necessity of constructing a branching system of export pipelines with output to international sea ports became evident. Separate stages of this task, representing enormous potential for the development of international co-operation between Europe and Asia, have already been successfully realised. In November 1997, for example, the oil pipeline Baku–Grozny–Novorossiysk began to transport millions of tons of oil.

Azerbaijan and the international transport corridor TRACECA – the principal component of the Great Silk Road

The Great Silk Road branched out into two routes that reached up to the west: the China–Middle Asia–Persia–Mediterranean route and the China–Middle Asia–Caspian Sea–Kura–Black Sea route. The route known today as 'TRACECA' is the international transport corridor Europe–the Caucasus–Asia that is the main component of the Great Silk Road.

In Brussels, May 1993 a meeting was held with the representatives of Azerbaijan, Georgia, Armenia, Kazakhstan, Kyrgyzstan, Tadjikistan, Turkmenistan and Uzbekistan as well as with representatives of Russia, Ukraine, Romania, Bulgaria, Turkey, Iran, China, Pakistan and countries of the EU. The aim of this meeting was to investigate various east–west routes connecting countries of Europe, the Caucasus and central Asia. As a result of this meeting, the Brussels Declaration was signed – a pledge of technical assistance from the EU for the development of the Transcaucasian international transport corridor TRACECA (Transport Corridor Europe–Caucasus–Asia). This marked the beginning of the Technical Assistance Tacis TRACECA project. The project's main tasks are to ensure:

- uninterrupted fast and reliable transportation of freight from Europe to central and South East Asia and back;

- the integration of the states participating in the transport corridor into a uniform economic space; and

- the formation of regional centres of manufacture and services to form part of a Eurasian market of manufacture and consumption.

In order to provide support for the international oil consortiums operating in Azerbaijan, there is a need for facilities to transport large volumes of freight from Europe, the USA and South East Asian states to Baku. In this respect, TRACECA represents a magnificent alternative opportunity to transport through the Russian Federation.

On 13 May 1996 in Serakhsa, in an effort to develop the transport corridor Europe–the Caucasus–Asia through Azerbaijan, the Presidents of Uzbekistan, Azerbaijan, Georgia and Turkmenistan agreed to co-operate to regulate transit and transport between these states. Other states have since joined this agreement, which provides state guarantees for the safety of freight, the simplification of customs procedures and a 50 per cent tariff reduction on freight transport. As a result, the volume of cargo carriage was 2.5 times higher in 1997 than it was in 1996.

The Tacis TRACECA programme includes many projects that are all directed at rehabilitating and developing transport and communication links. These include staff training, development of legislation and transport codes, reconstruction and rehabilitation of rail and sea transport facilities, highway improvements and forecasting of regional traffic on multimodal transport systems. Funding for these projects has been obtained from the EU through the Tacis programme and from inter-national financial institutions such as the European Bank for Reconstruction and Development.

Conclusion

Azerbaijan is at the heart of the global economic integration process and, as an essential participant in global power and transportation projects, it has good reason to soon be considered one of the world's advanced indus-trialised countries. Social and political stability, as well as a strong base in terms of social, economic, technological, ecological and legal matters, will guarantee the harmonious and purposeful development of an interna-tional transport system for the 21st century – TRACECA and the restoration of the Great Silk Road.

Part 3

Business Development

3.1

Understanding the Market

Soheil Ramanian, Trade Development Limited

Business culture

Azerbaijan is a country where knowing the right people is very important and you will not be successful unless you understand the business culture and make the right connections and the right moves.

Azeri people, being very close to the Middle East, have a Middle-Eastern attitude and approach. They like foreigners and are very courteous and pleasant towards them. Be warned therefore that a good meeting with officials and the fact that they have been very forthcoming does not necessarily mean that you are getting the business.

In order to do business, you must first win the trust of the decision-makers. This can be achieved through several meetings where you can show your commitment to doing business with them and perhaps by inviting them to visit you at your headquarters. You also need to ensure that you are talking to the right person, ie the one who holds the decision-making power, and not wasting your time negotiating with those who do not make the decisions.

Having been dominated by the Soviet Union for over 70 years, naturally, many Soviet-style business methods remain in practice. Therefore, any experience you may have of dealing with other republics of the former Soviet Union will also be of help.

Although everyone communicates in the Azeri language, the technical and business language remains Russian and communicating in Russian is therefore an added advantage. However, it is preferable to have Russian-speaking western staff than representatives from your offices in Moscow or other parts of the former Soviet Union.

Building relationships

It is important to build relationships with both Azeri organisations and western companies that operate in Azerbaijan. Flying visits to the market do not really achieve very much. You are expected to visit the market frequently and regularly so that a client becomes convinced that you can be trusted, that you are not going to disappear and that you are committed to the marketplace. Starting up a representative office, if you can afford one, would also provide further proof of your commitment to Azerbaijan. On many occasions, your faxes and letters may remain unanswered but a reply would be rapidly obtained if you were to visit the market. It is therefore important to understand the need for and benefit of frequent visits and of establishing relationships.

As already mentioned, do always ensure that you are talking to the decision-maker. An introduction to that person through mutual friends and contacts, whenever possible, is also preferable to cold-calling.

The market

In principle, the Azeri market can be split into two main sectors. The Azeri sector, mainly comprising the Azeri ministries and some new private sector clients, and the western sector, comprising oil and service companies operating in Azerbaijan.

Azeri sector

The Azeri sector of the market is mainly driven by projects initiated by various Azeri ministries, projects relating to the refining, petrochemical and manufacturing industries, and by the small private sector. Azeri ministries generally have small and confined budgets. Generally, there is little foreign currency available to finance significant procurement from the West. Some organisations such as SOCAR (the State Oil Company) and oil-related organisations have better access to foreign currency.

It should be noted that priority projects can be backed by a government guarantee, which in turn can be offered to western organisations such as ECGD to raise finance. A typical example of this form of financing is the development of the Baku airport, which was jointly financed by the UK and Turkish governments, based on an Azeri government guarantee. Although government guarantees are not easily available, having the right project and the right contact will make such financing a more realistic possibility.

It is very important to verify early on that the projects you are considering and discussing will be funded properly as there are many projects that sound interesting but are unlikely to start or succeed for lack of foreign currency financing.

The private sector in Azerbaijan is relatively young. The majority of the well-known private companies are involved in the supply of various consumer products, vehicles and tourism. Private sector companies normally look for favourable payment and credit terms from western suppliers.

It is important to note that the Azeri government generally welcomes western investment in Azerbaijan's economy. If you have the possibility of investing in any industry through a joint venture with a local ministry, you will find many more opportunities become available to your company.

Western sector

A good number of western oil companies are established in Azerbaijan and are involved in various oil consortia. There are also a number of engineering and service companies providing services to the oil and gas industry. There were over 5,000 expatriates living in Baku, mainly involved in the oil sector. In many instances, procurement decisions are made in Baku by the local office rather than by headquarters in the West. Therefore, it is important to establish good contacts with Baku-based procurement officers and project managers and also keep a regular check on projects being considered for development.

Although there are a few newspapers and newsletters generally advising you of what is going on in the oil and gas sector, it is important to keep in regular contact with the key personnel of western organisations to make sure that you are well-placed for various tenders and enquiries.

Short-term market potential

There are a number of projects financed by the World Bank, the European Bank for Reconstruction and Development (EBRD), the Islamic Development Bank, the European Union's Technical Assistance for the Commonwealth of Independent States (TACIS) and similar organisations. You should regularly check on these projects through World Bank publications, through the commercial section of the British Embassy or by using the internet. Once you become aware of a project that could be of interest to you, it is important to start building relationships. Make contacts with key personnel and decision-makers within the ministry or committee that will be the beneficiary of the loan.

Typical projects as of summer 1999 were in the following areas:

- road construction;
- land decontamination;
- sturgeon hatchery;
- ferry terminal upgrade;
- development of the banking sector;

- railway modernisation;
- educational reform;
- restoration of historic buildings/sites;
- farm privatisation;
- irrigation.

There are a small number of key projects that can be supported by government guarantee. These projects can also materialise in the short term. Generally, inward investment projects in infrastructure or in the manufacturing sector can be set up and formulated rapidly.

The western oil industry in Azerbaijan is going through a revival. This will lead to the development of export oil and gas pipelines, the development of semi-submersible drilling rigs, the development of fixed production platforms in the Caspian and many other service- and logistics-related opportunities.

Long-term market potential

Generally, Azerbaijan requires a great deal of modernisation in every area of its infrastructure, its manufacturing industry, especially that related to the oil and gas sector, its telecommunications and its power sector. As various consortia start producing oil, the government will begin receiving oil revenues and that means that there will be funds with which to rebuild the country. It is in this context that many people compare the future development of Azerbaijan to that of the small Persian Gulf Arab countries.

The market sectors that will make a significant contribution to the development of Azerbaijan are expected to be building construction, road construction, water and sewage, transport, telecommunications, power, servicing of the oil and gas industry, refining and petrochemicals, agriculture and tourism.

It is worth noting at this point that Azerbaijan has great agricultural potential; at one stage during the Soviet era, Azerbaijan was the second largest producer of cotton. The agricultural potential of the country has recently been overshadowed by the oil industry, but it is worth exploring.

There are also great opportunities in the environmental sector. Land decontamination, cleaning up of coastal waters, improvements to marine life (especially sturgeon) are all projects that have begun and are expected to develop.

Setting up

After your initial visit, if you decided to set up in Azerbaijan, you could be interested in the following:

- It is possible to register your Azerbaijani set-up as a representative office. This means that you would not get involved in any trading activity, which in turn means less involvement with the local tax authorities. It is always possible to register as a trading entity at a later date, should you decide to become an active trader in Azerbaijan.

- Azerbaijanis generally are educated and bright. It makes sense to employ good local staff and university graduates and to provide training and language courses to help improve their skills. It is also important to recognise that, in the initial stages especially, thorough and regular supervision is required. Salary levels very much depend on the level of activity of the oil companies as this has an impact on the labour market.

- For your accommodation and office needs, it is sometimes better to rent an apartment for joint living and working use rather than to rent separate office space elsewhere. It is important to be accompanied by a local when negotiating the rent on an apartment. The less you show your face as a western company, the less your rental will be. You should also make sure that your rental contract and agreement are properly registered and that your landlord is well aware of his commitments under the contract.

  There are also a number of new office buildings developed by Turkish companies and by western companies that can provide a reasonable operating base. If you are forming a joint venture with an Azeri organisation, your joint venture partner should be able to assist you with local staff and accommodation.

  If you are in the process of taking on an apartment as your base, do also check the situation with water and electricity, as in some areas there are disruptions to these services.

Living in Baku

In general, Baku is a pleasant place to stay. People are friendly, general security in the city is relatively good, although there have been some recent incidents in the way of mugging and burglary, but Baku is usually considered a safe place.

There are a number of western-style shops providing for the majority of expatriates' requirements. There is also a wide range of restaurants with very good quality food. The entertainment industry is very young; there are a number of places such as health clubs and nightclubs, but generally Baku is a little lacking on this front.

There are many expatriates already living in Baku, so other expatriates moving there would not consider it a lonely place, or a difficult place to live. Among the western banks, HSBC has a branch in Baku. Car rental companies can also be found, and in principle, whatever you need to set up your home or office is generally available. Baku is also well served by international airlines and connections.

3.2

The Foreign Investment Regime

Ledingham Chalmers

Introduction

In order to encourage the influx of foreign capital that is required to fuel Azerbaijan's future economic growth, the country's foreign investment policy must address adequately the reasonable concerns of foreign investors. While the exploitation of Azerbaijan's extensive hydrocarbon resources provides a limited windfall, it cannot be relied upon in isolation. Oil price fluctuation and technical uncertainties make it necessary for Azerbaijan to plan for long-term sustainable development of all its resources. Foreign capital is an essential component of that planning.

With some specific exceptions, particularly in relation to insurance companies and to the ownership of land, there are few restrictions on foreign ownership of or participation in Azerbaijani enterprises and foreign investors are provided with the same protection under the law as Azerbaijani nationals and legal entities.

Political and economic stability

The government has enacted several measures intended to promote a stable investment climate. Structural economic reforms are making steady progress and the privatisation programme, though delayed, is continuing.

Official statistics showing continued low inflation and stability of the national currency against the US dollar suggest that a degree of sustainable economic stability has already been achieved. This was doubtless assisted by President Aliyev's re-election to office for a second term in October 1998.

Prospective investors in Azerbaijan face issues that are common to many countries in the relatively early stages of their development. Examples of these are as follows:

- While the country has in recent years enjoyed relative internal political stability, the failure of Azerbaijan and Armenia to find a peaceful solution to the future of Nagorno-Karabakh and the continued political unrest in Dagestan and other neighbouring areas of the Caucasus provide an unpredictable geopolitical backdrop.

- President Aliyev has taken steps to eliminate corruption particularly within state institutions but this will not be achieved immediately.

- State agencies do not yet have the 'service charter' approach adopted by government departments in other countries such as the UK for example and, as a result, investors may experience both delay and difficulty in dealing with state officials.

- Legislation is not yet drafted to western standards and can be contradictory and internally inconsistent. Lack of certainty in the rules and application of the law are a major concern for inward investors.

- Public accessibility to legislation is limited.

- Legislation may be imposed retrospectively, although under the Constitution such legislation should not have a negative impact on foreign investors.

- Practice and procedure often differ.

Tax legislation and foreign investment

Prior to making an investment a foreign investor should, as a priority, undertake a full assessment of the effect of the local taxation regime. This should cover the taxes applicable, any relevant exemptions, the methods of charging and rates as well as whether the system in place provides a stable environment for sustained medium and long-term investment. This will form part of any economic feasibility study. The current Azerbaijani system fails to meet many of the expectations of a foreign investor although some improvements are expected with the adoption of the new Tax Code. Meanwhile two points should be noted:

1. There are no general tax incentives specifically designed to encourage investment in Azerbaijan. Some advantages have been gained by the exploration and production sector operating under production-sharing agreements; these have their own ring-fenced tax regimes and some benefits are passed on to their contractors.

2. Penalties for delay or non-compliance are not consistently applied and may be out of proportion to the default. Penalties may also be imposed on local managers. It is worth noting that the State Tax Inspectorate operates an incentive scheme for its officials based on a proportion of

the penalties collected by the Inspectorate thus creating a clear incentive on officials to impose penalties.

Pre-investment due diligence

Any potential investor is encouraged to commence due diligence on an investment target at a very early stage. Issues of concern are similar to those pertaining in other jurisdictions but the following matters may require particular attention in Azerbaijan before investing in an Azerbaijani legal entity:

1. Investigation on title to property including confirmation of compliance with registration procedures. In a recently reported case, the Economic Court declared the privatisation of certain land null and void as the relevant privatisation procedure had not been adhered to despite the relevant state body having issued the appropriate certification to the prospective land user. The court upheld the claim of the prior user that it should have had the opportunity to compete in the land's privatisation process.
2. The existence of any secured claims or charges over property should be investigated.
3. The company's accounting procedures and policies in relation to the recognition of liabilities and accruals should be ascertained. International accounting principles are only now being introduced in Azerbaijan.
4. The exact number of employees registered on the company's payroll should be determined. It is not uncommon in Azerbaijan for this figure to be in excess of those actually working in the company. There are a number of essential criteria to be fulfilled for redundancy, and redundancy payments may be as high as five months' salary. In addition, a number of classes of employee cannot be made redundant by law.
5. In common with other republics of the former Soviet Union, there may be little distinction between company assets and the personal assets of the company's shareholders.
6. If a company has taken a lease over any state property, the authority of the signing state official should be checked. Generally, all state property is now vested in the State Property Committee and a lease must be granted by it.

3.3

Investment Strategy

Ernst & Young

Introduction

As with any of the countries of the former Soviet Union, private ownership of business has only recently been introduced. Many business principles common in the West are new to Azerbaijan. Nonetheless the country has made significant progress in creating a stable economic and political environment for the foreign investor. The infrastructure necessary to support business is in the relatively early stages of development, and this is especially apparent in the gradual establishment of the legal framework in Azerbaijan, where business often focuses more on personal relationships than on contractual texts.

This chapter focuses on some of the main areas of concern to foreign investors planning an initial investment in Azerbaijan.

Key factors in developing a new venture

Culture

Azerbaijan has encouraged foreign investment, initially and predominantly in the oil and gas sector, but more recently in other sectors of the economy. However, Azerbaijan is taking a cautious approach that arises from its desire to maintain autonomy over its economic future. As a result, the foreign investor must be prepared to enter into agreements with the Azerbaijani government and state-controlled companies. However, in many of the key sectors of the economy (especially the oil and gas industry), there has been great reluctance to cede complete control to foreign investors, though foreign investors have been permitted operational control over their investments. As the local partners may be able to provide immediate access to local brands, local business knowledge and first-hand experience, these partnerships are generally of mutual benefit.

Personal relationships

The Azerbaijani business environment continues to evolve but still relies heavily on the development of personal contacts. It is often advantageous to identify the key decision-makers and nurture relationships with them to secure support for the implementation of a new venture. However, this can be difficult as there can be frequent changes or rotations of government personnel, and the members of a government negotiating team may not be the individuals with whom foreign investors work during a project implementation. Therefore, investors are cautioned to document in writing any agreement that they reach with any governmental official.

Poor condition of assets and low productivity

On an initial visit to a prospective project site, the poor state of facilities and equipment and inefficient production processes may strike the foreign investor. The emphasis in Soviet times, was on the need to achieve production goals in absolute terms rather than on the efficient and effective use of resources to achieve a quality output. In addition, since Soviet times there have been insufficient resources to properly maintain assets and inadequate training to bring production up to global standards. However, the workforce is generally well-educated and eager to learn western-style manufacturing techniques and operation methods. Therefore, the groundwork exists for a workforce that takes pride in its work and offers the necessary human resources to achieve investment objectives.

Market research

In the Soviet system production was centrally planned and imposed from above. The concept of production based on consumer demands was not common, and producers rarely solicited market opinion on the desirability of a particular product. Producers in the current marketplace are well advised to conduct market research to determine the desirability of their product, and whether demand would be sufficient to make an investment in Azerbaijan viable.

Reliance on previous investor experience

Azerbaijan's desire to attract western investment and its abundance of natural resources, particularly in the energy sector, are significant incentives for investment in the country. However, investors will face a number of impediments. These are best identified through the experience of other foreign companies already operating in Azerbaijan. Most companies with a presence in Azerbaijan are glad to discuss their experiences, both positive and negative, with other potential investors to work towards improving the state of the economy. A number of organisations, such as the American Chamber of Commerce and the British Business Group, have been established as a means of sharing information and facilitating operations in the country. In addition, many countries have set up embassies in Azerbaijan with on-site commercial officers who are available to assist foreign investors and address their problems.

Qualified advisers

Azerbaijan can be a challenging place to do business. As in other emerging economies, legislation is evolving rapidly as Azerbaijan makes the transition to a market economy and investors may find it difficult to stay apprised of the frequent legislative changes. Therefore, the services of qualified advisers are critical in order for an investor to understand the business environment and comply with the legal requirements on a business venture operating in Azerbaijan.

Start-up costs

The costs of starting up a business in Azerbaijan can be quite high and foreign investors should determine such costs as accurately as possible before making an investment. The main factors that lead to such high costs are as follows:

- Local infrastructure is not fully developed, so additional time and money must be expended to overcome this shortfall. In many cases this may mean importing skilled workers to service machinery and equipment, build facilities, train local staff, and otherwise impart their expertise;

- International management support is necessary for investors seeking to operate according to western business styles and practices. The key areas requiring support are in finance, marketing and sales, technical services, engineering, project management and the various aspects of petroleum project coordination;

- Due diligence and market analysis are necessary in order to identify potential contingent costs such as unpaid taxes, penalty assessments, pollution and contamination clean-up costs, existing supply contracts, and unsanctioned payments to officials;

- Communication costs are quite high. Within Baku, there is a well-established provider of international telephone services. However, outside

Baku, telephone communication channels are poor. In addition, mail services are unreliable, and therefore courier costs should be taken into account.

Conclusion

Azerbaijan has tremendous potential, and actively seeks to conduct business with foreign investors. With 19 signed production-sharing agreements (and additional blocks being negotiated) in the oil industry, and the continued privatisation of other sectors of the economy, many opportunities exist for investors. However, as with any emerging market, there are a number of issues to be considered in developing a successful presence in the country. By understanding and taking into account the key factors listed above, the foreign investors will have taken the initial steps towards establishing a successful venture in Azerbaijan.

Legal Overview of Investment in the Energy Sector

James E Hogan, Salans Hertzfeld & Heilbronn

Introduction

On 17 February 1999, the new Law of the Republic of Azerbaijan, On Energy, dated 24 November 1998 (the Energy Law) was published. The objective of the Energy Law was to provide an overall framework for the regulation of a wide range of activities falling broadly within the energy sphere. These include activities in the exploration, production and development of petroleum and natural gas, as well as the operation of energy transportation systems and electrical energy distribution. In spite of their obvious importance to participants in all sectors of energy activity, issues arising within these spheres are still governed primarily by specific legislation. With respect to the exploration, development and production of hydrocarbon resources and minerals, the Law of the Republic of Azerbaijan, On the Subsoil, dated 13 February 1998 (the Subsoil Law) would apply. For the most part the Subsoil Law regulates in great detail the procedures and requirements for activity involving the subsoil, while the Energy Law can be viewed as a more general framework for activity in all facets of the energy sector. There is also a Law of the Republic of Azerbaijan, On Electrical Energy (the Electricity Law), dated 13 June 1998, which is of importance to investors in this sector.

The Energy Law

The stated objectives of the Energy Law are:

- to ensure the effective development, production, transportation, distribution, storage, use and safety of energy materials and production;

- the creation of an effective and reliable energy supply to consumers, infrastructure and new workplaces;

- the conversion of energy resources, the reduction of the level of waste, the efficient use of energy and the use of renewable energy resources;

- the reduction of negative effects on the environment;

- the provision of subsidies to producers and consumers for the purpose of increasing energy efficiency;

- the composition of a state energy programme.

The Energy Law recites the constitutional principle that the state has an exclusive right of ownership over deposits of all primary energy materials (without infringing upon the exclusive rights of physical persons and juridical entities having exclusive rights under concluded energy contracts or pursuant to legislation). The Law is clear that the state shall exercise such rights, in accordance with law, for the purpose of ensuring safety and the energy independence of the state.

In a manner similar to energy laws of other states in the region, the Energy Law established the concept of setting mandatory norms of energy usage, with a timetable for complying with such norms and sanctions for failure to do so. Also, for the first time, the law establishes the principle that the consumer is responsible for paying for the energy used, and mandates the installation and use of individual meters to calculate energy consumption at consumer level.

The Law sets out strict provisions with respect to environmental protection, including the mandatory performance of state expert examinations of environmental impact for activities in the energy sphere. Moreover, liability is established for loss of life, bodily injury and damage to the environment.

All physical persons and juridical entities wishing to commence activity in the energy sphere must first obtain special permission for such activity from the corresponding governmental authority. Such permission may be granted pursuant to a concluded energy agreement or on the basis of an application to such authority. In this regard, such permissions are not to be withheld without cause.

The Energy Law sets out certain regulatory parameters for various types of energy agreements concluded between contractors and the appropriate governmental authority. These include exploration agreements, development and production agreements, main energy transportation system agreements, energy distribution agreements and underground storage agreements.

The Law imposes limits on the allowable duration of such agreements. For example, exploration agreements are to be concluded for terms not to exceed two years, subject to a possible extension of one year. It also provides: 'the term provided in an energy agreement for development and production may be divided over several periods or extended in total by not more than eight years from the date of the entry into effect of the agreement'. The law provides that while such terms may not be exceeded, they may be extended in certain circumstances, and ultimately the contractor would be eligible to participate in a tender for a new energy agreement (though apparently no preference to such existing contractor is envisaged).

Given the huge investments and lengthy cost recovery periods that apply in most hydrocarbon projects, it is odd that such short contract terms were established. These time limitations are all the more curious, in that they contradict the terms established by the Subsoil Law for exploration contracts (5 years), for production and development contracts (25 years) and for combined contracts (30 years). Moreover, there is a conflict between the two Laws in that the Energy Law establishes that rights are acquired as from the moment of the signing of the energy contract, while the Subsoil Law provides that subsoil rights arise as from the moment of the granting of the licence.

Resolution of these conflicts is difficult, in that Azerbaijan civil legislation applies the common norm of specific legislation prevailing over general, but it also applies the norm that a provision that is later in time prevails. In any event, for existing contractors, including those that have concluded production-sharing agreements which themselves have generally been enacted into law, these provisions of the Energy Law would not affect existing rights.

In the electrical energy sphere, the Law establishes a maximum term of 20 years, which may be extended by an additional period of 10 years.

All rights extended under an energy agreement are subject to registration, by application of the holder, with the appropriate government authority. Any changes in the information set out in an existing registration are themselves subject to registration.

As a general principle, the contractor under an energy agreement has the right to set prices independently. However, an exception is made for those contractors that are monopolists in accordance with their energy agreement. Monopolists are subject to control under the state energy policy and their prices or tariffs require approval by the corresponding governmental authority.

The Energy Charter Treaty

Apart from the Energy Law and the subsoil code, an often overlooked but extremely important document that also constitutes part of Azerbaijan

Energy Law is the Energy Charter Treaty, which was opened for signature in December 1994. The Energy Charter Treaty has been ratified by nearly 40 Organisation of Economic Cooperation and Development (OECD) countries and newly independent states, including Azerbaijan (23 December 1997) and the UK (16 December 1997).

The original concept of the Energy Charter Treaty was to create an energy community, based on the complementarity of western markets and the natural resources of the East. It was also intended to assist the economies of the newly independent states and strengthen security through close cooperation in the key energy sector. The energy sector is broadly defined in the treaty to include all economic activities concerning 'the exploration, extraction, refining, production, storage, land transport, transmission, distribution, trade, marketing or sale of energy materials or products'.

The Energy Charter Treaty was drafted at a time when the foreign investment and energy legislation of the newly independent states was in a very nascent state, and it was intended to serve as a regulatory framework that could apply in the energy sector until appropriate national legislation could develop. Even though the legislative infrastructure of countries like Azerbaijan has developed enormously in the past several years, the Energy Charter Treaty still offers important protection to foreign investors in the energy sector.

Among the protective measures offered by the Energy Charter Treaty are standard state obligations that are commonly set out in most bilateral investment protection treaties. These include:

- fulfilling all obligations agreed with an investor of another contracting state;

- permitting an investor free choice of personnel without restrictions as to nationality, national treatment concerning investment;

- free repatriation of invested capital and associated earnings;

- the payment of prompt, adequate and effective compensation in the event of expropriation.

Other important provisions of the treaty help foster transparency in legislation by requiring the publication of laws, regulations, decisions and administrative rulings, as well as the responses to be given to requests for information about relevant legislation. Finally, the Energy Charter Treaty sets out important dispute resolution provisions, which guarantee the right of a foreign investor to refer disputes to international arbitration before specifically listed forums, including the International Centre for the Settlement of Investment Disputes (ICSID), United Nations Commission on International Trade Law (UNCITRAL) and the Stockholm Chamber of Commerce.

SALANS HERTZFELD & HEILBRONN

Salans Hertzfeld & Heilbronn is a full service international law practice with offices in Paris, New York, London, Warsaw, Moscow, St. Petersburg, Kyiv, Almaty and Baku. For more than three decades partners in the firm have been pioneers providing legal advice in the CIS and Eastern Europe. Today, a team of over 90 lawyers are specifically dedicated to advising clients in the region.

In Azerbaijan, the firm has been active in counselling companies, financial institutions and government entities in the legal aspects of investment, trade and finance since 1990. It opened its Baku office in 1999, when the Wicklow Group became an integral part of the firm's worldwide practice. The Wicklow Group was established in Baku in May 1996, and was the first foreign law firm to be licensed in Azerbaijan. Its Managing Partner, Mr. Alum Bati, is a U.K. lawyer with more than 20 years of legal experience who has been based in Baku since 1993.

In the Baku office we strive to combine detailed knowledge of Azerbaijan law and practice with the firm's experience elsewhere in the CIS in similar legal specialisations and industry groups. As a result, the Baku office works closely with lawyers in other offices of the firm on a client-by-client basis in order to deliver high-quality legal services which take advantage of the expertise of the entire firm. The office currently consists of six lawyers, almost all of whom speak fluent English, Azeri and Russian, plus legal support staff. Partners in the Paris, London, New York and Moscow offices support the office on a daily basis.

With lawyers qualified to act on the whole spectrum of legal issues in Azerbaijan, the particular specialties of our Baku office are:

- Financial Services
- Oil and Gas: Natural Resources
- Corporate Services
- Privatisation
- Employment
- Real Estate
- Taxation

For further information about our experience and capabilities in Azerbaijan, please contact:

Mr. Alum Bati
Salans Hertzfeld & Heilbronn
Hyatt International Centre
Hyatt Tower 2
1033 Izmir Street
Baku 370065
Azerbaijan

tel: **(99 412) 907 565**
fax: **(99 412) 971 057**
Email: **abati@salans.com**

Full details are also available on our website: **www.salans.com**

Salans Hertzfeld & Heilbronn

Providing a full range of legal and tax services to financial institutions and investors in Azerbaijan.

For further information please contact:

BAKU

ALUM BATI

TEL: 99412 90 75 65

FAX: 99412 97 10 57

LONDON

ROBERT STARR

TEL: 44 20 7509 6000

FAX: 44 20 7726 6191

NEW YORK

JAMES BOYNTON

TEL: 1 212 632 5500

FAX: 1 212 632 5555

PARIS

JAMES HOGAN

TEL: 33 1 42 68 48 00

FAX: 33 1 42 68 15 45

www.salans.com

LONDON PARIS NEW YORK WARSAW MOSCOW ST. PETERSBURG KYIV ALMATY BAKU

Financing with the European Bank for Reconstruction and Development (EBRD)

European Bank for Reconstruction and Development (EBRD)

Introduction

The EBRD is one of the largest foreign investors in Azerbaijan. Through its projects, the Bank aims to assist the country in developing a market economy and works alongside other foreign investors to achieve this. By helping to mitigate project-financing risks, the EBRD can help foreign investors achieve commercial success in Azerbaijan.

The role of the EBRD

The EBRD was established in 1991 in response to major changes in the political and economic climate in central and eastern Europe. Inaugurated less than two years after the fall of the Berlin Wall, the Bank was created to support the transition to market economies in the region following the widespread collapse of communist regimes.

Based in London, the EBRD is an international institution with 60 shareholders (58 countries, the European Community and the European Investment Bank). Each shareholder is represented on the EBRD's Board of Governors and Board of Directors.

The EBRD finances projects in both the private and the public sectors, providing direct funding for financial institutions, infrastructure and other key sectors. Its investments also help to develop skills, to improve the efficiency of markets and to strengthen the institutions that support these markets.

A strength of the EBRD is its in-depth knowledge of its region of operations. As the largest foreign investor in the region's private sector, the EBRD is aware of the problems and the potential of each of its 26 countries of operations. Working closely with private investors, the Bank's staff recognise the investors' concerns about investment in the region and the political and economic uncertainty.

The Bank operates according to sound banking principles in all of its activities and promotes good business practices. It is careful to ensure that it is 'additional' to the private sector, complementing rather than competing with other private sources of finance.

The EBRD's initial capital base was e10 billion, which was doubled to e20 billion in 1997, allowing it to continue to meet the growing demand for its services and to maintain its commitment to financial self-sustainability.

EBRD financing

The EBRD is keen to encourage co-financiers to take part in its operations – in fact it usually limits its own involvement in private sector projects to 35 per cent. Apart from private sector companies, the main co-financing partners for the EBRD are commercial banks and other financial institutions.

The principal forms of direct financing provided by the Bank are loans, equity and guarantees. Loans are tailored to meet the particular requirements of the project. The credit risk may be taken entirely by the Bank or partly syndicated to the market. An equity investment may be undertaken in a variety of forms. When the EBRD takes an equity stake, it expects an appropriate return on its investment and will only take a minority position. Guarantees are also provided by the Bank to help borrowers gain access to financing.

Mitigating risks for investment partners

One of the Bank's main advantages is its ability to bear risk, allowing it to extend the boundaries of commercial possibilities in its countries of operations. Where possible, it shares the project risk by acting with other private sector bodies, such as commercial banks and investment funds as well as multilateral lenders. With its AAA credit rating, the EBRD is able to raise funds at the best rates from the international capital markets.

By utilising its experience in the region and its advantages as an international financial institution, the EBRD is able to mitigate certain risks, making it an attractive partner. The Bank's participation in a project can help to ensure that the operation is well prepared and implemented. For example, the EBRD will make sure that the project complies with local laws and regulations and that it is financially viable. To help a client attain the required levels of corporate governance and project preparation, the Bank is able to provide technical assistance funding made available by donor governments.

The EBRD's involvement in a project indicates to the market that the project meets rigorous technical, legal, financial and environmental standards. The Bank is able to structure projects in a way that is likely to attract other financing partners and thereby minimise the risks and costs for the parties involved. One of the main ways of achieving this is by co-financing with private banks, allowing participating banks to benefit from the Bank's preferred creditor status.

The sound management and profitability of a project can be enhanced by the EBRD's presence in an operation. When the Bank takes an equity investment in a company, it uses its influence on the company's board to promote good management and to mediate where necessary between local and foreign partners.

A major concern to potential investors is political risk, which again the EBRD can help to mitigate. Since all the Bank's countries of operations are represented on the Board of Directors, each member country has the opportunity to object to the approval of any EBRD-financed project. This helps to reduce the threat of any subsequent political risk.

Activities in Azerbaijan

As of January 2000, the EBRD had signed loan agreements totalling €242.3 million to finance eleven investment projects in Azerbaijan. Of these, just over 40 per cent are in the private sector. The Bank's private sector pipeline started to grow significantly in 1997–8 driven by:

- large foreign investment in the development of the oil and gas sector;
- restructuring of transport and social infrastructures;
- support for small and medium-sized enterprises (SMEs) through local banks.

Case study

The EBRD and the International Finance Corporation (IFC) have agreed to invest up to US$200 million each in a project to develop the offshore Chirag oil field in the Caspian Sea. Up to US$100 million of this is to be syndicated.

The two institutions are making five separate loans to affiliates of BP Amoco, Exxon, Russia's LUKOIL, Turkish Petroleum and Unocal, all of which are members of the Azerbaijan International Operating Company (AIOC). This is the first international consortium to have started operations in the country and includes six other oil companies from Azerbaijan, Japan, Saudi Arabia, the UK and the USA.

The early oil project undertaken by the AIOC and SOCAR, the State Oil Company, is the first stage of the development of the Chirag, Azeri and Deepwater Guneshli field complex. It is estimated that the overall cost will be between US$10 billion and US$12 billion and will result in the recovery of over 4 billion barrels of crude oil. Production got under way in November 1997.

The project includes the refurbishment of an offshore platform and drilling wells and the construction of undersea pipelines. It also comprises the repair and completion of two oil pipelines through Azerbaijan to the Russian border and Georgia.

The commitment of the EBRD and the IFC is expected to encourage private investment and to increase the country's oil production. Citibank, Dresdner Bank and Société Générale have participated as co-arrangers, each contributing US$25 million to the syndicated loan. It is hoped that the success of this project will lead to the implementation of other production-sharing agreements in Azerbaijan.

Key objectives

The EBRD's activities in Azerbaijan are focused primarily on the development of a strong private sector and on financing critical infrastructure investments in priority areas, in close cooperation with the government and other international financial institutions (IFIs). The emphasis in the financial sector is on providing financial assistance to the rapidly growing local private business sector. The EBRD's involvement in legal reform is designed to accelerate the transition to market economies and to boost foreign direct investment in Azerbaijan.

Privatisation and private sector development

As well as assisting foreign investment through projects with international sponsors, the EBRD seeks to support emerging local private businesses through equity and special instruments. The private sector initiatives under way include:

- financial sector projects to support SMEs, such as the Multi-Bank Framework Financing project;

- a project to participate in the privatisation of the International Bank of Azerbaijan; and

- a feasibility study on establishing a post privatisation fund, which will provide new capital to privatised and other private enterprises.

Financial sector

The EBRD is actively pursuing the development of a sustainable, competitive financial sector, working with representatives of the National Bank, the Ministry of Finance, the President's Office and IFIs as well as targeted local financial institutions. Under the Multi-Bank Framework Financing project, about €17 million will be made available to one or two qualifying banks for on-lending to SMEs. Participation in the privatisation of the International Bank of Azerbaijan is expected to take place within the framework of this facility. The EBRD is also introducing its Trade Facilitation Programme to local banks with the aim of developing intra-regional and international trade among the EBRD's countries of operation.

Agriculture and agribusiness

As the business environment in Azerbaijan becomes more attractive, the EBRD is hoping to develop projects in the agricultural processing sub-sector. Other operations in the sector will need to follow the government's reform programme. Additional economic policy reforms are required in the cotton, grain and wine sectors before viable Bank investments can be developed. Cotton growing, ginning and processing are likely to generate other good business opportunities.

Energy and natural resources

Oil

In addition to the Chirag oil project (see Case study above), the EBRD has held preliminary discussions with various companies involved in onshore oil development, with a view to financing small upgrading projects. The Bank is also continuing to monitor developments concerning additional export pipelines.

Oil services

The EBRD has a significant role to play in the restructuring of the sector by identifying potential joint-venture partners and structuring risk-sharing arrangements. The Bank is continuing to monitor developments in the industry in order to identify viable private sector investment projects.

Electric power

The EBRD's loan for the completion of the Yenikend Hydropower Station is now disbursing, while a loan agreement for a second hydropower project at Mingechaur was signed in June 1997. The Bank strongly supports the government's plan to privatise the management, and possibly ownership, of power distribution in a region to be selected as a pilot project. The EBRD will consider other projects that would improve energy efficiency in Azerbaijan.

Critical infrastructure

Telecommunications

The EBRD is exploring options for private investment in the telecommunications sector with the government and hopes to participate in the development of the sector. Meanwhile, the Bank is processing a private sector cellular telephone transaction.

Transport

The EBRD's priorities for transport emphasise the need for a reliable transport infrastructure as well as institutional reform to support the transition process and to establish a framework for private investors. The EBRD is working with transport authorities as well as other IFIs to define a programme of investment and is considering financial support for road upgrading. In the railway sector the Bank is contemplating a ₤18 million investment programme, mainly for upgrading wagon workshops and track renewal. The Bank is also committed to financing an upgrade of the Baku port ferry terminal. The EBRD's projects in the transport sector are part of the European Union- (EU) sponsored TRACECA (Transport Corridor Europe, Caucasus and Asia) initiative.

Legal reform

In an effort to address legal deficiencies, the EBRD has conducted three technical cooperation projects aimed at assisting the government with the development of a Secured Transactions Law, a Bankruptcy Law and a Foreign Investment Law. These projects are intended to lay the legal foundations for a system that allows local and foreign investors, including the Bank, to create effective security in private sector lending operations and to ensure that investors are well protected in the event of a borrower's bankruptcy.

The EBRD is continuing its involvement in legal reform to encourage and facilitate the creation of the optimal legal environment for the conduct of commercial transactions, helping to accelerate the transition process and foreign direct investment in Azerbaijan.

Additional information

Further information about the EBRD's activities in Azerbaijan and its projects with investment partners can be found on the Bank's web site (www.ebrd.com). The site contains the full text of the Bank's key publications, such as the *Annual Report* and *Financing with the EBRD*, which details the Bank's lending requirements. More information about the investment climate in Azerbaijan and its latest progress in the transition process can be found in the EBRD's *Transition Report*, published each November, and the *Transition Report Update*, published each April/May.

The *Azerbaijan 2000 Country Investment Profile*, published for the EBRD's Annual Meeting in Riga, May 2000, can be ordered for £10.00/$17.00 through the EBRD Publications Desk, Tel: +44 20 7338 7553 Fax: +44 20 7338 6102 E-mail: pubsdesk@ebrd.com Website: www.ebrd.com.

Establishing a Business Presence

Arthur Andersen

There is no one law in Azerbaijan which sets out the various forms of business presence. Rather, there are numerous laws, which must be referred to in order to come up with an overall summary of legal formations. Older laws drew differences between local entities formed with foreign capital and local capital, and granted special privileges to companies with foreign capital. However, such privileges have now been repealed.

The current legal environment makes the distinction between two general forms of entities operating in the country. The first is that of an Azerbaijani legal entity (ALE), which in itself can come in several forms, or that of a foreign legal entity (FLE), which generally comes in the form of a representative office. These two general forms of operating within Azerbaijan are discussed below in more detail.

Azerbaijani legal entities

Current legislation provides for the following forms of ALEs:

- General Partnership
- Limited Partnership
- Limited Liability Enterprise
- Joint Stock Company

General Partnership (GP)

A GP is established by at least two legal entities or physical persons with all partners having unlimited liability.

Limited Partnership (LP)

A LP is established by at least two legal entities or physical persons with at least one partner having unlimited liability.

Limited Liability Enterprise (LLE)

A LLE is established by at least two legal entities or physical persons with founding members actually owning shares in the enterprise. Each owner's liability is limited to the amount invested in the LLE.

Joint Stock Company (JSC)

A JSC is established by at least three legal entities or physical persons with each founding member subscribing to shares in the enterprise and each owner's liability limited to the amount invested in the shares. A JSC can either be 'open', with shares being freely traded between any investor, or 'closed', where its shares can only be owned by its funding members.

Foreign legal entities

Many foreign companies beginning their operations in Azerbaijan choose to register in the form of a FLE, which is generally effected through a representative office (RO). A branch office, although it has registration (and documentary) requirements very similar to those of a representative office, will be allowed to carry out commercial activities, ie it will enable the generation of income through the conduct of activities in Azerbaijan.

An official registration of a RO is required, which must be done with the Ministry of Justice. Registration with the tax inspector is also required. A RO is considered a non-resident for Azerbaijani tax and legal purposes. While a RO is traditionally thought of as an entity, which merely provides support and auxiliary services on behalf of its head office, in practice Azerbaijani legislation does not appear to prohibit a RO from conducting commercial activity. Local tax legislation clearly provides for the filing and payment of profits tax by a RO which conducts commercial activity, and in practice many foreign companies currently conduct commercial activity through a RO.

However, local authorities now will disallow the registration of a RO for entities which are thought to be engaged in commercial operations and will require the registration of a branch office.

A foreign investor can conduct business in Azerbaijan through either an ALE or a FLE (or representative office). Joint Ventures (JVs) are contemplated within earlier legislation as 'wholly foreign-owned Azerbaijan legal entities' (WFOALEs). Neither of such actually represents forms of legal representation and both are, for tax and legal purposes, considered ALEs. As stated above, all earlier tax privileges given to certain JVs and WFOALEs no longer exist.

Protection for foreign investments

The principles of foreign investment and the legal protection afforded to such investment in Azerbaijan are embodied in the 1992 Law on Protection of Foreign Investment.

The basic principle of this law is that foreign investment may be made in any type of activity unless Azerbaijani law prohibits it. The legislation provides that foreign investment will not be subject to nationalisation other than in exceptional circumstances (ie to prevent harm to the people and damage to the state interests of Azerbaijan). Furthermore, requisition of the foreign investment is possible only in the circumstances of natural disaster, epidemics and other extraordinary situations.

Such a requisition may be made only by a decision of the Cabinet of Ministers. In any case the foreign investors are entitled to compensation commensurate with the value of investment and paid in foreign currency, to be remitted abroad at the instruction of the foreign investor.

There is also some protection offered by the law against adverse changes to the foreign investor. In the case of a change in legislation adversely affecting an investment, the application of the legislation shall be on moratorium for a period of ten years.

However, there are a number of exceptions to the kind of legislation that will be the subject of this type of moratorium. These excluded areas include legislation governing defence, national security, public order, morality, public health, environmental protection and, most importantly, the tax regime.

An agreement for the promotion and protection of investments has been signed between the governments of Azerbaijan and the United Kingdom. This agreement provides that neither state shall subject the other's citizens, companies or investment to treatment less favourable than that accorded to its own or any third parties. The agreement also provides for specific recourse to international centres for settlement of disputes as against the Azerbaijani courts. A similar bilateral trade agreement has been signed between Azerbaijan and the USA.

It is pertinent to note that the following are considered to be foreign investors in Azerbaijan:

- foreign legal entities and citizens

- foreign states and international organisations

- registered citizens of Azerbaijan who are permanently resident abroad

- individuals with no citizenship.

PSA considerations

The PSAs provide for additional certainty of operations and investment protection. They are each established as separate laws and contain their own guarantees of the performance of certain obligations by the State Oil Company (SOCAR) as the representative of the government of Azerbaijan. The main protections include a stable regime for taxation, etc, for the period of the PSA (generally 25 years).

Other considerations

Employment laws

The Labour Code and allied laws regulate labour relations in Azerbaijan. The laws provide, *inter alia*, for regular working hours, leave entitlements, and the procedures for redundancies and termination.

It is mandatory for employers in Azerbaijan to be registered with the tax and social security authorities. Employers are legally bound to withhold and remit to the relevant authorities all necessary taxes and social security payments. Stringent penalties are imposed for non-deposit of such moneys within the stipulated timeframe.

Recently there has been legislation introduced for the issuance of work permits for foreign nationals in Azerbaijan. Although the decree is effective at the current time, there have been no detailed regulations produced and issues such as the form of application and the application fee have not yet been determined.

Language

The official state language of administration is Azeri. Legislation, court proceedings and record-keeping in all state agencies are generally conducted in Azeri.

Seals and stamps of entities operating in Azerbaijan must be in Azeri. Certifications and instructions for goods produced in Azerbaijan must be provided in Azeri and another language where applicable.

However, having said that Azeri is the official language, there are many instances in which Russian continues to be used in a business context. In a number of areas, Russian is the more favoured language of communication even within official agencies.

Currency

Trade within Azerbaijan may be carried out only in Azeri manats (in other words, manats is the only legal tender recognised within Azerbaijan).

Only authorised banks or specially authorised non-banking institutions may carry out foreign currency dealings.

Permission from the National Bank is required in cases where an Azerbaijani entity wishes to use an offshore account. Non-residents may, however, open offshore bank accounts without restrictions, deposit funds offshore, and they are not bound to sell foreign currency proceeds or submit a report upon withdrawal of foreign cash. Non-resident legal entities may purchase foreign currency in the domestic foreign currency market in stipulated cases. Advance overseas payment by non-residents for goods and services is not permitted.

There are no limitations on the amount of foreign currency that a non-resident individual can bring into the country, provided a customs declaration is completed. Foreign currency equal to the amount brought in may be carried out of Azerbaijan by non-residents. Non-resident individuals may also open and operate foreign currency accounts at Azerbaijani banks.

The Law on Protection of Foreign Investments guarantees the repatriation of profits in foreign currency for non-residents, subject to tax withholding and other applicable deductions.

3.7

Opening an Office in Baku

Tarik Fatheldin, Royalton

The whys

With Azerbaijan's enormous energy resources, especially in the oil and gas sector, the business environment can be very lucrative if care is taken to understand the influences working on an individual market at any one time.

The legal background

Azerbaijan's legal system is still in a state of transition; procedures required for registration are laborious and lengthy and should be arranged with the advice of competent lawyers. The need for a local attorney will obviously be determined by the size, complexity and nature of the business to be conducted.

First step: legalities

Companies must decide on the purpose of the office they wish to establish as this will determine the choice of ownership structure. There are a limited number of ways in which a foreign company can establish a business in Azerbaijan: a wholly foreign-owned company; a joint venture with a local company; or a representative/branch office. Companies are required to register with the Ministry of Justice as one of these entities.

The language

As the official language is Azerbaijani and certain documents have to be translated into Azerbaijani rather than Russian, business should be conducted with bilingual translators, experienced attorneys and accounting professionals.

Location, location

Where to locate? The old city offers a certain ambience and charm, and some companies such as architectural firms, design engineers and petroleum corporations are already located there. Disadvantages include insufficient parking facilities and inaccessibility.

The Landmark Office Plaza is a class A building and is the most prestigious office address. The building incorporates classic architecture with modern facilities, offering large floor space. It also houses the Old Mill Café, a stylish restaurant with a list of clients that reads like *Forbes Top 100*. The ISR Plaza is another class A building, again offering high standards with all the facilities; the building is located in the heart of the city. The Radisson SAS Hotel is also located in the building. The Hyatt Hotel also offers office space, with an enormous extension that has recently been completed. This new complex offers state-of-the-art facilities, including a health club, nightclub, etc. This area is rapidly becoming very cosmopolitan with the opening of a very popular Italian restaurant, Scalini.

The easy way

Foreign companies coming into the market can let someone else do the locating for them, by taking advantage of business facilitation services offered by various companies. For a fee, newly arrived companies can quickly move into fully furnished offices, equipped with computers, printers and the latest telecommunications. Western-style office space can be rented for US$30–US$50 per square metre per month in Baku.

The hard way

The alternative is to rent an apartment (either renovated or not renovated). This requires a great deal of time and patience as the local owners must first be located. Having done that, perseverance in bargaining and negotiation skills will also be required.

Employees

It is relatively easy to locate English-speaking local employees in Baku, but finding management with western work experience is rare. For any start-up operation, training facilities are an important consideration, and an opportunity to gain exposure to western ways of doing business is well received by Azerbaijani employees. Employment agencies can save a great deal of time by short-listing potential employees and most of agency workers speak English. The alternative is to advertise in local news-papers, some of which are published weekly in English – *The Baku Sun*, the *Azeri Times* and the *Daily News*.

Commercial intelligence

Use the local contacts and consult the many sources of commercial intelligence, including embassies, and chambers of commerce and business groups, which are non-profit, voluntary associations of individuals and companies operating in Azerbaijan. Keeping an ear to the ground and maintaining a steady physical presence is invaluable. The best source of information, and the ideal person in a business development role, is usually someone with excellent contacts in the local business community. Given the right high-level contacts, it is possible to hear of projects ahead of competitors and long before tender documents can be officially purchased. In addition to personal relationships, price most often remains the essential factor.

The Azerbaijan Chamber of Commerce

The Azerbaijan Chamber of Commerce has a list of local companies that can act as potential agents/distributors, but this is a market where personal contacts and relationships are critical and business is not easily done long-distance.

Part 4

Building an Organisation

Establishing a Presence

Ledingham Chalmers

There are three main ways in which a foreign investor may establish a direct trading presence within Azerbaijan:

1. Establish a joint venture involving foreign and local participation.
2. Create an Azerbaijani corporate entity that is wholly foreign-owned.
3. Establish a permanent presence in Azerbaijan such as a branch office of the foreign legal entity. These entities are treated differently under the current legislation especially in such areas as tax, ownership of land, currency regulations and the obtaining of certain licences and consents.

Of fundamental importance is that joint ventures and wholly foreign-owned legal entities incorporated in Azerbaijan are considered as Azerbaijani legal entities, whereas branch offices are considered 'non-resident' legal entities, involved only in trading activities in Azerbaijan on behalf of the foreign company.

There is little difference between a branch office and a representative office in Azerbaijan. Given that the state registration fee for opening a branch office (approximately US$215) is substantially less than that for opening a representative office (approximately US$2000), most companies now opt to open branch offices rather than representative offices. Accordingly, for the purposes of the remainder of this chapter, we will refer only to branch offices. It should, however, be borne in mind that the possibilities of opening a representative office still exist.

Azerbaijani legal entities as vehicles for foreign investment

In order to establish a joint venture or a wholly foreign-owned entity, various documents must be submitted to the Ministry of Justice. These include the draft charter and founding agreement of the new entity, extracts from the foreign company's register such as the Certificate of Incorporation and Memorandum of Association, documents confirming the local address of the Azerbaijani entity and extract board minutes confirming the establishment of the Azerbaijani entity.

Both joint ventures and wholly foreign-owned Azerbaijani entities may be structured as follows:

- limited liability company;
- closed joint-stock company;
- open joint-stock company.

Both the limited liability and the joint-stock companies share some basic characteristics in that liability for shareholders is limited to the extent of the charter fund and shareholders are severally liable to the extent of their respective unfunded portions of the charter fund. Shareholders in open joint-stock companies are free to transfer their shares. Shareholders in limited liability companies and closed joint-stock companies may transfer their shares provided that any pre-emption rights of existing shareholders are waived.

Joint-stock company (JSC)

JSCs are governed by the law on 'joint-stock company' and can either be closed or open but must have a minimum of three founders. In a closed JSC 50 per cent (in an open JSC 30 per cent) of the nominal stock value must be prepaid prior to the founding meeting. The amount of the declared charter fund must be in place within a year of the date of the company's registration. Currently the minimum charter capital for a closed JSC is approximately US$1,250 and for an open JSC, US$2,500. It should be noted, however, that it is not uncommon for foreign participants to be required to contribute any amount from US$5,000 to US$20,000 to the charter fund to meet local requirements. Closed JSCs' shares may only be held by the founders and/or by a predetermined group of persons.

Open JSCs have additional formation requirements including an obligation to produce an annual report and to offer shares to the public. Shares can thereafter be publicly issued and freely traded. Shares in JSCs are considered to be securities after registration of such with the Ministry of Finance. There are provisions and regulations relating to preferred and common shares, requirements for shareholders' meetings, procedures and powers of the management board and the establishment of an audit committee.

Limited liability company

There are no restrictions on the number of shareholders in limited liability companies and nor is there a minimum charter capital amount. The shares are not classed as securities. Apart from these differences the structure of the limited liability company is broadly similar to the closed joint-stock company.

Branch office

The concept of a branch office in Azerbaijan is different from that in many other countries in that the branch office may conduct commercial activities in the country on behalf of the foreign company. It has a status akin to that of a separate entity. Branch offices may be established by obtaining permission and a Registration Certificate from the Ministry of Justice. In order to register a branch office various documents need to be filed and certain formalities need to be completed. These include:

- an application letter stating basic details about the company, any business connections with Azerbaijani organisations and details of commercial transactions entered into in Azerbaijan;

- a notarised and legalised Certificate of Incorporation and Memorandum of Association (or equivalent);

- a company director's decision to set up an office in Azerbaijan;

- a decision on appointment of a manager;

- a copy of the passport of the proposed manager together with three passport photographs;

- a reference letter from bankers of a company;

- a copy of the lease agreement or other document of title verifying the address of the branch office;

- the regulations of the branch office setting out provisions as to the purpose, objects and obligations of the branch office and detailing the powers of the general branch;

- sample seal of a branch office;

- the appropriate fee (currently around US$200);

- any powers of attorney (as appropriate) duly notarised and legalised to enable any formalities in Azerbaijan to be undertaken by individuals on behalf of the foreign company in establishing and operating their office.

The branch office is deemed to have permission to be open on the issue of the Registration Certificate. If the office does not physically open within six months of that date, then the permission automatically expires. Permission will also be withdrawn on the liquidation of the foreign firm, if the branch office has breached the terms of its permission, the laws of Azerbaijan or any international agreement relating to its establishment or if the firm requests its own closure.

The branch office must register with the Azerbaijani tax authorities within ten days of the date of its registration with the Ministry of Justice. Such registration should be effected before the commencement of the activities of a branch office in Azerbaijan. If the office is not registered before that date, then it is deemed that the office is concealing income for the purposes of tax avoidance and penalties will be incurred.

Logistics

Premises

At the end of 1999 there was a surplus of office and residential premises of various standards in Baku. When entering into a lease, one should ascertain at an early stage whether rent is being negotiated on a net or gross basis. If a lessee is leasing from an Azerbaijani individual and the lessee is a legal entity, then that legal entity must withhold the relevant amount of income tax and pay it to the relevant Tax Department on behalf of the lessor. If the lessee is an individual then he is obliged to pay the gross rent to the individual lessor and the latter is responsible for payment of his own taxes.

All rentals must be paid in Azerbaijani manats, although most lessors will request payment in US dollars.

Not all residences offered for rent have been privatised and a potential lessee should request to see the purported owner's Registration Certificate and passport at an early stage in the rental negotiations.

There are no standard terms and conditions in practice and each lessee may negotiate the period of lease and notice for termination.

Owners of private property rarely insure their property and this should be borne in mind if a lessee is planning substantial investment in it.

Communications

In the centre of Baku, there are no real problems in obtaining telephone lines, although the cost can be as high as US$600 per line.

Recruitment

Azerbaijan has a surplus of English-speaking well-educated graduates. Secretarial and administrative staff can expect to earn approximately US$300–US$600 net per month and professional and management employees over US$1,000. While these net salaries are still low in comparison to western standards, the tax burden for the employer can be as high as 220 per cent of net salaries.

4.2

Agencies and Distributorships

Ledingham Chalmers

Introduction

The law on agency and distributorship is still governed by the old Soviet Civil Code. In this chapter we look at the salient issues that will be of concern to a foreign investor in the process from the establishment of a contract to its termination.

Agencies

General

Under Article 394 of the Civil Code, an agency agreement is defined as:

An agreement whereby one party (the agent) shall execute certain legal actions on behalf and on account of the other party (the principal). The principal shall pay the agent compensation if this is stipulated by the law or by the agreement.

An agency agreement can be non-exclusive and there is no requirement for an agency contract to be registered with any authorities.

The Civil Code stipulates two types of agency contract:

- agency contract

- commission agency contract.

Although both types of contract contain a number of similarities, the major differences between the two are that the first does not establish any privity of contract between a customer or third party and agent, whereas a commission agency agreement establishes such privity. Secondly, a simple agency contract may be terminated at will whereas a commission agency contract may only be terminated in certain cases, as discussed below. Under Article 407 of the Civil Code, the commission agent shall acquire rights and duties on a transaction that was executed by the commission agent with a third party. These rights and duties are upheld even though the principal may have been disclosed in the transaction and even though the principal may have had direct relations with the third party during the performance of this transaction. Confusingly, Article 411 stipulates that the commission agent shall perform all duties and realise all rights that stem from a transaction with a third party.

The commission agent shall not be responsible to the principal for performance by a third party of the transaction executed by him on account of the principal except for cases when the agent guarantees performance of the transaction by a third party (*del credere*).

Should a third party breach a transaction that has been executed with the agent, the agent shall notify the principal without delay and collect and provide the principal with all necessary evidence of such breach.

The principal having been notified of the breach by a third party of the transaction executed with the agent shall be entitled to require the transfer to himself of the agent's claims against the third party under the given transaction.

The law is unclear, but there is a possibility that an employment relationship could be created by the actions of an agent and a principal. Clearly, an agency contract should expressly stipulate that such a relationship will not be established.

Obligations of principals and agents

On a practical basis, an agent can acquire rights to customers by virtue of the agency contract only. Under Article 395 (Scope of Authorities of the Agent) of the Civil Code, an agent shall perform certain actions according to the instructions of the principal. The agent shall be entitled to deviate from these instructions if a particular situation requires it and if doing so is in the best interests of the principal, if the agent could not obtain additional instructions from the principal, or if the agent has not received a timely response to a query. In this case the agent shall inform the principal of the deviations as soon as possible.

Under Article 398 (Responsibilities of the Principal) of the Civil Code, the principal shall accept without delay from the agent performance by the latter of his duties according to the agreement. If not stipulated otherwise by the agreement, the principal shall:

1. provide the agent with all facilities necessary for the performance by the latter of his duties;

2. reimburse the agent for all his expenses that were necessary for the performance of his duties;

3. pay commission to the agent upon performance of his duties if this has been agreed (Article 394 of the Civil Code).

Termination

Under Article 399 (Termination of the Agency Agreement) of the Civil Code, it is provided that in addition to general rules of termination of obligations the agency agreement shall be terminated due to the following circumstances:

1. termination of the agency by the principal;

2. termination of the agency by the agent;

3. death of a person who is a party to the agency agreement or if he is recognised to be legally incapable or partly capable or missing;

4. liquidation of a legal entity that is a party to the agency agreement.

The principal and the agent shall be entitled to terminate the agency at any time. Any agreement or waiver from this right shall be considered invalid.

Under the Civil Code, termination indemnities shall be paid by the agent to the principal as follows. Should the agent terminate the agency agreement under conditions whereby the principal cannot protect his interests in any other way, the agent shall compensate any losses incurred by the principal by the termination of the agency agreement. At the same time, under Article 400 of the Civil Code, if the agency agreement is terminated prior to the fulfilment of entrusted duties, the principal shall reimburse to the agent all incurred expenses and pay the agent compensation due pro rata to the performed duties. This provision shall not be applied to the performance by the agent of duties after the agent has become aware or should have become aware of the termination of the agency.

Given these provisions, there is no limitation as to the agent's ability to solicit orders or collect such orders from customers. An agent is also entitled to handle customs clearance acting on behalf of a principal. Please note that in the event of a commission agency contract, a commission agent will receive goods in its own name, ie the customs declaration must indicate the name of the commission agent as an importer of commodities.

A commission agent shall not be entitled, unless otherwise stipulated in the contract, to refuse to perform an undertaken commission, except in the case when it is caused by impossibility to perform such commission, or the commission contract is breached by the principal.

A commission agent is obliged to notify the principal of his refusal in writing. A commission contract shall remain in effect for two weeks from the date of receipt by the principal of a notice of refusal to perform the commission from the commission agent. Under the Civil Code, the following indemnities for termination of a commission agency agreement apply:

1. Should the agent refuse to perform his duties due to a breach of the agency agreement by the principal, the agent shall be entitled to receive reimbursement of incurred expenses as well as commission due.

2. Should the principal terminate the commission agency granted to the agent wholly or partially prior to execution by the agent of certain transactions with third parties, the principal shall pay to the agent commission for transactions that were executed prior to the termination of agency as well as reimbursing the agent for the expenses incurred prior to the termination of agency.

Distributorships

There are no specific provisions in Azerbaijani legislation to regulate distributorship agreements. However, the relevant provisions of the Azerbaijani Civil Code concerning agency contracts and commission agency contracts would apply equally to a distributorship agreement.

A distributorship agreement can be non-exclusive.

A distributor may acquire all rights to customers subject to certain restrictions that may be imposed by a principal in a distributorship agreement.

The circumstances indicated in Article 399 of the Civil Code (see pp 223) can serve as the grounds for termination of a distributorship agreement.

Generally, there is no requirement for distributorship contracts to be registered with any authorities. However, some approvals should be obtained from local authorities if a distributorship contract envisages the import of certain goods to the Azerbaijan Republic.

4.3

Accounting Regulations

Arthur Andersen

All entities registered in Azerbaijan (Azerbaijani legal entities, representative offices and branches) are required to maintain their books and records on the territory of Azerbaijan, in local currency, and in accordance with Azerbaijan Accounting Legislation (AAL). This includes the use of a mandatory and rather rigid chart of accounts. In most cases, this will necessitate the employment of a full-time, experienced Azerbaijani chief accountant.

PSA considerations

The maintenance of accounting records is one of the chief differences between the PSA regime and non-PSA operations. PSA participants are able to maintain their accounts in accordance with the accounting guidelines specified within the PSA documents themselves. Generally, this means that their accounting requirements are more closely linked with international practices.

In order to demonstrate some of the issues that are prevalent in Azerbaijani accounting, we set out below some of the major differences between Azerbaijani accounting and international accounting systems.

Differences between AAL and IAS

Azerbaijani accounting rules differ substantially from International Accounting Standards (IAS) and general accepted accounting principles (GAAP) in other countries (eg the USA). A summary of the more significant differences follows:

Accounting policies

AAL does not require the detailed disclosure of accounting policies used in the preparation of the financial statements or footnote disclosures that provide additional information, analysis and clarification of the financial statements.

However, there is an Azerbaijani law on accounting other laws that specifies the chart of accounts. These laws provide examples of the nature of the entries that can be made in specific accounts as well as a description of those accounts.

Property, plant and equipment

Azerbaijani financial information is maintained in historic manat terms, and property, plant and equipment are recorded at acquisition price or cost of production including transportation and assembly costs. At various times since 1992, fixed assets were revalued in accordance with government decrees (most recently in 1996). Indices used for these revaluations did not necessarily account for the changes in the value of manat, nor did they result in the value of the underlying fixed assets to which they were applied being revalued to a current market value. Revaluations of property, plant and equipment are generally not allowed under IAS.

Depreciation

Under AAL, depreciation rates for various classes of assets are provided irrespective of industry classification. Rates often tend to be significantly lower (ie the assets are depreciated over a longer period of time) than those normally used under IAS. IAS requires all property, plant and equipment to be depreciated on a rational and systematic basis over the economic life of the related assets.

Impairment of assets

AAL does not permit an allowance against the carrying value of an asset, which may be impaired. This includes setting up an allowance for tangible assets as well as inventories, accounts receivable and other assets.

IAS requires, among other things, that long-lived assets and certain identifiable intangibles that are held and used by an entity be reviewed for impairment whenever events or changes in circumstances indicate that the carrying amount of an asset may not be recoverable. In addition, allowances may be made upon the carrying value of short-term assets (for example, accounts receivable) when it is likely that the full carrying value of the asset will not be recovered.

Deferred taxes

Under AAL there are no provisions regarding deferred tax accounting, even though Azerbaijani financial statements are currently prepared on the accrual method and taxes are paid on the cash method. Many of the items accounted for through equity, under AAL, are not tax-deductible (eg training, insurance, certain business travel costs).

Deferred tax assets and liabilities under IAS are recorded for the expected future tax consequences of existing differences between financial reporting and tax reporting bases of assets and liabilities, and loss or tax credit carryforwards.

Equity

In the balance sheet of an Azerbaijani company, equity is represented by charter capital, paid-in-excess capital, reserve capital, appropriated earnings, revaluation funds, social funds and retained earnings for the current and previous years. Deductions can be made directly from reserve funds for certain items such as non-tax-deductible expenses.

Under IAS, equity is generally represented only by capital stock, additional paid-in capital and retained earnings for the current and previous years.

General

In general, the Azerbaijani system reflects its historic evolution from a Soviet system. There is a focus on substance over form with respect to the documentation and recording of accounting information and transactions. Accounts prepared under Azerbaijani accounting principles generally do not provide adequate management information.

In addition, it is important to note that all accounting documents are required to be maintained in the Azeri language and generally in Azerbaijan. This can cause difficulties for a foreign investor with the requirement to either maintain translations of all accounting information or risk penalties for incorrect accounting.

Administrative penalties for incorrect accounting, which can be imposed for any number of small and rather inconsequential violations of Azerbaijani rules, can very quickly become an expensive issue. Administrative penalties are issued as a fine of one or two months' salary of the general director and/or the chief accountant. These penalties can apply irrespective of whether the error was accidental or deliberate, or whether or not it caused an understatement of the taxable income of the accounts. Furthermore, there is no discretion with respect to the imposition of such penalties, the Administrative Code does not provide for any mitigating circumstances.

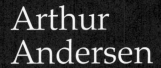

Arthur Andersen

Serving the Caspian

For more information on doing business in the Caspian please contact the individuals listed

Baku Peter Burnie
994 (12) 98 2486
994 (12) 98 2487 Fax

Almaty Rick McArthur
7 (3272) 60 8520
7 (3272) 60 8521 Fax

London Julian Small
44 (171) 438 3000
44 (171) 831 1133 Fax

Ashgabat Donald James
993 (12) 51 2405
993 (12) 51 2403 Fax

4.4

Tax Regime

Arthur Andersen

As with other parts of the Azerbaijani economy, there are two different systems currently in operation. With respect to taxation the difference between PSA and non-PSA treatments is even more distinct than the differences in other areas. In this chapter, we deal first with the system applicable to non-PSA activities and non-PSA contractors.

A range of taxes, duties and other burdens are provided for in the law such as:

- profit tax;
- property tax;
- VAT;
- road use tax;
- land tax;
- payroll tax and social charges;
- mineral fields tax (royalties);
- personal income tax.

In general, all legal entities registered in Azerbaijan are subject to the taxes discussed below (unless protected by the PSA tax regime). All foreign legal entities engaging in activity in Azerbaijan through a permanent establishment are required to register with the tax authorities.

Profit tax

All legal entities engaged in commercial activities in Azerbaijan are subject to profit tax. The current rate of profit tax for commercial or production activities including the oil sector is 30 per cent.

Profit tax is computed on the entity's taxable profits. Taxable profits are computed by deducting business expenses, VAT, excise tax, and the cost of production. The Azerbaijani chart of accounts regulates the quantum and the nature of deductible business expenses. However, only amounts of few types of deductible expenses are constrained by various Azerbaijani instructions.

For Azerbaijani legal entities, the following tax concessions are available:

- Amounts expended on capital investment on production and repayment of bank loans obtained and used for such purposes. Capital investment on production is interpreted as capital outlay for new objects, reconstruction, expansion and modernisation of existing enterprises and also purchase of fixed assets for this purpose;

- Donations to charitable and such other funds up to a maximum of one per cent of taxable profits;

- Tax losses can be carried forward for a period of five years and may be used to offset future taxable profits.

For foreign legal entities: a foreign legal entity operating in Azerbaijan through a permanent establishment is charged to tax in Azerbaijan on Azerbaijani source income. Profit tax is calculated as income less expenses attributable to the permanent establishment in Azerbaijan.

Unlike Azerbaijani legal entities, foreign legal entities are not permitted to carry forward their losses for profit tax purposes. Foreign legal entities are also unable to enjoy the same concessions and incentives as described in the above paragraphs as applicable to Azerbaijani legal entities.

Taxpayers make quarterly payments of profit tax in advance, computed from the anticipated profit for the quarter concerned. Filing requirements for Azerbaijani legal entities, joint ventures and foreign legal entities differ slightly with foreign legal entities having fewer reporting obligations than Azerbaijani legal entities in some circumstances.

The income of a foreign legal entity from foreign trade operations is not subject to tax in Azerbaijan. In the event that the tax authorities are unable to estimate profits of a foreign legal entity from Azerbaijani sources, they (the tax authorities) may deem 25 per cent of expenses or 20 per cent of incomes as taxable profit.

Foreign legal entities with no permanent establishment are subject to withholding tax on income derived from Azerbaijani sources at the following rates:

Lease payments	20%
Management fees	20%
Freight income	6%
Interest	15%
Other income	20%
Dividends (transferred out of Azerbaijan)	15%

In the case of double tax treaties the rate of withholding tax varies depending on the contents of the particular treaty.

Property tax

All entities are subject to a property tax at the rate of 0.5 per cent of the cost of their fixed assets. Tax is calculated on the average annual value of the fixed assets on the statutory balance sheet, ie the depreciated cost of property as per the statutory balance sheet.

VAT

The standard VAT rate in Azerbaijan is 20 per cent. Sale of goods and services, including imported goods (at customs) is subject to VAT. Input VAT paid for fixed assets can generally be offset against output VAT. It cannot be capitalised as part of the asset's cost. Services rendered by international organisations (eg the United Nations), companies dealing with housing construction and construction of social facilities, consulting services on the basis of governmental agreements, as well as credits and loans, are not subject to VAT.

The VAT system operates in a similar way to the basic European Union (EU) Sixth Directive systems. Input VAT can be offset against output VAT, and any excess VAT is available for refund. In practice, of course, refunds are generally not available, although refundable balances can sometimes be offset against other tax liabilities.

Road use tax

Several different taxes are paid to the road fund by legal entities. These include:

- 15 per cent of the sale price (after VAT) of fuel or lubricants (not crude oil);

- 0.05 per cent of an entity's turnover (applicable to all entities, both Azeri legal entities and foreign legal entities, irrespective of whether the entity has vehicles or uses roads); a rate of 0.3 per cent applies to trade companies;

- 2 per cent of the purchase price of vehicles;

- an additional vehicle owners' tax is paid annually based on the vehicle's horsepower (110 manats per horsepower for physical persons and 225 manats per horsepower for legal entities);

- transit tax paid on entering the country at a rate based on the type of vehicle, its load and load weight.

Land tax

All enterprises utilising land are subject to a land tax calculated as a percentage of the minimum wage on 1 May each year. In Baku, the rate of tax is one per cent of the minimal salary per square metre, while in other parts of the country it varies from 0.4 per cent to 0.8 per cent.

Payroll tax and social charges

All Azerbaijani registered enterprises must make payments to social insurance and employment funds. Payment to the social insurance fund is 33 per cent of gross wages; in addition, one per cent of the employees' salaries is withheld and paid in.

An amount of two per cent of gross wages is paid by the employer to the employment fund. Thus, the employer's total payroll tax liability is 35 per cent. Generally, for foreign employees only a contribution to the employment fund is required. A payment of one per cent of the tax base for profit tax purposes is made to the invalid fund.

Mineral fields tax (royalties)

Enterprises and individuals engaged in mineral extraction are subject to a mineral fields or subsoil tax. The tax is applied to the net income received from the sale of the product at rates ranging from 3 per cent to 26 per cent.

According to the list approved by the Cabinet of Ministers in June 1996, the tax is applied to the extraction of crude oil, natural gas, ferrous metals, rare metals, non-ore minerals, processed and decorative stone, cement, barium, clays, volcanic ash, sand and other construction materials inputs, salt, gravel, precious and semi-precious stones, iodine and mineral water.

The level of royalty payments for crude oil is set at 26 per cent of the wholesale price less transport, and at 20 per cent for gas. Royalty cost is included in the cost of production (ie it is tax-deductible for profit tax purposes).

Personal income tax

Foreigners physically present in Azerbaijan for 183 days or more during any calendar year are subject to personal income tax in Azerbaijan on their total worldwide income. Those present for less than 183 days are subject to tax only on Azerbaijani source income.

Virtually all forms of compensation are taxable to an employee including hardship and cost of living allowances, payments by employer for employees' children's education and payment of taxes on behalf of an employee. However, employer-provided reimbursements for housing and cars are not taxable. There are no other material personal deductions or allowances available.

Foreigners expecting to be in the country for more than 183 days of any given year are required to file a preliminary tax declaration, showing expected worldwide income. An annual tax declaration must be filed by 1 February of the following year.

Employers are required to compute and withhold taxes from the salaries of all employees in accordance with the tax rates in force. Taxes withheld are to be remitted to the government immediately. Local employees whose taxes are withheld have no further tax filing obligations.

Personal income tax rates are applied on a graduated basis, the top marginal rate being applicable at relatively low gross income levels. The top marginal rate is 35 per cent. A table of rates applicable to annual incomes is attached.

Table 4.4.1 Personal income tax rates

Annual income (AZM)	Tax rates (AZM)
Up to 1,200,000	Free
1,200,001–7,200,000	12% on the amount exceeding 1,200,000
7,200,001–16,800,000	720,000 + 20% on the amount exceeding 7,200,000
16,800,001–36,000,000	2,640,000 + 25% on the amount exceeding 16,800,000
36,000,001–60,000,000	7,440,000 + 30% on the amount exceeding 36,000,000
More than 60,000,000	14,640,000 + 35% on the amount exceeding 60,000,000

Source: Tax Rates as of 2000, Azerbaijani Government

Penalties

Azerbaijani legislation provides for severe penalties for failing to comply with the applicable tax, accounting and currency rules in an accurate and timely manner. Fines can be imposed up to 110 per cent of disputed amounts. In addition, penalties can be imposed for late payment at 0.1 per cent per day.

The PSA system

Within the PSA system it is also appropriate to distinguish between PSA contractors (ie the signatories to the PSA) and PSA subcontractors (those providing services to PSA contractors).

Contracting parties

Oil and gas contractors are only subject to profit tax and social fund contribution for local employees. Other major payments include bonuses and acreage fees. The PSA parties are exempt of all other taxes including royalties.

Profit tax
Under the PSAs currently effective, contracting parties carrying out business in Azerbaijan in connection with petroleum operations are subject to tax on profit. The profit tax rate is negotiable and varies from 25 per cent for consortia PSAs signed in 1994 and 1995, to 32 per cent for PSA consortia signed later.

Social charges
Under PSAs, it is normally required that the contracting parties make contributions of Azerbaijan state social insurance and similar payments. These include contributions to the pension fund, the social insurance fund and the employment fund, totalling 35 per cent of gross local payroll. These contributions are made only with respect to employees who are citizens of Azerbaijan.

Bonus payment, acreage fee
The terms of bonus payment and the size of the bonus are negotiable and vary for each individual PSA. Starting with the second consortium signed, there has been an acreage fee for the contract area during the exploration period and additional exploration period. An annual acreage fee is negotiable and for some PSAs the range of the acreage fee is US$1,200 to US$2,000 per km^2.

Royalties
Under existing PSAs, the parties are not subject to royalties existing for extraction of hydrocarbon resources in Azerbaijan.

Sub-contractors

Both Azeri legal entities and foreign legal entities can register as sub-contractors to PSAs. Azeri legal entities will be subject to tax in accordance with general taxation rules. However, registered foreign sub-contractors are only subject to withholding tax, in addition to social fund payments in the same manner as contracting parties.

Withholding tax
Foreign sub-contractors carrying on business in Azerbaijan in connection with hydrocarbon activities shall be deemed to earn a taxable profit of

20–25 per cent, depending on the particular PSA, of the payments received in respect of work or services performed in Azerbaijan. These sub-contractors are subject to tax on such profit at the rate of 25—32 per cent, resulting in a total withholding tax obligation of 5—8 per cent, depending on the particular PSA.

Social charges
Under PSAs, it is normally required that the parties involved shall make contributions of Azerbaijan state social insurance and similar payments as described for PSA contractors.

Road fund tax
Several different taxes are paid to the road fund by sub-contractors. Road fund tax includes only 2 per cent of the purchase price of vehicles; an additional vehicle owners' tax is paid annually based on the vehicle's horsepower (110 Manats per horsepower for physical persons and 225 Manats per horsepower for legal entities).

VAT

Contractors and sub-contractors are 'exempt with credit' from VAT (ie a zero per cent rate is applied) in connection with petroleum activities on all:

- Goods, works and services supplied to or by them.

- Exports of petroleum and all products processed or refined from such petroleum.

- Imports of goods, works and services.

Additionally, any supplier of works and services (including sub-contractors) to each contractor should treat those supplies as being exempt from VAT with credit.

Residency rules

For employees of PSA contracting parties and sub-contractors, special residency rules apply. A person who spends more than 30 consecutive days or a total of 90 days in a calendar year in Azerbaijan will be considered as tax resident.

Customs and Excise Regulations

Arthur Andersen

The area of customs is perhaps one of the most difficult areas to deal with in respect of any investment in Azerbaijan. There are a large range of different documents and rules applicable to the area and a large number of small departments dealing with individual parts of the customs process. Therefore it can be difficult to receive consistent and transparent treatment in dealing with customs issues in Azerbaijan.

Once again there is a difference between PSA and non-PSA operations. PSA contractors and subcontractors are exempt from all customs duties under the respective PSAs. Therefore they pay only the customs processing fees discussed below.

Customs storage facilities

Goods may be imported and stored in ordinary customs warehouses in Azerbaijan. The customs code provides that goods and equipment stored in customs warehouses with no release into free circulation shall be free of any import duties for up to three years. Duties and taxes are payable on removal of such equipment and goods from the customs warehouse, unless specifically exempt from payment of import duties.

Processing of goods within customs area

Goods can be imported into Azerbaijan under the processing regime. Under this regime, import duties and VAT are payable upon import of the goods. The imported goods should then be processed within the customs area. At the time of export of these goods from Azerbaijan, all import duties and VAT paid on import are to be refunded.

For the purpose of operating under this regime, a licence needs to be obtained from the customs committee. No formal procedure has been laid down for the purpose of obtaining this licence. The licence is granted by the customs committee on a case-by-case basis. The code also stipulates that the processing of goods and their export has to be accomplished within two years of their import into Azerbaijan.

Temporary import

Until recently, goods could be brought into Azerbaijan under the temporary import regime. However, as of 1 April 1999 the decree that provided for this regime has been withdrawn. Therefore it would appear that temporary import is no longer available.

However, the actual position with respect to temporary import regimes and their availability is unclear. It is expected that some form of regime will continue to be available; the specific format and requirements will be released when the replacement decree is available.

Import tax

Import tax is now 15 per cent for most goods. Different rates apply in the case of countries with which trade agreements have been concluded. Assets brought in by a foreign investor as part of its capital contribution to charter capital are exempt from import tax. In addition, exempted goods include:

- goods for re-export and processing;
- other materials imported under intergovernmental agreements.

No import tax is due on goods imported by foreign employees for their personal needs, or for humanitarian and technical aid, as long as it is to be distributed free of charge.

Customs charges of 0.15 per cent or 0.3 per cent are payable on the customs value of imported goods as a customs processing fee. This fee is applicable to all imports.

Export tax

As of 28 October 1997, all exports are free from export tax. Several categories of exports are prohibited however – such as barter, commercial credit or consignment basis sales.

Excise tax

Excise tax, in the range of 5–90 per cent, is applied to a number of goods and services. The list of these goods is approved annually by the Milli Majlis (National Assembly) when submitting the annual budget and is subject to revision by the Cabinet of Ministers. In 1997, it included many petroleum products, in addition to luxury and other goods such as alcohol and tobacco.

Exported goods and services are not subject to excise tax.

4.6

Intellectual Property

Ledingham Chalmers

Introduction

As the markets in Azerbaijan open up to increased foreign investment activity through direct sales, the establishment of joint ventures with Azerbaijani companies or through other forms of cooperation such as franchise or licensing agreements, the protection of established and often valuable intellectual property rights should be given appropriate consideration. The failure to protect such rights adequately in a new market or to evaluate the rights of others can have far-reaching consequences for the success and profitability of a business.

The current legislative structure relating to trade marks, patents and copyright in Azerbaijan has been adopted over the last few years to provide for the national registration and protection of intellectual property rights. Article 30 of the Constitution of Azerbaijan recognises the ability of persons to own rights in relation to intellectual property. Additionally the 1992 Foreign Investment Protection Law specifically gives protection to intellectual property rights providing that the legal regime in respect of foreign investors should not be less favourable than that provided to Azerbaijani nationals who hold intellectual property rights under Azerbaijani law.

The principal regulations are laid out in:

- 1996 Law on Copyright and Associated Rights
- 1997 Law on Patents
- 1998 Law on Trade marks and Geographical Indicators.

Copyright

The Law on Copyright and Associated Rights became effective in October 1996. Under the law, copyright may exist in scientific, literary and artistic works as well as artistic performances, sound recordings and television programmes. It appears that there need be no aesthetic appeal or artistic quality for copyright to exist in such artistic works. Copyright is also recognised for computer databases and programmes.

The legal ownership of copyright in any work is automatically vested in the author of the work and as such there is no requirement to formally register copyright of any work in Azerbaijan.

The law does, however, provide for a registration mechanism for copyright with the Copyright State Agency of the Azerbaijan Republic. The Agency will issue a Registration Certificate to the author and such a certificate will serve as proof of the authenticity of the author's right to copyright unless such a presumption can be refuted.

The law generally provides that copyright of any appropriate work ends after a period of 50 years after the death of the author. Within that time period the author or his permitted assignees enjoy exclusive rights to the work including the author's copying, publishing, performing and broadcasting of such works. A copyright owner may assign such rights to any persons or legal entities in Azerbaijan or abroad both within or outside the territory of Azerbaijan.

Where the author's copyright is infringed, then the author has the right to demand either repayment by the infringer of all income gained by the infringer from the violation of the copyright or, alternatively, compensation in lieu of damages up to a total amount of 275 million manats (approximately US$68,750).

Azerbaijan is a signatory to the 1998 Berne Convention for the Protection of Literary and Artistic works, which became effective in Azerbaijan in February 1999.

Patents

The Law on Patents has been in force in Azerbaijan since 1997 and governs the issue, licensing, registration and regulation of patents in Azerbaijan.

In order to establish the patentability of an invention the applicant must establish that the invention is new and is capable of useful industrial application.

For patents to gain protection under the Law, they must be registered with the appropriate State Agency and a patent in respect of the invention must be issued. The State Committee for Science and Technology is the principal agency which issues patents for appropriate inventions. Following the issue of any patent certificate, the State Committee will within three months of that date officially publish the patented invention.

On the issue of a patent, the patentee has an exclusive right to make use of the patent for 20 years from the date of filing of the patent with the State Committee in respect of inventions and 10 years in respect of industrial design rights or manufactured utility models.

A patentee may grant an assignment on sale or license the use of his patent and no other user may make use of the product patented without the consent of the patentee. Such assignments or licences must normally be registered at the State Committee for Science and Technology in order to be legally effective.

Any person who infringes a patent duly registered in Azerbaijan as an unauthorised user may be subject to various civil and criminal penalties as set out in the law.

In practice it is often the case that inventors in Azerbaijan may simply seek copyright or trade mark protection over their works rather than seek to register a patent. This situation is principally a result of the more stringent formalities that are in place with respect to the issuing of patents, coupled with the fact that enforcement proceedings are often more complicated given the nature of the legislation.

With respect to the international protection afforded to patents, Azerbaijan became a signatory to the 1970 Washington Patent Co-operation Treaty in September 1995 and the Eurasian Patent Convention.

The Washington Treaty enables an applicant to submit a single international application in one language and to file one application at one office of a signatory state. The signatories of the Treaty will therefore respect the date of first registration of that patent at the first office.

Trade marks

Trade marks are used to protect the goodwill and reputation of a business by preventing exploitation by unauthorised third parties.

The principal legislation concerning trade marks is contained in the Law on Trade marks and Geographical Indicators, which became effective in August 1998.

To gain protections under the law, trade marks must be registered and must be sufficiently distinctive and novel.

Application for registration is made to the appropriate state committee (usually the State Committee on Science and Technology). Successful registration confers on the holder the exclusive right of use and exploitation of the mark and protects against infringements of that mark.

First registration is for a period of ten years from the date of filing of the application letter. Subsequently, and upon further application by the trade mark owner, such a term may be extended for a further period of ten years.

The registered owner of a trade mark may permit other parties to use it provided that the license agreement is registered with the appropriate state committee. Under Azerbaijani law, a license agreement implies that the quality of the products protected by a trade mark under a licence must be equivalent to that quality produced by the licensor. In addition, the licensor has an implied right to control the quality of the licensed product.

Azerbaijan is a signatory to the Madrid System on the International Registration of Marks which recognises the role of the World Intellectual Property Organisation in Geneva in handling international trade mark applications.

Property Law and Security Aspects

Ledingham Chalmers

Introduction

For foreign investors, a clear and efficient system of law is required to deal with title to land and buildings and take security in order that badly deeded development, infrastructure and construction project risks are minimised. Azerbaijan has made a start towards achieving such a system; however, there is much work still to be done.

Land and buildings

The principal legislation governing land law in Azerbaijan is the Land Code, as ratified by the Milli Majlis (National Assembly) on 25 June 1999 enacted by the Presidential Decree of 4 August 1999 and published on and therefore effective from 8 August 1999. Under the Land Code, land formerly in the ownership of the state may be deemed sold to constitute private property by the appropriate Regional Executive Authority or municipality. The executive authorities and municipalities have the power to grant natural persons and legal entities plots of land for three different uses:

1. lease and temporary use (the latter is to be granted to persons of Azerbaijani nationality only) for either a short term of up to 15 years or for a long term of up to 99 years (although such terms are renewable);

2. permanent use (effectively in perpetuity);

3. private ownership.

Foreign citizens or legal entities do not have the right to own land or take it for use, although they are legally entitled to lease land under Article 48 of the Land Code and the Land Lease Law of 11 December 1998.

Despite the restrictions imposed on land ownership, foreign investors may purchase, with full title, property such as buildings and other constructions. The Law, On the Protection of Foreign Investments of 15 January 1992, specifically provides that foreign investors may make investments by way of acquisition of buildings and constructions. Where a piece of land with buildings is transferred from an Azerbaijani national to a non-Azerbaijani, the land will be transferred to the relevant executive authority or municipality and the non-Azerbaijani entity is required to conclude a lease with that authority. A long-term lease on the land may be granted to the non-Azerbaijani. Full title for the building itself would be transferred to the non-Azerbaijani entity.

Despite the fact that under Azerbaijani law nothing prevents foreign investors from owning residential premises or buildings in the city of Baku, the Baku Executive Authority has issued a decree requiring all natural persons to meet certain residency requirements in order to obtain title. Practically, such restrictions have been overcome on occasion through negotiation with the Baku Executive Authority and/or by court order.

Under the Civil Code, proprietary rights in a property take effect from the moment of physical transfer of legal possession of the property to the buyer unless law or contract provides otherwise. If a transfer contract is subject to state registration, transfer of the proprietary rights to the property will take effect from the date of registration of such contract.

Land registration

A regulation of 27 August 1992 states that the State Land Committee was established in order to perform a number of functions of the regional executive authorities; however, the necessary mechanisms for its effective operation have not yet been established. The recently enacted code has not altered this position. In the meantime, all transactions relating to land in Baku are entered in the Land Registry books of the Baku Executive Authority. The State Land Committee maintains the Land Registry for lands outside Baku. Any land transaction that has not been registered in the appropriate land registry may be declared void and invalid by the relevant authority. In addition, the State Property Committee's permission is required for use, lease, pledge and other alienation of state property or rights to state property and such state land transactions are registered with the State Property Committee.

Taking security

Azerbaijani law provides for the following forms of security: pledge, suretyship, guarantee, liquidated damages and earnest money. There are no restrictions imposed on foreigners in acting as the creditor. Securities and debts may be specified in foreign currency and in the event that a sale of Azerbaijani assets takes place in manats, the amount will be converted to foreign currency at the official exchange rate of the National Bank of Azerbaijan on the date of sale.

Pledge

The Pledge Law of 3 July 1998 states that any goods, securities, valuable materials, plots of land in private ownership and other proprietary rights may be pledged except where prohibited by Azerbaijani law (for example for reasons of national security). In order for a pledge agreement to be legally binding, it should be in written form and specify the following:

- the names and addresses of the parties;
- description, location and value of the pledged assets;
- details of the secured transaction including value;
- reference to an agreement of which it is a security;
- date and events upon which the pledger's obligations become due;
- whether the pledge is possessory or registered and general or specific;
- any other agreed terms between the parties.

Under Article 10 of the Pledge Law, a pledge agreement cannot be free-standing but must be dependent on another agreement (for example the underlying loan agreement) in order to validly constitute the pledge and consequent obligations. State property generally may be pledged only with the consent of the State Property Committee. Generally, where the pledged assets are registered, then the pledge agreement must also be registered, such a registered pledge becoming effective from the date of registration. However, there are a number of conflicting provisions between the Pledge Law and specific laws on various types of property. Advice should be taken to ensure a valid pledge has been created.

The pledge of enterprises or buildings and objects directly related to land must be registered in a 'hypothecate book'. However, there is as yet no developed legal mechanism for hypothecates and land mortgage registration in Azerbaijan.

In the event that the pledger defaults in the performance of its secured obligations, the pledgee shall have the right to a first priority claim over the secured assets ahead of non-secured creditors. In the event that receipts from the secured assets are insufficient to cover the pledgee's claim under the pledge agreement, then the pledgee will have a right of claim against other assets but will stand on an equal footing with ordinary creditors.

The pledgee may enforce his rights over the pledger's assets by serving a notification of enforcement on the pledger, with a copy of such notification to be submitted to the relevant registration authority within seven days of the date of notification to the pledger. Enforcement is possible 30 days after notification.

Suretyship

In terms of the Civil Code, if the principal defaults in the performance of his obligations under a suretyship agreement, the principal and the surety shall be jointly liable to the obligee for interest payments, indemnification for loss and liquidated damages unless the parties have agreed otherwise.

In the event that the surety is sued by the obligee, under Article 194 of the Civil Code, the surety shall be obliged to join the principal in the action. If the surety fails to join the principal, the principal shall have all defences available to it against the surety as would have been available to it as against the obligee. The surety has the right to utilise all defences available to the principal against the obligee's claim even where the principal has accepted liability. The surety also has the right to proceed with a claim against the principal for the amount paid by the surety to the obligee in satisfaction of its obligations. As part of this process, upon performance of the principal's obligations by the surety, the obligee must submit to the surety all documents certifying the claim against the principal as well as transfer the rights securing such claim.

A principal that has performed the obligations secured by the suretyship must immediately notify the surety of such performance without delay. Otherwise, the surety who has also performed the same obligations reserves the right to proceed with a claim against the principal. In such an event, the principal is entitled to claim from the obligee any additional benefit received by the obligee.

Under suretyship, the obligations of the surety cease upon the fulfilment of the obligations that have been secured. The suretyship also ceases if the obligee does not file any claim against the surety within three months of the date when the obligations were due. If such date and/or the period for filing a claim have not been specified by the parties, the suretyship shall cease one year from the date of execution of the suretyship provided there has been no other agreement signed between the parties.

The suretyship must be concluded in written form and the absence of such formal requirements may invalidate the suretyship. Enforcement of suretyship is possible through the courts.

Guarantee

The concept of 'guarantee' is similar to that of suretyship and is in fact treated as a form of suretyship.

The main difference between suretyship and guarantee is that under the guarantee, the responsibility of the guarantor to the obligee is additional to the responsibility of the principal, whereas under the suretyship the surety and the principal are jointly responsible to the obligee.

In practice, the guarantee is the most commonly used form of security between Azerbaijani legal entities.

Liquidated damages

Liquidated damages (for example penalties or fines) are recognised under Azerbaijani law as monies that a debtor is obliged to pay to a creditor in the event of non-performance or improper performance or delay of the former's obligations.

A liquidated damages clause may be incorporated into a general agreement to secure the direct obligations of the parties under that agreement.

Earnest money

The Civil Code recognises 'earnest money' as any deposit payment made by one party to the other at the time of entering into a contract as part payment for the total amount due under that contract. The deposit serves as proof of the existence of the contract. It should be noted that the party that has received the earnest money must pay to the other party double the amount of such money should the former fail to perform its obligations under the contract. This form of security must also be executed in written form.

4.8

Employment Law

Ledingham Chalmers

Introduction

As increasing numbers of western companies build up their operations in Azerbaijan, the country's laws relating to employment become of increasing relevance to both employers and to their local and expatriate employees. The Labour Code (effective from 1 July 1999) provides the main source of employment legislation in Azerbaijan and regulates the employer/employee relationship, irrespective of the nationality of the employees.

The employment contract

There are certain legal requirements that must be included in any employment contract. These include:

- full details of the parties;
- the location of employment;
- employee's obligations and conditions of work, including working time, remuneration and allowances, duration of leave, labour protection conditions, social insurance and others;
- commencement date and date of execution of the contract;
- mutual obligations of the parties;
- term of the contract;
- any other terms agreed between the parties that do not place the employee in a worse position than that laid down in statute.

Failure to include any of the above provisions in an employment contract will nullify the whole contract. The contract should also stipulate the employee's salary as a gross amount, inclusive of the employees' income tax or social insurance fund contributions. The tax authorities consider that if a contract indicates the employee's net salary, then there may be an implication that the employer is bearing the individual employee's tax liability. This is specifically prohibited under Azerbaijani tax regulations. Nonetheless, the employer must withhold and remit to the relevant tax authorities all necessary taxes and make the appropriate contributions to the Social Insurance Fund and the Employment Fund so that, in practice, payment is made net to the employee.

Generally, an individual labour contract should normally be for a non-fixed term unless the nature of the employment is short term or seasonal. Where an employment contract is for a fixed term, evidence must be shown of the employee's consent to enter into the contract.

Employment conditions

Minimum salary

The minimum salary in Azerbaijan is 5,500 manats per month (approximately US$1.30).

Maximum working week

The statutory maximum hours in the working week is 40. Depending on the age or physical condition of employees or under certain working conditions, this maximum may be reduced to 36 or 24 hours. On the basis of a 40-hour working week, employees are not allowed to work more than eight hours a day in a five-day working week. Where a six-day week is being worked, employees are not allowed to work for more than seven hours a day and the last working day before a weekend should not exceed five hours. On the day before a national holiday and/or the National Mourning Day, the working day should be reduced by at least one hour.

At the end of each working week, employees are entitled to continuous rest of not less than 42 hours.

Overtime

The basic premise is that overtime (which is defined as any working period in excess of the fixed duration of working time) is prohibited and should not be a condition of employment.

In certain circumstances, however, overtime is permissible, on the grounds, for example, that the work being carried out cannot be suspended for technical reasons. Overtime cannot exceed four hours during any consecutive two-day period and two hours a day.

The overtime payment rate is stipulated at a rate of twice the base salary, calculated on an hourly basis.

Shift work

Generally, shift work should be no longer than eight hours, excluding any lunch break, and payment should be increased by minimum levels of surplus remuneration due to be established by the appropriate executive authority. The night shift is defined as any shift that either wholly or partly falls within the period from 10 pm to 6 am. The evening shift is defined as the shift that immediately precedes the night shift. Certain categories of employees may not be involved in night shift work.

The rotation regime

The rotation regime applies to all workers who are either based offshore or on-site at remote industrial projects, where the employees work for a specific period on-site and then return periodically to the base where their enterprise is principally located. The maximum 40-hour week should still be observed while on rotation.

A schedule, approved by the management and the trade union (if any), should stipulate the timings of the start and end of the working day, designated lunch breaks and other rest periods together with non-working periods and a weekly day off (either Saturday or Sunday). The working day cannot exceed 12 hours (inclusive of overtime).

Termination and dismissal

An employment contract may be terminated by the employer in the event of the liquidation, reorganisation, transfer of ownership of the employer or redundancy on two months' notice and must be accompanied by compensation of not less than one month's salary. The employment contract may also be terminated on one month's notice following a decision by a competent body that the employee is unable to meet the job requirements. Termination without notice is only possible following a material breach of the employment contract by the employee.

The employee may give notice to the employer to terminate a non-fixed contract on 15 calendar days' notice.

Probationary periods

The probationary period for a new employee before the issue of a permanent employment contract cannot exceed three months, during which time the employee is entitled to three days' notice of termination.

Leave

Annual leave

Azerbaijani legislation stipulates not less than 21 calendar days' annual leave for most workers, although managers and 'experts' (this includes lawyers, accountants and certain grades of secretaries) are entitled to 30 days. In addition, there are 14 public holidays and a National Mourning Day in Azerbaijan, although in the event that an employee is on leave during a public holiday or during the National Mourning Day, no additional day is given in lieu. However, under the relevant International Labour Organisation Conventions, which take precedence over the provisions of the Labour Code in case of conflict, such additional days in lieu should be granted. No monetary compensation is payable in place of annual leave, except upon termination of employment. Extended leave must be granted to certain categories of employees under certain circumstances.

Additional annual leave is granted to those employees with regard to their length of service as follows:

- for more than 5 years' service – an extra two days;
- for more than 10 years' service – an extra four days;
- for more than 15 years' service – an extra six days.

Maternity leave

Maternity leave is granted for 126 calendar days where the employee is entitled to full pay and an employer may be required to keep the post open for the employee for a period of three years after the employee goes on maternity leave. Two minimum salaries (approximately US$2.60) are payable per month during this time. Another person may be employed in lieu of the woman on maternity leave on a fixed term basis subject to immediate termination of employment when the woman on leave wishes to return to work.

Sick leave

Employees who have produced satisfactory documentary evidence that they are unfit to work are entitled to payment for up to six months from the date of their absence from work. After six months of absence, the employee may be dismissed.

Of further interest

Penalties for employers

A company's manager can be held both civilly and criminally liable for breaches of labour legislation and penalties can include statutory fines and even imprisonment or hard manual labour for up to a maximum of one year for serious breaches. It is therefore essential that full and up-to-date legal advice be obtained before potential employers consider expanding their operations in Azerbaijan.

Production-sharing agreements in the oil and gas sectors

Under the standard terms of the various production-sharing agreements entered into between the State Oil Company (SOCAR) and western oil companies (which must by law be undertaken), contractors, operators and subcontractors are given some latitude. They are free to implement, *inter alia*, recruitment and dismissal programmes and practices that are customary in international petroleum operations and that are best able, in their experience and judgement, to promote an efficient and motivated workforce. These provisions are clearly contrary to the general law and where there is conflict between any of the production-sharing agreements and the general law, the former prevails. In a recently reported case involving a major western oil company, the courts did not apply the provisions of a production-sharing agreement. It is unclear what the courts' basis was for such action.

Dispute Resolution

Ledingham Chalmers

Introduction

The domestic court system and enforcement procedures are of paramount importance to many international investors. This chapter looks at the Azerbaijani courts, the role of international arbitration and enforcement procedures.

The Azerbaijani court system

The experience of the Azerbaijani courts in litigation involving foreign investors is limited. Uncertainties within the present court system are widely recognised within Azerbaijan by both foreign and Azerbaijani parties, and contracts involving foreign parties tend to provide for an arbitration procedure in a third country.

In commercial matters between legal entities, the courts of first instance are the district economic courts, the economic courts of the Azerbaijan Republic and the Supreme Court of Nakhchivan Autonomous Republic (although this court also performs the function of a court of appeal in Nakhchivan). Civil matters involving individuals must be heard by the district courts of general jurisdiction. The Court of Appeal and the Economic Court of the Azerbaijan Republic are the civil courts of appeal, and the Supreme Court of the Azerbaijan Republic acts as the Court of Cessation, being the highest court in the country.

At present, no special courts of appeal or courts of cessation exist. These will only be created once the new procedural codes (both criminal and civil), currently at the stage of elaboration, are enacted. This requirement is provided for by Section 4 of the Presidential Decree of 10 June 1997, enacting the Law On Courts and Judges. Currently, the court system that exists in practice differs significantly from the one stipulated by this Law. In practice, in Azerbaijan, unlike in many other countries, the courts are divided into economic courts, military courts and courts of general jurisdiction, empowered to decide upon all kinds of cases. A new Law (which at the time of writing had been adopted but not implemented) envisages a further division of the courts according to the nature of the cases to be reviewed. This new Law states that with respect to the economic courts, there is a division between the Economic Court for Disputes arising out of international agreements and the Economic Court of General Jurisdiction. However, such a division does not exist in practice. Currently, all cases are being considered by the Economic Court of General Jurisdiction.

Under Azerbaijani law, civil proceedings should not exceed 37 days (7 days for the preparation of the case and 30 days for its resolution). Under the new Civil Procedures Code the term of consideration of a claim is three months after it has been lodged with the court. However, in practical terms, the average duration of civil proceedings is around six months in the first instance. International disputes have rarely been considered by the Azerbaijani courts but it is unlikely that litigation would be a quick and efficient method of solving disputes.

To date, Azerbaijan has not enacted any specific legislation devoted exclusively to the issues of international commercial litigation. References may be found, however, in other laws that affect this matter indirectly. For example, Article 3 of the Code of Economic Procedure provides that any waiver of a party's right to apply to the arbitration courts is invalid. The Code does not stipulate whether this provision prohibits a waiver of the right to apply to the Azerbaijani arbitration courts or whether it prohibits a waiver of the right in general (ie either Azerbaijani or foreign arbitration courts).

Nowadays, arbitration courts in Azerbaijan have been transferred to economic courts, which are specialised courts, and no longer depend on arbitration tribunals. In fact, there is no institutional arbitration in Azerbaijan nor is there a mechanism providing for the establishment of an ad hoc arbitration procedure. Further, the decision of the Board of the High Economic Court adopted on 27 December 1994 states that any party to a contract where an arbitration forum that is other than the Economic Court has been chosen is free to object to the transfer of proceedings to such a forum. There appear to be no mandatory provisions in Azerbaijani legislation directing the enforcement of such arbitration proceedings.

From a practical point of view, and taking into consideration other indirect provisions contained within the legislation, there is some support to indicate that the choosing of a foreign forum and of foreign law is recognised as valid for arbitration proceedings. This process is certainly widespread in international contracts signed in Azerbaijan. For example, the Azerbaijan Civil Code generally recognises the choice of law concept in respect of cross-border agreements. Article 571 of the Civil Code stipulates that the rights and obligations of the parties to a foreign trade transaction will be regulated by the law of the country where the transaction is concluded, unless otherwise agreed between the parties. The phrase 'foreign trade transaction' includes any agreement on export/import of products, insurance, distribution and delivery of goods and services from abroad where one of the parties is a foreign legal entity located abroad. There are, however, a number of areas where Azerbaijani law is exclusively applicable, including proprietary rights related to property located within the territory of Azerbaijan.

International judgments, awards and enforcement

Conventions

The Republic of Azerbaijan is a party to bilateral agreements on legal assistance with the Russian Federation, Ukraine, Georgia, Kazakhstan, Turkmenistan, Uzbekistan, Kyrgyzstan, Turkey, Bulgaria and Iran. Azerbaijan is a signatory to the Minsk Convention on Legal Assistance along with the other members of the Commonwealth of Independent States (CIS) and to the European Convention on International Commercial Arbitration of 1961. Azerbaijan is a party to the 1958 New York Convention. Azerbaijan is also a party to the 1996 Interim Agreement on Trade and Trade-related Matters between itself and the European Community, the European Coal and Steel Community and the European Atomic Energy Committee. This last agreement states that each of the parties shall encourage the use of arbitration for the settlement of disputes arising out of commercial and cooperation transactions concluded by economic operators of the European Union (EU) and Azerbaijan. Arbitration procedures are to be governed by the use of the UN Commission on International Trade Law (UNCITRAL) rules of arbitration and the selected arbitration centre should be a state signatory to the 1958 New York Convention on the Recognition and Enforcement of Foreign Arbitral Awards.

In January 1999 Azerbaijan became a party (with certain reservations) to the Moscow Agreement on the Mutual Recognition of Decisions of Arbitration and Economic Courts of Members of the Commonwealth of Independent States of 6 March 1998.

International arbitration

Generally, the practice of the appointment of independent arbitrators to settle disputes between parties in Azerbaijan is not widely recognised on the domestic front.

The first large international contracts that were entered into following Azerbaijan's independence from the Soviet Union consisted principally of production-sharing agreements relating to the exploration and development of the vast oil fields in the Caspian Sea. These contracts were entered into by consortia of western oil firms and the State Oil Company of Azerbaijan (SOCAR) and were ratified by the Azeri Parliament. These contracts brought into focus the need for arbitration clauses in international contracts.

Further foreign investments have been made in the country and it is now established practice to provide for arbitration in international contracts in a third country. The UNCITRAL rules and the rules of the International Chamber of Commerce are the most frequently used framework for providing the rules of arbitration.

As far as forums are concerned, Stockholm has historically been viewed as a popular location for arbitration proceedings involving the countries of the CIS although London, Geneva, New York and Paris also feature prominently in current contracts.

Practicalities of enforcement

As already mentioned, the practice of independent arbitration is not widely recognised in Azerbaijan. In addition, there is no precedent to indicate whether a foreign arbitral award would be enforced by the Azerbaijani courts. Azerbaijani law states that arbitration decisions rendered abroad are enforceable in the Azerbaijan Republic in accordance with the relevant international treaties. In other words, it seems that the Azerbaijani courts would enforce arbitration decisions from countries with which Azerbaijan has entered into mutual treaties and would not recognise a decision where no treaty has been entered into. As overriding law, any foreign arbitration decision would only be enforceable in Azerbaijan provided that such a decision were final and enforceable in the courts where the decision was made and did not contradict the public policy of the Azerbaijan Republic.

New Civil Code

Azerbaijan has adopted a new Civil Code that will come into effect on 1 September 2000. This Code will substantially alter the civil framework of the Azerbaijani legal system as it continues its development from a socialist controlled economy to a free market economy. As this chapter does not take account of the new Civil Code, specific advice should be sought on its potential impact on any of the matters referred to herein.

Part 5

Case Studies

5.1

AMEC

Pauline Guest and Chris Bond, AMEC

Why Azerbaijan?

Experience and success in North Sea operations have led to oil and gas service companies looking further afield. The Caspian Sea currently contains reserves between one to two times those of the North Sea, thus making the area commercially interesting to major oil companies such as BP Amoco and Exxon Mobil. The industrial city of Baku, with its population of almost 3 million inhabitants, is a natural regional hub that used to be the most international city in the former Soviet Union. It has been the recognised focus for Caspian oil production since the last century, and is core to present-day exploration and production (E&P) activities in the region.

The success of events such as the Caspian Oil and Gas Exhibitions – there have now been seven in total – is testimony to the high level of interest in the region from various industrial sectors interested in overseas investment, including hydrocarbons, banking and telecommunications.

In the UK, AMEC is a major player in the oil and gas services market and, like many proactive companies in the industry, we are constantly looking for opportunities to expand our activities beyond our traditional North Sea market.

Following the collapse of the Soviet Union, AMEC, along with a number of operators and other service companies, decided to examine how North Sea experience could be utilised in revitalising the Caspian as a leading oil and gas province.

Our North Sea experience is the foundation of our success in Azerbaijan. Established technical expertise and proven methods of working in an environment where cost drivers are constantly being reviewed and new practices introduced has proved invaluable.

Nature of opportunities

The type of work available in Azerbaijan's oil and gas industry – support services, engineering projects and major developments – fits well with

AMEC's expertise and our long-term strategy of internationalising the business.

Our strategy for Azerbaijan is to provide our full range of services to the oil and gas market by progressively building a local operation. This is crucial and derives from our success in Aberdeen where we opted for organic growth rather than 'parachuting-in' to fulfil the requirements of specific projects.

However, businesses in the Caspian must look to the future with realism, rather than blind optimism or pessimistic gloom. This is AMEC's approach, as Alan Hall – late Divisional Director with AMEC – recently pointed out:

> The Caspian was full of expectation a few years ago, but things have slowed down, and we have to accept this. Companies like AMEC must appreciate that the development is a gradual process, overnight successes rarely happen – and there's no such thing as an instant return.
>
> Hence, companies must approach the Azerbaijani market with their eyes open and understand that success takes time, planning, commitment and a lot of effort.

Getting established

The most important thing is to establish your organisation in Baku and then open for business. If your company is not registered in Azerbaijan, you cannot have a bank account and cannot employ people.

Registering for business

New entrants to the market in Baku have to go through a lengthy process in order to get started. Patience is required as the process is highly bureaucratic and involves the Minister of Justice issuing registration papers and the business producing a whole list of documents – it can take a couple of months for registration to be finalised.

It will be to your advantage to engage professional help in terms of a legal adviser or accountant in Baku, preferably, a Scots or English law company that is also registered in Baku.

Leasing an office

After registering the company, the next issue is finding suitable premises and setting up your office. Having a working office in Baku is essential, rather than trying to handle work from a UK base in Aberdeen or London.

Leasing itself is not difficult in Azerbaijan but does require the assistance of a professional. Ironically, it is actually easier to arrange than in the UK, as leases can be of a short-term nature (from as little as six, or 12 months). A large range of offices is available at favourable prices, considerably cheaper than at home, and lease documents are prepared in English and Russian.

After opening our office in November 1996, the next step was to develop initial contacts in Baku and get a foot in the door of our potential clients.

As our activities began to progress, a larger office was procured in 1997, allowing us to begin trading in earnest and to recruit more people. We have since relocated to an even larger engineering office to accommodate new team members migrating from Aberdeen to work on the Chirag 1 Water Injection Project. The new office is situated close to our key clients, in the heart of the old city.

In less than three years, our Azerbaijan business has progressed from just a single AMEC manager travelling to Baku with little more than the contents of a suitcase to become a thriving operation employing around 40 personnel – 35 of whom are Azerbaijani nationals.

Being prepared

The basic premise for securing work in Azerbaijan – apart from being the best company for the job in question – is to be registered and based in the country. Trying to secure work when you are based in the UK is almost impossible. At AMEC we have found that since opening our office, we have been successful in obtaining a steady stream of work.

The British and US Embassies lent much-needed moral and physical support and our employees made many normally impossible things happen. Key factors that emerged were that a wide network of relationships is essential and Azerbaijani employees are an absolute necessity.

Success does not come easily in Azerbaijan and competition is fierce, so it is essential to market your company actively and really sell what you have to offer.

Setting up communications

To succeed in Azerbaijan you must invest in IT and in telecommunications, as these are your links to the rest of the world, including to expertise in the UK and elsewhere. There are various methods for setting up communications and several British telecommunication companies as well as a number of local firms operate in Baku.

Although Azerbaijani telecommunications systems are now more modern and reliable than in the past – when phone connections had a habit of cutting out at various intervals – they remain very expensive. When setting up communications, it is also necessary to bear in mind that a considerable lead time is required for installation – it can take months rather than weeks, so be prepared.

It is worth noting that calls from Azerbaijan to the UK cost four times as much as they do in the opposite direction, and are approximately US$5 per minute from Azerbaijan. However, local calls are usually free.

Pitfalls

There are certain pitfalls which businesses ought to be aware of, when considering entry into the Caspian market.

- **Lack of planning**: It is vital to ensure that all the important market research has been carried out, that the company has been registered, an office located, and contingency plans made in the eventuality of there being no immediate work. Before jumping on the plane to Baku serious planning is required, and a clear business strategy is a must.

  Chris Dovell, the current AMEC President for Baku Operations, recognised this when he stated: 'The lack of outstanding problems is a tribute to the work done by my predecessor in establishing the company and to the support of the local staff.'

  Everything was well planned in advance.

- **Winning work can take time**: Companies need to appreciate the importance of gaining a foot in the door first, rather than hoping to jump into a large contract within minutes of arriving. It must be remembered that operations here are very different to those at home: success in the UK market does not necessarily guarantee success in the Caspian. Local conditions *must* be assessed on their own merits.

- **Taxation**: It is imperative that companies are adequately briefed on the pitfalls of taxation, as both company tax and income tax are very complicated in Azerbaijan. The reason for this is that Azerbaijan is neither Soviet nor western, but is still building up new legislation. Much guidance is required, particularly with respect to import duties. In fact, professional help is essential to ensure that no mistakes are made, as mistakes can literally be costly – those who default may be subject to heavy penalties or fines. It should be noted by companies that a new law has recently come into being, whereby licences must be purchased for each employee – rather like a work permit. These licences cost approximately US$200 each.

- **Lack of local knowledge**: It is essential to recruit, as quickly as possible, a local office manager. He must be a very competent, multi-lingual, streetwise person, well connected in Baku, who knows where all local authority offices are, who can get things done, and even offer advice on local customs and culture. A man on the ground to set up and run the business with you, and who knows how things tick is not a luxury, but a necessity. Ask any company in Baku.

Life for expatriate managers and skilled workers

Baku will be an enlightening cultural experience for new arrivals as it is, after all, a relatively poor country emerging from 70 years within the Soviet Union. However, it is important not to be confused by lack of recent investment. Azerbaijan's history and culture are long and rich, including being the oil production centre of the world long before the UK had dreamt of hydrocarbons beneath the sea.

It is advisable to fill in a British citizen's registration card on arrival – these are available from the British Embassy. Once you have arrived in Baku, the first thing you will notice is its lack of western sophistication. Andy Bannerman, Chirag Construction Manager, has commented: 'I have personally visited Baku on several occasions and the first thing that hits you is the general condition of the infrastructure and the buildings. These obviously suffer due to a lack of investment. Another shock is seeing so many derricks and nodding donkeys around.' It cannot be denied that certain areas require refurbishment, such as pavements and streetlights, but building work in the form of new modern office blocks is taking place, and whatever the place does lack in western sophistication, it more than makes up for in friendliness. Andy went on to add, 'Local people are generally friendly and during my stays I was put up in the Crescent Beach Hotel where accommodation, food and facilities are on a par with, or exceed, UK standards.'

Alan Hall and others also commented on the friendliness of the people, whom, he stated, are 'a cultured and intelligent people'. Alan believed that Baku, like Abu Dhabi, has the potential to become a holiday destination, with its hot climate, and splendid beaches – once oil revenues come flowing in to fund faster refurbishment. After all, much of Azerbaijan is beautiful and green, and there are more and more organised tourist trips arranged to explore the countryside.

Expatriates must get used to a very different culture – Azerbaijan is, after all, a Muslim country. Expatriates must be respectful of religious customs or may risk hostility from Azerbaijanis.

Accommodation

Things have improved on the accommodation front over the past couple of years. There is a range of hotels from expensive western-type complexes (which are often full) to local, cheap hotels which are not to be recommended for western tastes as they lack facilities and often house extra non-paying unwelcome guests in the form of cockroaches. Aim for a western-standard hotel, regardless of the cost.

For long-term residents in Baku, an apartment is a sensible option. Apartments can vary in size, are fairly plentiful and western facilities are now more or less standard. Admittedly, the furnishings are simple and functional and the faded elegant entrances to buildings may have seen better days, but do not let this put you off. Many apartments are fairly central and available on short-term leases. Tenants should be aware that power and water cuts in apartments are not unknown. (NB Expatriate companies are required to pay a 66 per cent tax on apartments.)

On a large project, skilled workers would normally be set up by the client in a camp. Such camps are generally of a good standard as they are provided and paid for by the oil companies.

Food

In the city, restaurants which cater for many palates are widely available, from Chinese to Indian, Italian, Mexican, and of course local cuisine. Prices for international restaurants tend to be similar to those in the UK, and this also applies to pubs and bars where the British will find prices similar to home. If feeling homesick, there are a couple of pubs (including a good Irish pub) with British landlords and English-speaking staff to put you at ease.

If you wish to do your own catering, there are a number of super-markets that sell most western products. For those who wish to sample shopping the Azerbaijani way, there are markets every day throughout the city that supply fresh fruit and vegetables at cheaper prices than those charged in the supermarkets.

Transport

The city of Baku is fairly spread out, so transport other than a strong pair of legs is required to get around. Taxis are readily available – you can hail them from the roadside – and quite cheap, but the cars have often seen better days and drivers tend not to speak much English. The best option is to acquire your own vehicle with a local chauffeur who knows the geography of the city. Driving is challenging, as the standard is 'robust', with motorists travelling fast according to traffic rules not readily apparent to the uninitiated.

Health

Falling ill is seldom desirable and even less so when far away from home. However, there are several clinics (such as AEA for expatriates) run by western companies and staffed by western staff. It is advisable to register with one of these clinics as soon as you arrive in the country. It is also essential to have an arrangement set up with one of the international emergency response companies such as SFA. These companies offer a 24-hour emergency response service, with a contact number in the UK. They act as intermediaries if anyone is injured, and can arrange air ambulances if required. (NB You must have good medical insurance and a procedure in place for accidents and emergencies.)

Drinking tap water is not recommended, but bottled water is readily available at most local shops.

Climate

For expatriates or visitors anxious about temperatures, Baku's climate is one of heat and humidity in the summer – air conditioning is desirable – with cool, wet and windy winters.

Leisure and recreation

Life for any worker must include some leisure and relaxation. Baku could make a great holiday resort but leisure facilities are a bit sparse. At the moment, leisure facilities include:

- tennis courts;
- sandy beaches (which are beautiful, but you do pay US$5 for those located north of the city);
- swimming pools in hotels (local pools are not recommended);
- health clubs at the expensive hotels;
- tenpin bowling;
- football pitches;
- cricket pitches.

The leisure market, as we know it, is not yet established. However, with more and more businesses opening in Baku, the situation is constantly improving.

Personal safety

Crime is not a great problem in Baku, perhaps due to the zeal of the local police but obviously, like anywhere else, it is better to be safe than sorry. Doing the following will go some way to prevent you becoming a victim of crime:

- do not leave valuables on display in your apartment or hotel room;

- lock anything of value away securely;

- dress down rather than going for glamour – it is a poor country so do not flaunt ostentation;

- stay in groups, especially at night, around bars in certain parts of town, to avoid falling victim to opportunistic muggers. Street lighting is not great and pavements, like roads, are often in need of repair;

- use taxis at night;

- never carry wads of cash around on your person;

- always carry a photocopy of your passport and a list of emergency numbers.

Language

The linguistic challenge for newcomers is coping with the national language of Azeri, or with Russian, which is used for business and technical purposes. It is worth making the effort to scale the language barrier by learning Russian rather than adopting the British stance of assuming that everyone understands English if it is spoken slowly and loudly. The Cyrillic alphabet may not be the easiest to master but it is worth it in the end, even if learning Russian only allows you to converse with taxi drivers.

As most business is conducted in English, language is not normally a problem. When recruiting local personnel, you should aim to employ people who speak two or three languages (which many Azerbaijanis do), or else provide training to facilitate this. There are plenty of administrative personnel around who speak good English, and interpreters are needed to assist with any tricky business meetings. It is worth noting that government officials prefer to conduct business in Azeri rather than Russian.

Working

Staff development for future growth.

At AMEC we are committed to staff development and skills enhancement – our slogan 'winning with people' applies to all employees, regardless of race, gender, position or location. To assist with cultural and skills differences, we have had a team of six Azerbaijanis – engineers, designers, document controllers, and a translator – from our Baku office travelling to Aberdeen for their third visit. The aim is to benchmark their current skills and knowledge levels against UK standards and enhance their engineering knowledge, so that AMEC can attain the long-term objective of having a highly skilled, cost-effective and fully integrated workforce in Baku. We were fortunate in having recruited over 30 local personnel for our first big contract – the BP Shelf 5 Istiglal Project – who have remained with us on our current job. And it is not all work: in addition to learning about AMEC operations and our design standards and procedures, the visiting Azerbaijanis gain exposure to our sophisticated culture of football, pubs and fish suppers, among other things! Fuad Ragimov, the translator for the group, commented that Azerbaijanis and Scots get on really well together, and communication has been excellent. 'We really didn't expect to visit here, but Ray [Fox] had promised to arrange a familiarisation visit and a chance for us to see AMEC's activity in Aberdeen, particularly as regards safety and engineering. It has been a very useful exercise.'

On the whole, it is advisable to maximise local involvement by directly employing local personnel for two reasons: reduced labour costs and to 'give something back' to the area and the people.

On the first point, manpower costs are greatly reduced. As a rule of thumb, for every expatriate employed, it would be possible to employ seven/eight local engineers. With tradesmen, it is worth employing Azerbaijanis for high turnover work, due to costs. Companies who invest in local hire will have a competitive advantage over those who use only expatriate labour.

Secondly, using local personnel is actively encouraged by the government and endorsed by major companies, and steps are in place to eradicate exploitation (Azerbaijani oil workers have no wage agreements in place). Utilisation and training of local labour is essential if you want to be in the market for the long term.

When it comes to assessing local versus expatriate activity, the ideal scenario for all parties is for the company to have access to its home knowledge base, but to use local personnel to execute the work in hand, at fair rates of pay.

Contracts in place and beginning to deliver

AMEC is presently involved in the project management, detail design, procurement, onshore fabrication, offshore installation and commissioning of a water injection system for the Chirag 1 platform, which is located 120km east-south-east of Baku, in the Caspian Sea. The platform is operated by BP Amoco on behalf of the Azerbaijan International Operating Company (AIOC), and the water injection system has been designed to maintain reservoir pressure and hence continue production at 100,000 barrels per day. This requires the installation of new equipment around the platform, including a 250-ton package which houses the turbine-driven water injection pumps. Kicking off with the design in the middle of December 1998, construction started in October 1999, and the system was running on the platform by the end of May 2000.

The challenge for AMEC was how to balance reduced costs with matching the client specification for a package that will withstand the challenging demands of working in the Caspian; fortunately a good working relationship with the client allowed this.

Project Manager Ron Malone sums it up thus: 'The client–supplier relationship has been more of a partnership at times, because we are all working towards the common goal of producing the best product at the keenest possible price.'

Workplan: Aberdeen to Baku

The project kicked off in Aberdeen where systems design and procurement is carried out, but work has recently transferred to the office in Baku. As already mentioned, there has been a regular transfer of personnel between Baku and Aberdeen, with the Azerbaijani engineers working in our Aberdeen office to assist in engineering works and to familiarise themselves with UK methods, and Aberdeen personnel also making regular visits to Baku to ensure feasibility and operability.

At present, detail design is well on its way and fabrication in Baku is due to start shortly. The module and packages will be assembled in Azerbaijan although many of the constituent parts have been procured internationally.

Setting up excellent health, safety and environmental performance

Here in Baku, we aim to adopt the same health and safety standards as in the UK, by implementing established AMEC HSE (Health and Safety

Executive) policies that apply to AMEC personnel anywhere in the world. When bidding for work in the Caspian, it is very important to demonstrate total commitment to safety, as a change in location cannot mean a slipping of standards.

On the current project, risk and hazard assessments are undertaken during work scope development and prior to commencement of any work. Key safety documents in English must be translated into Russian and translators are always on-site to provide clear and precise safety instructions to the workforce and supervisors. We have a dedicated HSE adviser to provide advice and support at all times.

Working with local goods and services suppliers

As regards supply of goods, we tend to buy specialist goods (eg computer hardware, vendor packages, etc) elsewhere, as such items – if available in Azerbaijan – are not always certified to western standards. However, we do try where possible to use local companies for office consumables. Most local companies are competitive with UK prices, goods are readily available and are of the required standard. Companies in Baku are well used to bidding for work and carry this out in English.

Commercial terms are very different to those in the UK. Azerbaijan, which is in the process of developing its banking system, is very much a cash society, with cash on delivery being the norm rather than the 30-day invoice period we are accustomed to. It is not common practice to pay in advance. It is important to note that the manat is the currency required by the government for official business with local companies; however, business with western companies and western-managed hotels is normally conducted in US dollars. Taxi drivers accept either currency.

Delivery of local goods in Baku does not generally constitute a problem. Things tend to go wrong when it comes to delivery of imported goods, although the intentions are always good. Sometimes delays arise with customs imports, or else transportation can be difficult. Air transport is readily available but expensive, so many businesses use roads which can take anything from one to four weeks to deliver, even from Europe. Shipping goods is only really feasible during the warm weather months. The Volga Don canal stretches from St Petersburg in the Baltic to Astrakhan on the Caspian and is the main transport route for shipment of goods. Unfortunately, it is usually iced up from November to April, which means scheduled deliveries by sea have little room for delay. This can be crucial when transporting packages from Europe, and where delays can have serious cost implications on a project.

When it comes to hiring local personnel for various services, there is a large pool of local tradesmen for office services, painters, plumbers, etc. Most are very good but, as in the UK, it is worth checking skills level before use, as all work must be carried out without compromising on safety, quality or productivity. As stated above, it is both cost-effective and a way of meeting ethical obligations to provide employment to the area for as many members of the population as possible, working with companies committed to Azerbaijan and its people.

Summary

So, what have we at AMEC learned about operating in Baku that might be of use to companies who want to do business in Azerbaijan? In simplistic terms of dos and don'ts, we feel the following are important pointers:

- **DO make use of all available information and help**: There are plenty of organisations to offer you sound impartial advice on working in Azerbaijan, such as the DTI, the British Embassy, Scottish Enterprise, or the Anglo-Azeri Society to name but a few. Also *do* select all organisations' strengths. Take advantage of the 'UK plc' mentality and work with rather than for or against customers and competition.

- **DO recognise and respect the Azerbaijani culture, history and national pride**: Remember you are a guest in this country, and here to provide mutual benefit, as well as a growing profit for your business. Maximise local employment; get involved in the local community; provide training and skills enhancement for Azerbaijanis, and then rest assured that you are giving them something back. If you wish to survive, you need to think long term, and build a genuinely locally run operation, rather than foisting a western culture or colonial approach, which will inevitably be a short-term one.

- **DO provide a proactive UK back-up team**: This is essential, particularly in the early stages, for technical, admin *and* moral support.

- **DON'T assume that standards can drop because you're out of the UK**: For example, health, safety and environmental performance are rigorously adhered to – Baku is not a soft option.

- **DON'T forget: like our country, Azerbaijan is unique – a blend of former Soviet culture with many older, still partially prevailing cultures**: Listen, be flexible, learn and adapt to your surroundings.

Baku is a thriving regional hub, with friendly inhabitants, a great place to work and improving all the time. See you out there.

Acknowledgements

The authors wish to thank the following without whose contributions this chapter could not have been written: Alan Hall, Divisional Director; Ron Malone, Project Manager – Chirag 1 Water Injection Project; John Pearson, Engineering Manager – Chirag 1 Water Injection Project; Andy Bannerman, Construction Manager – Chirag 1 Water Injection Project; Ian Moir, Commercial Manager; Fuad Ragimov, Translator.

This chapter is dedicated to the memories of Ray Fox, AMEC President for Baku Operations, who opened our first office in Baku, and Alan Hall a Divisional Director.

Sadly, Ray died unexpectedly while in Azerbaijan before this book could be published. A charismatic figure, Ray is acknowledged for securing work and establishing AMEC as a leader in the Caspian oil and gas industry.

Alan Hall, another charismatic figure, who died suddenly in April 2000, played a major role from London, in promoting AMEC'S investment in Baku. He forged many very good friendships with leading figures in Baku's oil industry.

Morrison International Ltd

Morrison International Ltd

History

Morrison International Ltd's involvement in Azerbaijan dates back to 1991. At that time, our contacts with oil and service companies operating in the North Sea suggested that the time was right to establish a presence in Baku, so that we would be ready to provide a construction service to the oil and service companies that would soon be moving there. Initial visits served to reinforce this view and a local office with full-time expatriate management was set up in 1992.

Learning the system

Becoming familiar with the system proved very difficult as in the early days there just wasn't a 'system' to learn. Much of the legislation related to company formation, registration had not yet been established and the tax system was 'evolving' on a day-to-day basis.

Recruiting and training

It was clear from the early days that the recruitment and training of a local workforce would be a key issue if we were to succeed in Azerbaijan – and indeed, this has been one of the major factors in our success. It soon became apparent that the workforce was technically competent but lacked both the motivation to work efficiently and the knowledge of the quality and safety standards that are standard in the West.

We therefore embarked on an intensive training programme (constantly being reviewed and updated) that has enabled the company to gradually reduce its expatriate supervision staff to a minimum. This has improved efficiency and given us the ability to provide our clients with high standards of work and quality of service at competitive prices.

Integrating expatriate and Azerbaijani nationals

From the early days it has been our policy to have a totally integrated team – both in the office and out on site. This helps to avoid any feeling of 'us and them' and ensures that everyone is working together towards a common goal. Language is an obvious potential barrier here, and our UK staff have laboured long and hard (with mixed success) to learn some basic Russian – although Azerbaijani has now become the 'official' language and its use is therefore becoming more widespread. Fortunately, the local population is generally well educated and finding English-speakers for most clerical or managerial positions is not difficult.

To joint venture or not?

In most countries in which we operate, we have found a joint venture with a local company to be the most satisfactory way of operating. Azerbaijan has been somewhat different in that in the early days most of the 'companies' operating were either still state-owned or had recently been 'privatised', which meant that they were still structured in the same way as a state-owned organisation, but without the guaranteed support that had previously been given. The fact that our clients were mainly from the western oil companies meant that the 'political' benefits of being in joint venture with a local partner were not as important as they have subsequently become. If starting up now, some form of business relationship with a local company would be a much more important factor for success.

Becoming a local company

As the market in Azerbaijan has changed, it has become increasingly important to be seen as a local company, with local management, offering a quality service to all sectors – and not just as an oil industry 'specialist'. We have therefore now established Morrison Caspian Ltd, a locally regis-tered company undertaking a wide variety of industrial, commercial, retail and residential construction projects in a number of locations across Azerbaijan.

Providing a flexible service

The need for flexibility in our approach to securing workload over the years has been key to developing our business as the market has changed.

Being part of a large construction group with diverse interests has assisted in this, as it has been possible to import specialist expertise when necessary.

For example, when we first established a presence in Baku, our primary intention was to undertake civil construction work to support the oil companies as they developed their infrastructure and facilities. However, it soon became clear that their strategy was to undertake the minimum necessary infrastructure upgrading work, certainly until oil reserves were proven and income streams established. What they did need, though, was western-standard office space and accommodation for their personnel.

We therefore had to change our approach and personnel to those more experienced in building refurbishment and property management in order to meet this demand.

Our strong local connections also became useful as the need arose to find suitable building land to meet clients' needs, whenever existing buildings were not suitable. It has also been of benefit to have a property development arm within the Morrison Group, as the need for structured finance packages to assist clients defray capital costs has become a desirable added value benefit that we have been able to offer.

Giving value for money

The concept of a 'value for money' service, particularly when related to a construction product, is not always an easy one to sell, particularly in a country where any form of choice has long been denied to the customer.

Even the westerner, who would probably never buy a suit or a car for him- or herself on the basis of the cheapest model available, suddenly makes price the overriding criterion when it comes to 'buying' an office, apartment or manufacturing facility.

Our local labour force and efficient management does enable us to compete for price with our competitors when compared on a like-for-like basis, and we are confident that our higher standards of workmanship and quality of materials will give our clients a value-for-money product and service.

However, there are now many competitors from a number of countries that have been offering cheap construction prices/alternatives and it has been very frustrating to find ourselves being compared with some organisations for whom quality of service and building is not up to Morrison's standards. At the end of the day it will be the building owners and the country itself that could suffer, through inheriting a poor quality infrastructure and long-term maintenance problems. However, making a decision of quality over price needs foresight and immediate affordability (not always present) and a strong regulatory system.

Looking to the future

In theory, at least, there will be opportunities for construction companies in Azerbaijan for many years to come. There is certainly the need to upgrade most sectors of the country's infrastructure and to meet the social and leisure needs of an increasingly demanding population. There should also be the financial resources available to foot the bill, as oil revenues flow through to boost government budgets and thence into the private sector. The question on everyone's lips, though, is 'when will this start to happen?'

Certainly, low oil prices over the recent past caused the oil companies to review their plans and schedules – with at least a short-term cut-back on expenditure. The government will therefore have to continue to rely on foreign assistance, through bilateral and aid agency programmes, in order to fund the most urgent requirements. In addition, the private sector will not have adequate cash available and will increasingly be looking for creative and structured finance packages in order to fund the construction of housing, retail and leisure facilities to meet the population's growing aspirations. The recent increases in oil prices will hopefully help the country's cash flow situation to a degree and should bode well for the construction sector as a whole.

But it will be those organisations that are able to respond to changing demands and which are proactive in their approach to providing for their clients' needs that will be the ones most likely to reap the future rewards for 'sticking it out' through any difficult period. As we have always known, Azerbaijan will reward those who have made a long-term commitment to the country, whereas those seeking a quick return are likely to be disappointed.

5.3

Lukoil

Lukoil

The foundation of all Lukoil's present success in Azerbaijan was laid seven years ago. After precise and careful planning, Lukoil's president, Vagit Alekperov, was able to approach the State Oil Company of the Azerbaijan Republic (SOCAR) with a proposal for a mutually beneficial programme of co-operation for the joint exploration of hydrocarbon deposits on the Caspian shelf. The framework for an agreement of co-operation was signed by Lukoil and SOCAR in September 1993. Active business contacts between Vagit Alekperov and Natik Aliev, as presidents, and Ravil Maganov and Ilham Aliev, as vice-presidents, of Lukoil and SOCAR respectively, have been indispensable to the creation and development of branch ventures for Lukoil in Azerbaijan.

The experience of the past few years has confirmed the wisdom of choosing a strategy of consolidation of economic links between Russia and Azerbaijan.

The official starting point of Lukoil's economic activity in Azerbaijan, in addition to that of other foreign oil companies, should be considered the 'Contract of the Century' (Azeri-Chirag-Guneshli), which was signed on 20 September 1994. This agreement included exploration, development and production sharing, where Lukoil's participating interest is 10 per cent.

In addition to this major contract, Lukoil's activities include taking part in two oil consortia. The first is with Italian Agip in the exploration of the Shah Deniz structure (LUKAgip having 10 per cent of the participating interest) and the second is with American ARCO in D-222 (Yalama) consortium (LUKARCO having 60 per cent of the share). It should be noted that the D-222 (Yalama) Agreement, which was signed in the presence of presidents Boris Yeltsin and Heydar Aliyev on 3 July 1997 in Moscow, became the first agreement where SOCAR retained a considerable share of the project (40 per cent). Furthermore, Lukoil is planning to invite a number of Azerbaijani and Russian oil and gas enterprises to bid for contractual works.

But the sphere of interest of a vertically integrated company such as Lukoil is not restricted to co-operation in the oil and gas sector. The

LUKOIL-BAKU Trade House, in partnership with SOCAR and the Singapore-based FELS, participates in the modernisation of vessels, and in the construction and provision of services for drilling rigs. Lukoil has created a network of fuel stations corresponding to international standards and ecological norms. In future, our fuel stations network will be considerably enlarged. In order to ensure the regular supply of fuel stations with high quality oil products, Lukoil intends to build its own bulk plant.

It can be stated with confidence that Lukoil's day-to-day activity is a real economic bridge between Russia and Azerbaijan. During its seven years of activity, Lukoil has done much to consolidate not only political but also economic links between Russia and Azerbaijan. It can be said that some six years ago few foreign companies were ready to invest in Azerbaijan, but the situation is now very different. At present, co-operation with Azerbaijan is the target of interest of many leading world companies and Lukoil, as one of the first on the ground, has a strong advantage in the field. It is necessary to underline that the exploration for oil and gas is only one of Lukoil's activities in Azerbaijan. Other areas of activity include a variety of cultural, scientific and trade interests.

Working in Azerbaijan, where the country counts over a million refugees and where many families live in certain poverty, it would be inconceivable for Lukoil not to help where it can. On the Lukoil president's initiative, the Lukoil Charity Fund was created in April 1996. Among the many foreign companies in Azerbaijan, Lukoil is the only one to have a dedicated charity fund. In its few years of activity, the Baku division of the charity fund has spent over US$1.4 million.

Lukoil also takes part in scientific and technical programmes, and was one of the organisers and participants of the international scientific-practice seminar on 'Industrial and ecological safety of oil and gas operations in the Caspian Sea', held in Baku in May 1998. It is hoped that conducting these seminars will make Baku a centre where large-scale ecological surveys can be carried out for all states of the Caspian area. This is a real objective as Azerbaijan has huge scientific and human resources potential.

Lukoil intends to continue in its close co-operation with Azerbaijan in the oil industry and in other areas of the economy. New investments are being planned in different areas of the Republic's economy that will help expand our scientific, cultural and trade links with Azerbaijan.

Appendices

Appendix 1

Visitors' Information

HSBC (Business Profile Series)

Geography

Located in the Near East along the west side of the Caspian Sea, Azerbaijan has a total land area of 86,600 km². The country is bordered by the Russian Federation to the north, Georgia to the northwest, Armenia to the west, Iran to the south and Turkey, which shares a short border with the Nakhchivan Autonomous Republic. The capital of Azerbaijan is Baku.

Mountains cover approximately half the country: the Greater Caucasus in the northeast, the Lesser Caucasus in the southwest and the Talysh Mountains in the extreme southeast. Mount Bazar-Dyuzi, in the Greater Caucasus on the border with the Russian Federation, is the highest point at 4,466 metres above sea level.

The country has more than 1,000 rivers and some 250 lakes; however, the majority of the rivers and lakes are small. The Kura is the largest river, flowing through Azerbaijan from Georgia in the northwest and emptying into the Caspian Sea in the southeast. The country's largest lake is Lake Hajikabul, which covers just 16km².

Administratively, the country is divided into 65 districts, the Autonomous Republic of Nakhchivan (which is separated from the main part of the country by southern Armenia), and the region of Nagorny Karabakh (which has been occupied by Armenian forces since 1992). Armenians of Nagorny Karabakh declared their independence in 1991 but have yet to have their claim recognised internationally.

Climate

Azerbaijan's climate varies significantly from arid subtropical to tundra conditions. Precipitation varies greatly with the coastal regions receiving an average of 200–300 millimetres annually, while the southern slopes of the Greater Caucasus receive 1,000–1,300 millimetres.

In the summer months of June, July and August, temperatures can reach over 30°C and in the winter months of January, February and December they can drop to 0°C, although they are more usually around 5°C.

Language

Azeri (Azerbaijani) is the official language and is spoken by 95 per cent of the population. Russian is also widely spoken and still taught in local schools. English is making rapid inroads and primary, secondary and higher educational establishments offer curricula in English.

Visas

With the exception of nationals of members of the Commonwealth of Independent States (CIS), all visitors to Azerbaijan are required to obtain visas and carry valid passports. Visas are available through Azerbaijani embassies or consulates. However, as visa requirements are subject to change, visitors are advised to check with consular authorities before making final travel arrangements.

Work permits

The Azerbaijani authorities have introduced legislation requiring foreigners to obtain work permits. As these conditions are subject to change, visitors are advised to obtain up-to-date information from consular authorities prior to arrival in the country.

Health regulations

No mandatory immunisations are required for visiting Azerbaijan. Travellers are advised to take precautions against malaria, particularly in the southern areas of the country.

Customs regulations

Visitors entering Azerbaijan must complete a customs declaration form, which must be retained until departure. Articles intended for personal use (including currency and valuables) must be registered on the form. The importation of weapons and ammunition, narcotics, pornography and loose pearls is not allowed. Prohibited exports include precious metals and works of art and antiques – unless permission has been obtained from the Ministry of Culture.

Exchange controls

The import and export of manats (AZM) by non-residents is prohibited. All foreign currency must be declared on arrival and the export of foreign currency is limited to the amount declared on arrival. Funds changed into manats or Russian roubles can be reconverted upon leaving the country with the payment of a substantial commission and by producing proof of the original exchange transaction. Consequently, visitors are advised to change relatively small amounts of money, as required.

Access

The Bina International Airport is approximately 15 kilometres from Baku. State-owned Azerbaijan Airlines flies to some 55 destinations, including Dubai, Frankfurt, Istanbul, Karachi, London, Moscow, St Petersburg and Tehran. Services are also provided by British Airways, Emirates, Iranair, KLM, Lufthansa, Pakistan International Airlines, Transaero (a private Russian airline), and Turkish Airlines.

Via passenger ferries on the Caspian Sea, Azerbaijan is linked with the Russian Federation, Central Asia and Iran. Azerbaijan is also connected by rail to Tehran, Tbilisi in Georgia and various cities – such as Moscow – in the Russian Federation.

Local transport

The country has some 2,100 kilometres of railways and a road network that stretches more than 35,000 kilometres including over 31,000 kilo-metres of paved roads. Travel within some regions of the country is restricted and visitors must obtain special permission from the Ministry of the Interior to visit those areas. Traffic drives on the right.

Taxi fares should be negotiated before starting a journey. Baku also has an underground railway system – the Baku Metro – that has been in oper-ation for some 30 years.

Currency

Subsequent to the country's declaration of independence in 1991, Azerbaijan introduced a new currency in 1992 – the manat – to replace the Russian rouble. One manat equals 100 gapiks. Notes are issued in denominations of 50, 100, 250, 500, 1,000, 10,000 and 50,000 manats.

The US dollar is also widely accepted in hotels and restaurants, but not in shops or supermarkets, where payment must be made in manats. Acceptance of credit cards and travellers cheques is limited, but increasing.

Local time

Azerbaijan is four hours ahead of GMT and follows the daylight saving practice of putting the clock forward an hour in Spring and turning it back in the Autumn.

Religion

Islam is the main religion. About 70 per cent of the country's Muslims are Shi'a, with the remaining 30 per cent Sunni. Freedom of religion is allowed. Other religious groups include Russian Orthodox, Armenian Orthodox, Christians and Jews.

Social customs

The normal form of greeting is a handshake, and business cards are typically exchanged at initial business meetings.

Media

The main daily newspaper is the Azeri-language *Khalg Gazeti*, which is state-owned. Other newspapers include *Azadlig*, *Azerbaijan*, *Yeni Musavat*, *Bakinski Rabochy*, and *Mukhalifat*. Magazines include *Azerbaijan International*. Radio Baku broadcasts in Azerbaijani, Arabic, English and Turkish. Azerbaijan national television broadcasts in Azerbaijani, Russian and English. Several privately owned television companies are operating in Azerbaijan and there is a cable television package provider also.

Business hours

Government Offices	Monday – Friday
	9.00am – 1.00 pm
	2.00am – 6.00 pm
Banks	Monday – Friday
	9.00am – 3.30pm
Shops	Monday – Sunday
	9.00am – 7.00pm

Hotels

Major hotels in Baku include the Abseron, Europa, Azerbaijan, Intourist, and Hyatt Regency. Reservations are advisable at most of these hotels and essential at the Hyatt.

Tipping

Tipping is appreciated but not compulsory. Taxi drivers, waiters and hotel staff usually accept tips.

Electricity

Voltage in Azerbaijan is usually 220 volts, 50 Hz.

Medical

For visitors, emergency treatment is free with the exception of small payments for medicines and hospital treatment. Travel insurance is recommended. Should a visitor need to extend their stay due to illness, the traveller will have to pay for all treatment. Foreigners working in Baku are advised to use one of the two western-operated clinics (OMS and Western Medical).

Clothing

In general, business attire for men is a suit, shirt and tie; women typically wear skirts or trousers and jackets. In the summer months, lightweight clothing is recommended as Azerbaijan is quite warm. However, warm clothing is essential for the winter months.

Food and drink

The most traditional Azerbaijani dishes are *plovs*, which are made of rice, with different fish, meat, vegetable, or fruit seasonings. Other local specialities include: sturgeon, *pity*, a mutton soup with chickpeas, *dovga*, a yoghurt and spinach-based soup with rice and meatballs, *gutab*, pastries stuffed with pumpkin or spinach, and *dolma*, and a variety of kebabs. Azerbaijan is one of the least expensive places in the world to buy caviar.

Black tea is a favourite of the mostly male patrons of the *chaikhanas* (tea houses). Alcohol is widely available, including locally produced wines and Russian vodka. More restaurants and nightclubs are also being opened in Baku to cater to the local and foreign business communities. Western-style food is available at major hotels and restaurants.

Tap water should be boiled before drinking. Bottled water is widely available.

Shopping

Azerbaijani carpets are a good buy and it is worth a trip to the carpet-weaving centre at Nardaran. Locally produced silk, ceramics and other crafts can be purchased at the Sharg Bazary (covered market) in Baku. Items made before 1960 are subject to export tax and must be certified by the Ministry of Culture before they can be taken out of the country. Artefacts purchased at official tourist shops are already certified.

Public holidays

New Year's Day	1 January
Mourning Day	20 January
Ramazan Bayram*	In February
International Women's Day	8 March
Novruz Bayram*	In March
Gurban Bayram*	In April
Victory Day	9 May
Azerbaijan Republic's Day	28 May
Salvation Day	15 June
Army's Day	9 October
Independence Day	18 October
Constitution Day	12 November
Revival Day	17 November
Day of Solidarity	31 December

* Dates vary according to the Islamic Calendar

Appendix 2

Sources of Further Information

United Kingdom contacts

Association of British Chambers of Commerce
4 Westwood House
Westwood Business Park
Coventry CV4 8HS
United Kingdom
Tel: + 44 24 7669 4484
Fax: + 44 24 7669 5844

Azerbaijan British Trade and Industry Council (ABTIC)
Bay 757, Kingsgate House
66–74 Victoria Street
London SW1E 6SW
United Kingdom
Tel: + 44 20 7215 4881
Fax: + 44 20 7215 4817

British Council
10 Spring Gardens
London SW1A 2BN
United Kingdom
Tel: + 44 20 7930 8466
Fax: + 44 20 7839 6347

British Invisibles
Windsor House
39 King Street
London EC2 8DQ
United Kingdom
Tel: + 44 20 7600 1198
Fax: + 44 20 7606 4248

Confederation of British Industry (CBI)

Centre Point
103 New Oxford Street
London WC1A 1DU
United Kingdom
Tel: + 44 20 7379 7400
Fax: + 44 20 7240 1578

Customs and Excise

Dorset House
Stamford Street
London SE1 9PY
United Kingdom
Tel: + 44 20 7202 4687
Fax: + 44 20 7202 4131

East European Trade Council

Suite 10
Westminster Palace Gardens
Artillery Row
London SW1P 1RL
United Kingdom
Tel: + 44 20 7222 7622
Fax: + 44 20 7222 5359

Embassy of the Azerbaijan Republic

4 Kensington Court
London W8 5DL
United Kingdom
Tel: + 44 20 7938 3412
Fax: + 44 20 7937 1783
E-mail: sefir@btinternet.com

European Bank for Reconstruction and Development (EBRD)

One Exchange Square
London EC2A 2EH
United Kingdom
Tel: + 44 20 7338 6000
Fax: + 44 20 7323 0195

European Investment Bank
London office
68 Pall Mall
London SW1Y 5ES
United Kingdom
Tel: + 44 20 7343 1200
Fax: + 44 20 7930 9929

Export Market Information Centre
Trade Partners UK
1st Floor, Kingsgate House
66–74 Victoria Street
London SW1E 6SW
United Kingdom
Tel: + 44 20 7215 5444/5
Fax: + 44 20 7215 4231

The International Finance Corporation
European Office
4 Millbank
London SW1P 3JA
United Kingdom
Tel: + 44 20 7222 7711
Fax: + 44 20 7976 8323

London Chamber of Commerce and Industry
69 Cannon Street
London EC4N 5AB
United Kingdom
Tel: + 44 20 7248 4444
Fax: + 44 20 7489 0391

Technical Help to Exporters
British Standards Institute
389 Chiswick High Road
London W4 4AL
United Kingdom
Tel: + 44 20 8996 9000
Fax: + 44 20 8996 7400

Trade Partners UK
Transcaucasia Desk
Bay 758, Kingsgate House
66–74 Victoria Street
London SW1E 6SW
United Kingdom
Tel: + 44 20 7215 4771
Fax: + 44 20 7215 4817

Azerbaijan contacts

Azerbaijani Railways
230 Dilara Aliyeva Street
Baku 370010
Azerbaijan
Tel: + 994 12 98 44 67
Fax: + 994 12 98 42 80

Azerigaz
23 Yusif Safarov Street
Baku 370025
Azerbaijan
Tel: + 994 12 67 74 47
Fax: + 994 12 67 42 55

Chamber of Commerce and Industry
31–33 Istigliyyat Street
Baku 370601
Azerbaijan
Tel: + 994 12 92 89 12
Fax: + 994 12 98 93 24
E-mail: expo@chamber.baku.az

The International Bank of Azerbaijan
Head Office
67 Nizami Street
Baku 370005
Azerbaijan
Tel: + 994 12 93 00 91/93 41 59
Fax: + 994 12 93 40 91
Website: www.Ibar.Az

National Bank of Azerbaijan (Central Bank)
19 Bul-Bul Avenue
Baku 370070
Azerbaijan
Tel: + 994 12 93 50 58
Fax: + 994 12 93 31 06

State Oil Company of Azerbaijan Republic (SOCAR)
73 Neftchilar Avenue
Baku 370004
Azerbaijan
Tel: + 994 12 92 07 45
Fax: + 994 12 93 64 92

Tacis
Government House, Room 851
Baku 370016
Azerbaijan
Tel: + 994 12 93 60 18/93 95 14
Fax: + 994 12 993 12 76
E-mail: info@eccu.baku.az

World Bank
91–95 Mirza Mansur Street
Icheri Sheher
Baku 370004
Azerbaijan
Tel: + 994 12 92 28 07
Fax: + 994 12 92 14 79

Government ministries

Agriculture and Food
Government House
Azadlyg Meidany
Baku 370016
Azerbaijan
Tel: + 994 12 93 08 84/93 80 03
Fax: + 994 12 94 53 90

Communications
33 Azerbaijan Avenue
Baku 370139
Azerbaijan
Tel: + 994 12 93 00 04/93 09 96
Fax: + 994 12 93 44 80

Culture
Government House
Azadlyg Meidany
Baku 370016
Azerbaijan
Tel: + 994 12 93 43 98/93 74 24
Fax: + 994 12 93 56 05

Defence
3 Azizbeyov Avenue
Baku 370073
Azerbaijan
Tel: + 994 12 39 46 07/38 61 31
Fax: + 994 12 39 41 89

Economics
Government House
Azadlyg Meidany
Baku 370016
Azerbaijan
Tel: + 994 12 93 69 20/93 64 90
Fax: + 994 12 93 20 25

Education
Government House
Azadlyg Meidany
Baku 370016
Azerbaijan
Tel: + 994 12 93 72 66/93 19 66
Fax: + 994 12 98 75 69/93 80 97

Finance
6 Samad Vurghun Street
Baku 370601
Azerbaijan
Tel: + 994 12 93 30 12/93 05 62
Fax: + 994 12 98 79 69

Foreign Affairs
4 Shykhali Gurbanov Street
Baku 370078
Azerbaijan
Tel: + 994 12 92 34 01/92 64 75
Fax: + 994 12 65 10 38

Information and Press
12 Gara Garayev Street
Baku 370001
Azerbaijan
Tel: + 994 12 92 67 47/92 65 23
Fax: + 994 12 92 93 33

Internal Affairs
7 Husi Hajiyev Street
Baku 370005
Azerbaijan
Tel: + 994 12 90 92 22/90 95 15
Fax: + 994 12 90 99 29

Justice
13 Bulbul Avenue
Baku 370601
Azerbaijan
Tel: + 994 12 93 97 85/98 80 04
Fax: + 994 12 93 83 67

National Security
2 Azizbeyov Avenue
Baku 370073
Azerbaijan
Tel: + 994 12 93 18 00/95 04 91
Fax: + 994 12 93 62 96/93 14 27

Public Health
4 Malaya Morskaya Street
Baku 370014
Azerbaijan
Tel: + 994 12 93 29 77/98 50 94
Fax: + 994 12 98 85 59/93 46 46

Social Welfare
Government House
Azadlyg Meidany
Baku 370016
Azerbaijan
Tel: + 994 12 93 19 79/93 75 78
Fax: + 994 12 93 94 72

Trade
68 Mehti Husseinzade Street
Baku 370066
Azerbaijan
Tel: + 994 12 92 16 42/98 92 67
Fax: + 994 12 98 00 11

Youth and Sports
98a Fatali Khan Khoisky Avenue
Baku 370110
Azerbaijan
Tel: + 994 12 90 64 42/90 64 43
Fax: + 994 12 64 36 50

State committees

Anti-Monopoly Politics and Business Support
85 Salatin Askerova Street
Baku 370002
Azerbaijan
Tel: + 994 12 95 79 72/94 80 82
Fax: + 994 12 94 69 51

Construction and Architecture
67 Fizuli Street
Baku 370014
Azerbaijan
Tel: + 994 12 93 78 38/98 93 07
Fax: + 994 12 98 32 04

Ecology and Environment Protection
31 Istiqlaliyyat Street
Baku 370001
Azerbaijan
Tel: + 994 12 92 41 73/92 61 19
Fax: + 994 12 92 59 07

Ethnic Relations
68 Lermontov street
Baku 370066
Azerbaijan
Tel: + 994 12 92 54 31/92 33 73
Fax: + 994 12 93 07 29

Geodesy and Cartography
70 Ataturk Avenue
Baku 370108
Azerbaijan
Tel: + 994 12 62 88 21/61 71 94
Fax: + 994 12 61 84 00

Geology and Mineral Resources
100a Bahram Aghayev
Baku 370073
Azerbaijan
Tel: + 994 12 38 54 54/38 04 81
Fax: + 994 12 39 84 32

Housing
Government House
Azadlyg Meidany
Baku 370016
Azerbaijan
Tel: + 994 12 93 34 67

Hydrometeorology
3 Rasul Rza Street
Baku 370000
Azerbaijan
Tel: + 994 12 98 22 96/98 14 91
Fax: + 994 12 93 69 37

Improvement of Soil and Water Economy
Government House
Azadlyg Meidany
Baku 370016
Azerbaijan
Tel: + 994 12 93 61 54/93 51 65
Fax: + 994 12 93 11 76

Insurance Inspectorate of the Cabinet of Ministers
112 Chingiz Mustafayev Street
Baku 370009
Azerbaijan
Tel: + 994 12 94 59 24
Fax: + 994 12 94 09 41

Land
93a Alaskar Alakbarov
Baku 370141
Azerbaijan
Tel: + 994 12 32 20 50/32 20 52

Monitoring Safety Procedures in Industry and Mining
26 Samad Vurghun street
Baku 370601
Azerbaijan
Tel: + 994 12 94 12 77/94 19 41

Production of Special Machinery and Conversion
40 Matbuat Avenue
Baku 370141
Azerbaijan
Tel: + 994 12 39 40 30/39 23 07

Property
20 Yusif Safarov Street
Baku 370002
Azerbaijan
Tel: + 994 12 98 14 33
Fax: + 994 12 93 19 49

Protection and Restoration of Historical and Cultural Monuments
39 Asaf Zeinally Street
Baku 370004
Azerbaijan
Tel: + 994 12 92 19 18/92 22 25

Refugee and Displaced Persons
20 Rashad Street
Baku 370072
Azerbaijan
Tel: + 994 12 67 15 43/67 34 54
Fax: + 994 12 62 66 06

Science and Technology
24 Samad Vurghun Street
Baku 370000
Azerbaijan
Tel: + 994 12 95 54 94/94 05 40
Fax: + 994 12 94 08 81

State Customs
2 Inshaatchylar Avenue
Baku 370073
Azerbaijan
Tel: + 994 12 92 75 45/38 80 80
Fax: + 994 12 98 18 36

Statistics
24 Inshaatchylar Avenue
Baku 370136
Azerbaijan
Tel: + 994 12 38 11 71/38 77 25
Fax: + 994 12 38 05 77

Taxation Inspectorate
23 Alfred Nobel Avenue
Baku 370025
Azerbaijan
Tel: + 994 12 66 00 62/66 00 37
Fax: + 994 12 98 33 71

Veterinary Medicine
7a Najaf Narimanov Street
Baku 370106
Azerbaijan
Tel: + 994 12 62 76 13/62 18 76
Fax: + 994 12 62 66 06

Appendix 3

Contributors' Contact Details

Azerbaijan Environment & Technology Centre (AETC)
8 Khanlar Street
Baku
Azerbaijan
Tel: + 994 12 91 43 98
Tel/Fax: + 994 12 93 52 58

AMEC
City Gate
Altens Farm Road
Nigg
Aberdeen AB12 3LB
United Kingdom
Tel: + 44 1224 291000
Fax: + 44 1224 291001
E-mail: Info@apel-a.amec.co.uk

Aon-Azeri Insurance & Reinsurance Brokers Company
80 H Zardabi Street
Baku 370122
Azerbaijan
Tel: + 994 12 92 44 00
Fax: + 994 12 97 71 10

Arthur Andersen
96 Nizami Street
The Landmark
Baku 370010
Azerbaijan
Tel: + 994 12 98 24 86
Fax: + 994 12 98 24 87
E-mail: info@aa.baku.az

Azerbaijan Entrepreneurs' (Employers) Confederation
31 Istiglaliyyat Street
Baku
Azerbaijan
Tel: + 994 12 92 07 05
Fax: + 994 12 92 54 71
E-mail: info@azerinvest.baku.az

Commercial Section, British Embassy
Hyatt Tower
1 Bakikhanov Street
Baku 370065
Azerbaijan
Tel: + 994 12 90 72 43/47
Fax: + 994 12 90 72 42
E-mail: office@ukemb.baku.az

European Bank for Reconstruction and Development (EBRD)
One Exchange Square
London EC2A 2EH
United Kingdom
Tel: + 44 20 7338 6000
Fax: + 44 20 7323 0195

Ernst & Young (CIS) Ltd
2nd Floor, Hyatt Tower
1 Bakihanov Street
Baku 370065
Azerbaijan
Tel: + 994 12 90 70 20
Fax: + 994 12 90 70 17
E-mail: info@eycis.com

GlaxoWellcome
Apartment 5
22 Mardanov Brothers Street
Baku
Azerbaijan
Tel/Fax: + 994 12 97 66 01/97 66 26
E-mail: azglaxo@azeurotel.com

Dr Edmund Herzig
Department of Middle Eastern Studies
Manchester University
Oxford Road
Manchester M13 9PL
United Kingdom
Tel: + 44 161 275 3070
Fax: + 44 161 275 3264
E-mail: edmund.herzig@man.ac.uk

Improtex Group
115 Hazi Aslanov Street
Baku 370000
Azerbaijan
Tel: + 994 12 98 02 27/98 02 28
Fax: + 994 12 98 92 25
E-mail: info@impro.azerbaijan.su

Ledingham Chalmers
5 Melville Crescent
Edinburgh EH3 7JA
United Kingdom
Tel: + 44 131 200 1000
Fax: + 44 131 200 1080
E-mail: info@ledingham-chalmers.co.uk

Lukoil
13 Tagiev Street
Baku 370005
Azerbaijan
Tel: + 994 12 97 41 24
Fax: + 994 12 97 41 79

Morrison Construction Group plc
12 Atholl Crescent
Edinburgh EH3 8HA
United Kingdom
Tel: + 44 131 226 4666
Fax: + 44 131 200 4480
E-mail: info@morrcon.co.uk
or
Shand House
Matlock
Derbyshire DE4 3AB
United Kingdom
Tel: + 44 1629 734441

Murphy Shipping & Commercial Services Ltd
8 Rasul Rza Street
Baku
Azerbaijan
Tel: + 994 12 98 01 51
Fax: + 994 12 93 93 15
E-mail: freight@murphy.baku.az
or
Unit 3
Boeing Way
International Trading Estate
Brent Road
Southall
Middlesex UB2 5LB
United Kingdom
Tel: + 44 20 8571 5710
Fax: + 44 20 8571 5711
E-mail: murphyuk@compuserve.com

Royalton
10 Pushkin Street
Baku 370010
Azerbaijan
Tel: + 994 12 93 55 44
Fax: + 994 12 98 02 55
E-mail: ROYALTON@compuserve.com
        Royalton@azerhotel.com

RSK Environment Ltd
Spring Lodge
172 Chester Road
Helsby WA6 0AR
United Kingdom
Tel: + 44 1928 726006
Fax: + 44 1928 725633

Salans Hertzfeld & Heilbronn
4th Floor
Clements House
14–18 Gresham Street
London EC2V 7NN
United Kingdom
Tel: + 44 20 75 09 00 00
Fax: + 44 20 77 26 61 91
E-mail: info@salans.com

State Oil Company of Azerbaijan Republic (SOCAR)
28 Sabit Orujev Street
Baku 370025
Azerbaijan
Tel: + 994 12 98 66 53
Fax: + 994 12 93 36 38
E-mail: ferdsocar@azevt.com

Trade Development Ltd
20 Grosvenor Place
London SW1X 7HN
United Kingdom
Tel: + 44 20 7235 2808
Fax: + 44 20 7235 2802

Union of Insurance Companies of Azerbaijan
c/o Aon-Azeri
80 H Zardabi Street,
Baku 370122
Azerbaijan
Tel: + 994 12 92 44 00
Fax: + 994 12 97 71 10

Index of Advertisers